AF568086

Applied Diplomacy

Through the Prism of Mythology

WRITINGS OF
TP SREENIVASAN

EDITED BY
DIVYA S IYER

FOREWORD BY
JAGDISH BHAGWATI

First published 2014

ISBN 978-81-8328-381-6

Published by
Wisdom Tree
4779/23, Ansari Road
Darya Ganj, New Delhi-110 002
Ph.: 23247966/67/68
wisdomtreebooks@gmail.com

Printed in India

Media credits: *The Indian Express, The New Indian Express, Tribune, Rediff.com, India Ink, New York Times, Wall Street Journal, TEDx Talks*

Dedicated to Former Foreign Secretary Jagat Singh Mehta, who taught the author to think critically and creatively about foreign policy

CONTENTS

Ashwatthama—The United States

Parasurama—Weapons of War and Peace

Kripacharya—The United Nations

FOREWORD

The old tradition where senior Western bureaucrats wrote about their colonial experiences in India, Ceylon, Indonesia and elsewhere, is practically a lost art. Indeed, this was done sometimes with great grace, as by Leonard Wolf, whose second volume of autobiography titled *Growing* is a remarkable description and analysis of his stint in Ceylon; as are the essays of George Orwell, especially *Shooting the Elephant* when he was posted in Burma.

Ambassador TP Sreenivasan is a distinguished diplomat who has had wide-ranging experiences and has a pen, or should I say a PC, to match. He has written this wonderfully entertaining and acutely insightful set of short essays, what we call Op Eds, on the many subjects he has had to deal with; all helpfully classified by common threads which make it easier to see the interconnectedness of his thinking on related topics. Since this is a rich smorgasbord, which is a feast that almost paralyses you with indecision as to what to savour first, it is hard to pick and choose.

But I particularly enjoyed and learnt from his essays on trade policy and climate change, issues that the new government under Prime Minister Narendra Modi will have to turn to immediately.

His views on our relationship with Japan, with whom we plan to intensify our economic and political relationship, are particularly wise. Revealing also is his 'insider' analysis of India's bid for a permanent seat on the UN Security Council.

This collection of his writings shows why, when I receive a new essay from Ambassador Sreenivasan, I never reach for the 'delete' button. The reader of this collection will have that same pleasure and privilege, admittedly later than I have enjoyed, now that his gifted editor, Dr Divya Iyer has brought this collection together for a wider readership. She has also provided a prism of mythology to see the essays in a new light. With her depth of knowledge of mythology, she has evoked in each section of the book the attributes and tales of one of the Sapta-chiranjeevis. This fascinating and unique experiment makes the book a wonderful gift for the author, who has just turned seventy. Read and enjoy!

Jagdish Bhagwati
University Professor of Economics,
Law and International Affairs, Columbia University

INTRODUCTION

Ashwatthama Balir Vyasaha Hanumantha Vibeeshanaha
Kripa Parasuramascha Saptaitey Chiranjeevinaha

Diplomacy and mythology may appear to be two independent streams, flowing parallely, never seeming to merge. Scratch beneath the surface, look beyond the obvious and you recognise that the linkage is actually quite deep, entrenched in the legends and tales of all religions.

Mythology abounds in instances where the protagonists of the story engage in diplomatic missions. Lord Hanuman has been recognised as the first ever Indian ambassador, as portrayed in the eternal Hindu epic, *Ramayana* and Lord Krishna puts on the mantle of the ambassador of peace in the epic, *Mahabharata*. Deeds of King Solomon, Joshua and the diplomatic corps of the ancient Canaanite city of Gibeon bear testimony to the concept of diplomacy as revealed in the Bible. Ambassadors of Islam also served as political and diplomatic agents as portrayed in the Quran. The history of ancient India reveals a jewel in the crown of diplomatic studies in the form of the *Arthashastra*, a work attributed to the masterly statesman, Kautilya or Chanakya of the Mauryan Empire. He employs three categories of diplomats to execute his strategic policies, viz. plenipotentiaries, envoys entrusted with special missions and royal messengers, in addition to consular agents and espionage agents. *Arthashastra* even elaborates upon diplomatic immunities and regulations in a concise manner. Modern Indian history, too, has borne witness to many an exceptional diplomat like Ambassador Extraordinaire Swami Vivekananda. Thus religion, mythology and diplomacy seamlessly blend sans barriers.

Indian mythology is rooted in traditions and beliefs, both religious and cultural. Several families abide by many of those rituals and practices amidst the heft of the modern world. One such godly practice caught my attention a few years ago. Birthdays are occasions for celebration and rejoicing, irrespective of religion or nationality. It is especially considered to be auspicious for a *shishya* and is marked by a special puja and submission of *pranaam* to his guru. In return, the *shishya* will be granted the blessings of his guru by way of a wrist band which is an artistically hand-woven red thread, with seven sacred knots made on it. These seven knots are symbolic of the seven immortal beings in the Hindu pantheon—the Sapta-chiranjeevi. Each one of them is granted the boon of longevity for their noteworthy code of conduct. Hence, it is a sacred custom to invoke the blessings of Chiranjeevis on someone's birthday, uttering the words: '*Chiranjeevi Bhavah*'. Tweaking the tradition a bit, I decided to pay obeisance to the Sapta-chiranjeevis in an attempt to humbly beseech them to bestow their choicest blessings of joy, peace and longevity on my teacher and mentor who celebrates his seventieth birthday in 2014. I hereby invite every reader to join in spirit the celebration of this milestone birthday of a benevolent human being, who has climbed great heights through his arduous efforts and erudition.

***

Seven has been a unique number in all spheres of knowledge and tradition in this world. From the Homeric seven to Shakespeare's seven ages of man, from the primeval seven planets to the seven seas, from the *Saptaswaras* (The seven notes of the Indian musical scale—*Sa Re Ga Ma Pa Dha Ni*) to the *Saptarishis* (the scintillating constellation consisting of seven stars, The Big Dipper), from the seven days of the week to the seven colours of the rainbow, from seven flames of the God of fire, Agni, to the seven circuits of the Kaaba—the pre-eminence and paramountcy of 'all things seven' spans across Hindu, Biblical, Jewish, Zoroastrian and Islamic traditions and beliefs, not to mention the scientific and mathematical significance of the numeral.

The concept of Sapta-chiranjeevi or seven immortal beings also belongs to the same string of beliefs, although the *Bhagavat Purana* does mention the existence of the eighth Chiranjeevi—Markandeya. The etymology of the Sanskrit word 'Chiranjeevi' can be broken into two parts: 'Chiram' meaning 'long' and 'jeevi' meaning 'one that lives', thus imparting the literal meaning of 'long living' to the word. Implicit in the above description is the fact that 'sapta' is the Sanskrit term for the numeral 'seven'. However, linguists still contest the common perception that Chiranjeevi roughly translates into 'an immortal being'. The near-accurate meaning would be 'long living'—so long, that to a normal mortal being, it would seem like such a being will never die, or live unto eternity. Thus, a being with a prolonged longevity (*chiranjeevi*), one who will never die (*amartya*) and one who will live forever (*nitya*, *ananta*) are three different entities in Sanskrit and the Hindu scriptures. Human beings acquire prolonged longevity as a result of their benevolent acts, whereas demigods and devas are considered to be immortal, and gods are believed to be eternal beings.

The Sapta-chiranjeevis are supposed to be men who walked the earth, whose lives and legends have been extensively recounted in the *Puranas* and the epics, *Ramayana* and *Mahabharata*, and have been granted the boon of a prolonged life. Many believe that these seven men have been walking the earth for thousands of years and still do. Nevertheless, the fact that these mythical heroes continue to capture our attention ceaselessly, figure in our folklores and art forms prominently and dwell in our conscience vividly, truly makes them the Chiranjeevis that they are. This modest endeavour seeks to emulate their merit and learn invaluable lessons from their lives that resonates the accents of diplomatic adventures like the tolling of a bell.

Hanuman: The first ever diplomat that India sent abroad elaborates upon the current state of India's foreign policy. Vibheeshana: The virtuous sibling of a vile brother-enemy, who stands for righteousness in the midst of threats and fears, portrays India's pusillanimous yet positive take on its neighbourhood. Ashwatthama: The power-house of the Kauravas, who was cursed to live a prolonged life as he erred under the ire of humiliation, warns us about the wrongdoings that unquestioned power can instigate, as in a super-power like USA. Parasurama: The sage with the most destructive weapons ever that could annihilate life on earth warns us about the hazards of nuclear weapons and urges us to embrace disarmament. Kripacharya: The iconic preceptor who was granted immortality in recognition of his impartiality under all circumstances draws parallel with the United Nations of our times. Mahabali: The legendary ruler of Kerala in whose memory the festival of Onam is celebrated every year, invokes Kerala and Malayalees. Vyasa: The master storyteller of all times brings to us amusing tales, narratives and lives of yore in remarkable style. The lives of the seven icons have much in common with the art of diplomacy that is in vogue today. Their tales and TP Sreenivasan's trails intertwine to take the road less travelled, promising to be an intriguing journey for the reader.

***

Applied Diplomacy is a collection of fine writings by former Ambassador TP Sreenivasan, curated from a bunch of riveting articles published over the course of the last decade in leading national as well as international newspapers, magazines and electronic media and transcripts of speeches delivered at institutions of international repute and memorial lectures delivered to honour legendary men. He takes us through seven diverse streams of his career in his effortless and inimitable style. *Applied Diplomacy* consolidates the wisdom gained from the field notes in diplomacy and traces the footprints of the diplomat. More recently, post-retirement he has added several feathers to his cap; the most commendable of them being his accomplishments as the executive vice-chairman of the Kerala State Higher Education Council and as a television broadcaster, unveiling to the world, the information doorway to international affairs in the form of *Videsha Vicharam*, telecast every week on Asianet News channel. This book largely covers his works in the period since the publishing of his autobiography *Words, Words, Words*, which unravels the gripping realities of his life and career. He has shown a keen interest in mentoring students and inspiring them to join the Indian Foreign Service. Students who have been groomed and nurtured by him will always be grateful to him for the wisdom and inspiration bestowed upon them. This book is a humble *gurudakshina*—a respectful offering to the teacher from the student—to the great teacher in him. I have largely relied upon electronic sources for the collection of articles, and a systematic method of sorting them has been followed. Each of the seven diplomatic streams flows over the crust of values that one of the Chiranjeevis stands for. Here we start weaving the strands of mythology, diplomacy and gratitude in an attempt to immortalise the words of an astute diplomat; an ode to the Sapta-chiranjeevis, a solemn birthday prayer for the revered teacher!

Divya S Iyer

Hanuman
The Mascot of Indian Foreign Service

Lord Rama described his disciple, Lord Hanuman, after he met him for the first time in the following words, 'He has mastery over language. It is impossible for anyone to converse like him without attaining command over the *Rig*, *Yajur* and *Sama* Vedas. His proficiency in grammar is thorough; he has studied it many times over. And though he has spoken so much, he has not uttered a single word out of place or irrelevant to the context. There is no grimace on his face, eyes, forehead or brow, nor any inappropriate gesture from any other part of his body. His diction is neither expansive nor elliptical, neither too slow nor too fast. The thoughts in his heart, escaping his throat, are expressed in a medium tone. His language is cultured, attractive and beatific, and his manner, neither gushing nor tardy. How can the objectives of a king, who does not have such an illustrious emissary, ever be accomplished?'—*Valmiki Ramayana*, 4.3.26–34

An ideal diplomat could not have been described better. The role of a diplomat in war and peace is elucidated by the legends and parables portraying Hanuman and his army of monkeys. The story of Hanuman supervising the building of the rock-bridge across the sea for Lord Rama to reach Lanka, reveals that the duty of the diplomat is often not confined to ambassadorial functions alone. So does his readiness to use force to fight against an instance of injustice, as revealed by Hanuman burning the city of Lanka to ashes, when Ravana sets the emissary's tail on fire, to insult him. An envoy with the capacity to use force instantly in the event of an attempt to shoot the messenger is confined only to mythology though.

Indian foreign policy has evolved on the foundation of values and ethos stemming from such timeless legends and cultural norms. The Non-Aligned Movement (NAM) and the Panchsheel principles were amongst the first bricks laid for building the elegant castle that Indian foreign policy is today. Chiranjeevi Hanuman lives on as a graceful reminder of the victory of Indian diplomats throughout the world.

TP Sreenivasan has encapsulated in many of his writings and speeches the many charms and the innumerable challenges the Foreign Service faces. The experience he has gained from Tokyo, Thimphu, Moscow, New York, Yangon, Suva, Nairobi, Washington and Vienna was not devoid of hazards. He faced two military coups, an expulsion and an armed attack. But he continues to be an advocate of the IFS and convincingly argues that the charms far outweigh the challenges. To young Civil Services aspirants, his advice is to learn more about the IFS before they make their choice. This section is recommended as necessary reading for aspiring diplomats.

***

1

DIPLOMACY: CHARMS AND CHALLENGES

Like other professions, no single definition can capture the many facets of diplomacy. No single experience can reflect its many dimensions. The popular musings and definitions of diplomacy and diplomats state: 'A diplomat is an honest gentleman, who lies abroad for his country.' 'If a diplomat asks you to go to hell, he will say it in such a way that you look forward to the trip.' 'If a lady says "no", she means "may be", if she says "may be", she means "yes", if she says "yes", she is no lady. If a diplomat says "yes", he means "maybe", if he says "maybe", he means "no", if he says "no", he is no diplomat.'

When I joined the Service in 1967, I was told that Indian diplomacy was 50 per cent protocol, 30 per cent alcohol and 20 per cent TN Kaul (the then foreign secretary). Most definitions strengthen the popular perception that diplomacy is some kind of linguistic deception at worst and artful dishonesty at best. My father, who was instrumental in my choosing a diplomatic career, called me a 'diplomat' whenever he felt that I was less than honest or less than forthright with him. The popular image of a diplomat is still that of a man in sartorial splendour, who frequents cocktail circuits and engages in conversations, but says nothing.

In actual fact, diplomacy is the technical instrument for conducting business between states by peaceful means. Intelligence, tact, patience and judgment are essential tools of diplomacy. Communication skills are of paramount importance, but diplomacy is not made of words alone. A diplomat, posted abroad, finds out what his country requires from his host country by way of information and material, sifts and collates the information received, determines the options available to his government to secure what it needs and once the government's decision is known, uses his skills to secure it on the best possible terms. In the process, he has to project his country in the best possible light, fighting all the way with the media that provides images that may not always be palatable. What he secures may be modern technology, an industrial product, a traditional craft or simply a great idea. In certain cases, it may even be a strategic piece of land. Failure of diplomacy can lead to espionage, coercion or even use of force. War is, after all, diplomacy by other means. Humanity, therefore, has a great stake in the success of diplomacy.

The charm of diplomacy as a profession is on account of the honour involved in representing a nation in another country or a global forum. Living in world capitals itself is a privilege. To drive past the imperial palace in Tokyo, the Kremlin in Moscow, the White House in Washington, Empire State Building in New York, the Hoffburg Palace in Vienna, the Golden Pagoda in Yangon for work every day for years, as I have done, has an excitement of its own. When people from all over the world squander their life savings to spend a few days in these cities, diplomats are paid to live there. To be able to speak for the country in the UN chambers in New York, Geneva, Vienna and Nairobi is truly an enriching experience. Diplomatic successes are not always measurable or tangible, but there is a sense of victory every time the Indian point of view is accepted by the international community or when an anti-Indian move is thwarted. Instances of Indian successes in international diplomacy are many, particularly at the United Nations. Some years ago, an independent survey placed Indian diplomats just after those of the five permanent members of the Security Council in terms of influence and effectiveness.

Multilateral diplomacy, whether at the universal level at the United Nations or the regional level, has its own charms and challenges. It is only at the UN that the strengths and weaknesses of individual countries and the power equations of the world can be witnessed. The permanent members stand apart on account of their power of the veto. Their effectiveness has increased after the end of the Cold War, as they are able to work together, except in isolated cases. But while they have the ability to veto an action, the rule that any action has to be supported by nine positive votes in the Security Council gives even the non-permanent members a voice in decision-making. There are ways and means even for the non-members of the Security Council to influence the decisions of the body charged with the protection and promotion of international peace and security. Even during the decades when India has not been a member of the Security Council (1992-2011), it has succeeded, among other things, to keep the Kashmir question out of it despite efforts by Pakistan to rake up the issue. Indian diplomacy achieved another spectacular success by containing the fallout of our nuclear tests of 1998. India is not yet recognised as a nuclear-weapon state, but the world has learnt to live with India's possession of nuclear weapons and does not lose sleep over our capability.

The challenge, however, is to bridge the gap between the popular perception of our importance and the reality of the world situation. To us, it is totally illogical that India, with a population of over one billion, a civilisation in its own right and totally committed to the UN, is not yet a permanent member of the Security Council. The rest of the world has many other considerations in reforming the Security Council. Pandit Nehru had once declined an offer for India to take China's place in the Security Council, as he felt that India should take its turn in due time. But in today's global scenario, Indian aspirations in this regard remain unfulfilled. The unwillingness of the permanent members to share their privileges with others, the competing claims of other countries and our nuclear status are major hurdles. With the weakening of the Non-Aligned Movement, India does not have a solid constituency of its own and has to forge partnerships with different countries and groups of countries, based on the issues at hand. In this situation, Indian diplomats have to work even harder to attain their objectives in the United Nations.

The United Nations is neither a world parliament, nor a debating society. Delegations go there with specific instructions, forged by their governments. When we lobby hard with delegations, some of them actually say, 'You may be able to change my mind, but you cannot change my instructions.' But in reality, there is much that individuals can do to be friendly or unfriendly, even within their instructions. There are various ways in which delegations express their views in the event of a vote. They either vote positive or negative or abstain. But they can also 'not participate' or be absent to take nuanced positions for one reason or another. In the early years of its membership of the UN, the People's Republic of China had developed non-participation in votes as a policy position. According to one story, a Chinese diplomat happened to be absent when a particular vote was taken. When he returned to find that the vote was over, he took the floor and stated, 'Mr Chairman, I was absent at the time the vote was taken. I would like it to be recorded that if I was present, I would not have participated in the vote,' underlining the distinction between non-participation and absence. I had the experience of a friendly voting gesture from the Republic of Slovenia to which I was accredited as ambassador from Vienna (2000-04). In the General Assembly session, a resolution on self-determination, traditionally adopted by consensus, came up for a vote at our request as the Pakistan ambassador claimed that support for the resolution amounted to supporting Pakistan's position on Kashmir. Since the resolution itself did not mention Kashmir and in the earlier years, we had not asked for a vote, many delegations had no instructions and in the ensuing confusion, many abstained on it. Most countries do not want to take a position when India and Pakistan clash at the United Nations. The Slovene ambassador also abstained in the relevant committee, which made our delegation happy; as that was what we had requested friendly countries to do since the resolution itself was not anti-Indian. But when the matter was reported to the Slovene capital, Ljubljana, the government felt that Slovenia should change its vote to positive in the General Assembly, as Slovenia was a great champion of self-determination. When this came to be known in New York, I received instructions to ensure that Slovenia did not change its vote. I went up the ladder in the Slovene bureaucracy to find that a final decision had been taken to change the vote to positive, with the approval of the foreign minister. Foreign Minister Rupel, whom I knew well, initially stuck to his position, but when it became clear that it was a test of our friendship, he told me that he would do his best without revealing what Slovenia would do. On the appointed day, when the resolution came to a vote in the General Assembly, the Slovene ambassador went out for a walk, leaving his seat vacant. Foreign Minister Rupel was received with special warmth when he came to India later, on account of this gesture of friendship to India. We understood well his compulsion not to appear to be opposed to the principle of self-determination. Being absent was the only option he had, to show sensitivity to India's concerns.

Diplomacy is not just about doing business with governments; it is also about winning friends and influencing people. Common pursuits outside the professional sphere help to create bonds that eventually benefit work. Bridge and golf groups, theatre and music circles and others have been of immense value to cultivate people. Even the much-maligned diplomatic cocktail circuits are important in the diplomatic world as food and drinks often serve as lubricants for conversations. One ready-made constituency diplomats can use consists of compatriots settled abroad, either as expatriates or local citizens.

In countries where there are large communities of Indian origin, Indian diplomacy has special charms and challenges. India and her children abroad have rediscovered each other. On the one hand, India has begun to rely on the Indian communities in industrialised countries for technology and investment, and on the other, the communities abroad have realised that they need an Indian safety net in the event of unforeseen events in their countries of adoption like it happened in Burma, Uganda and Fiji. The PIO card (for People of Indian Origin) and dual citizenship have been accepted in response to these new phenomena. Indian diplomats enjoy special privileges in countries where there are large Indian communities. In Fiji, for instance, the Indian high commissioner was treated on par with the prime minister as half the population was of Indian origin. Even in the United States, the increase in the stature and profile of the Indian community has enhanced the prestige of the Indian ambassador. But our diplomats are caught between the high expectations in India and among the overseas Indians about what each can do for the other. The sensitivity of the host country is another important factor, which inhibits freedom of action for both.

In Fiji, I remember how the Indians there had unrealistic expectations about Indian intervention, when following the 1987 military coup, the first of several in the following decades, they were virtually disenfranchised. Our limited intervention in terms of trade sanctions and moral support had some impact, but it led to charges of interference in internal affairs. The military government overlooked our non-recognition of its authority for two years, but when the pressure mounted, it gave me exactly seventy-two hours to leave.

In Kenya, the so-called Asian community had a commanding position in commercial and economic activities, but its relative prosperity made it vulnerable to accusations of corruption and other evil deeds. They also came to be associated too closely with those in power. This sure recipe for hatred took the form of prejudices even about the Indian high commission. The prevalent atmosphere of crime provided the cover for a politically-motivated armed attack on my wife and me, which left us with some broken bones. I myself played down the political significance of the incident, to take the sting out of it and not to cause panic in the Asian community. Still, the incident had a profound impact on the migrant community in Kenya.

It is in the United States that the powerful Indian community has been making a significant contribution to Indian diplomacy. The India Caucus in the US House of Representatives, which has more than 115 members and the Friends of India in the Senate, which was formed in 2004, owe their origins largely to Indian American activism. No other country has been able to have such recognisable lobbies in the US Congress. More and more Indian Americans have become active in the electoral politics of the United States. Although many of them wish to remain distant from Indian positions as such, their agenda, like India's, is fostering of mutually beneficial relations between the two countries. Indian American support for India is neither automatic, nor uniform. They were totally opposed to the Emergency in 1975 (the nineteen-month long state of Emergency in the country declared by the Indira Gandhi regime), but they were solidly supportive of the 1998 nuclear tests. They were critical of the government when reports of harassments of Christians reached the United States in 1999. They were quite prepared to energise friendly US congressmen and senators to take up the issue with the US at a time when we were still dealing with the aftermath of our nuclear tests. Winning Indian American support on different issues is a challenge to Indian diplomacy in the United States, but once they are convinced of the merit of an issue, they are able to influence US policy in India's favour.

Diplomatic practices have changed over the years, but principles have remained constant. Resident missions are a modern phenomenon. In the ancient days, diplomats were dispatched on special missions to uncharted courses, with no guarantee of successful return; with nothing but a general brief about the objectives. They negotiated alliances, treaties and agreements and threatened use of force on behalf of their nations. They were left to their own devices to accomplish their missions and there were cases of some of them perishing either on the high seas or on enemy territory. According to one legend, a cannibal king told an ambassador that his predecessor was delicious!

Diplomacy is no less hazardous today. Even before terrorism began to threaten governments and their representatives worldwide, diplomats were targeted by disgruntled elements, criminals and crazy people. In April 1961, an eminent diplomat from Kerala, Shankar Pillai was shot dead by a mad man who was denied a visa by our high commission in Ottawa. Many diplomats around the globe have been victims of attacks, motivated by real and imaginary grievances against their governments. The charm of representing a nation inevitably carries with it the challenge of coping with threats to physical security. The messenger being held responsible for the message is not new. In the *Mahabharata*, Kauravas order the detention of Krishna for the message he brought from the Pandavas and in the *Ramayana*, Ravana tries to humiliate Hanuman, who went to Lanka to negotiate the release of Sita.

The skills that are required of diplomats vary from place to place. Knowledge of foreign languages is an obvious advantage, but the exigencies of service land our best Chinese experts in Brazil or Japanese experts in Bhutan. Some of us never got posted back to the countries where we went to learn the language. In any event, swift movement of diplomats from country to country is not particularly conducive to mastering any language. Some acquaintance of languages with the ability to exchange pleasantries can be useful, but use of inaccurate language can lead not only to misunderstandings but also embarrassment. A little knowledge of a foreign language is indeed a dangerous thing. I recall how a Soviet admiral said to an audience of Indian naval officers how happy he was that India always sent the cream of the Indian defence forces to the Soviet Union for training and expressed the hope that this practice would continue in the future also. An Indian naval officer, who prided himself in his knowledge of the Russian language, interpreted his words thus, 'I am glad that India exports good cream to the Soviet Union. I hope that you will send us better cream at least in the future.' No wonder that many seasoned diplomats prefer to speak in their native language even if they know the language of his interlocutor reasonably well. Needless to say, it is not only foreign languages that cause embarrassing moments, but also nuances in our own first language. There is a story about a party functionary in the old Soviet Union, who got jailed because of 'terminological inexactitude'. When he was asked why he missed the last party meeting, he said in all innocence, 'Oh, was it really the last party meeting? If I knew that, I would certainly have come.'

Language is not the only challenge that diplomats face in foreign lands. Mastering local customs and social graces to get accepted in different cultures can be even more demanding. Drinking the brew served at a tea ceremony in Japan, sipping tea with yak butter in Bhutan or gulping down kava, the bitter national drink of Fiji, with a straight face is no easy task. To compliment the hosts on the aroma and taste of these national delicacies is the real test of diplomacy. Being received in Papua New Guinea by men charging with spears and retreating at the last minute can be unnerving. They do that in memory of the old tribal custom of treating every outsider as an enemy till he is proved otherwise. In Solomon Islands, the high commissioner, on his first arrival, has to kill a huge pig with one hit at its head with a club and accept the carcass as a gift. I spent a couple of hours wondering how I would carry a dead pig in my baggage, but I was relieved to learn that it was served as lunch to the assembled guests in my name. I also learnt that my 'spokesman' had already acknowledged the compliments paid to me on the quality of the pork served.

No diplomat can be effective in Austria if he does not understand wines or cannot fathom the intricacy of the music of Mozart or Beethoven. The only way to secure access to people in power in Burma or the South Pacific is by spending long hours on the golf course. Culinary habits differ not only from country to country, but also from region to region. Imagine the challenges of a foreign diplomat in India coping with Indian languages, Indian cooking styles and social customs from Kashmir to Kanyakumari! There is a story of a head of state, who came to India and returned to his country with a bindi on his forehead, thinking that Indian women were brilliant as they had 'something up there', that he did not have.

Speaking of the possible bewilderment of foreign diplomats over the diversity in India, the challenge of reporting events and opinions from foreign countries comes to mind. With the availability of tons of news and views in English alone, not to speak of regional languages, it must be difficult to separate the grain from the chaff. I have been fortunate enough to serve in 'two-newspaper countries' such as the Soviet Union and Burma. In both these countries, it was sufficient to read one newspaper to know the official view as well as what passes off as public opinion. In Burma, even the choice between two newspapers was illusory as the two had identical content. Conversations with officials did not reveal any different perspective. On the other hand, in countries with vibrant media and open intellectual debates, diplomats have the additional challenge of analysing the massive amount of material to sense the pulse of the people. Diplomats are generally cautious about making predictions, but many diplomats in India must have predicted victory for the National Democratic Alliance government in the 2004 elections in India, on the strength of the media projections and astrological predictions! In the United States, it is an impossible task even to follow just the writings on India in the media, not to speak of the internal debate on domestic and foreign policies. In addition, there are the think tanks, the universities and others who provide in-depth analyses of events on a continuing basis. The advent of the internet has made this material available at home simultaneously and it is quite possible that the headquarters may be better informed than the diplomats on some of the events abroad.

The information revolution has indeed altered the nature of diplomacy beyond recognition. The days of diplomatic representatives acting on their own are long gone. The only occasion on which I had to act without instructions on an important issue was when Colonel Sitiveni Rabuka, my one-time golf partner, carried out a military coup in Fiji, declared himself head of state and invited me to meet him, with other ambassadors, to listen to his case. I had no way of consulting New Delhi as he had cut overseas communications before he marched into the Fijian parliament to take the entire treasury bench to prison. I was in a dilemma as the envoys of Australia and New Zealand, which had alternative communication channels, were instructed not to attend. I decided to go, particularly to voice my concern about the lives and property of the people of Indian origin, against whom the coup was aimed. Fortunately, New Delhi saw the wisdom of my decision as it gave us a central role in later events. On all other important occasions, I had clear instructions from home even when there was very little notice.

Today, heads of state and government meet more often than before, and they actually discuss business as against rubber-stamping agreements worked out by diplomats. Foreign ministers talk to each other at the drop of a hat and ambassadors get to know the outcome only subsequently. But even the information revolution has not rendered diplomacy redundant. There are many issues in bilateral and multilateral spheres that do not need to come to the attention of policymakers at home. Personal diplomacy still plays a role in explaining positions and implementing agreements. The consular problems around the globe are complex and it is only the resident diplomats, who can deal with issues such as illegal immigration, visas and passports. Diplomats have, of late, turned their attention to trade and economic matters to make up for lost political leverage. Then there is the need for public relations and personal conversations to focus attention on relevant facts and figures. For instance, even area experts and intellectuals are often surprised to learn in personal conversations that India has the second largest Muslim population in the world. It is not enough that statistics are available for reference; it is necessary to highlight them to drive home a particular point. Diplomacy as an art is, therefore, not likely to diminish in importance or die.

Pandit Nehru said in Parliament once that in the Indian Foreign Service, the government gets two people to work on one salary.

Spouses play an important role in diplomacy as visible symbols of their nation. Spouses have to remain intellectually alive and knowledgeable in order to be able to have intelligent conversations and to correct impressions about their culture. This was part of the reason for the government to discourage Foreign Service officers from marrying foreigners. Considering the stress and strains of their lives, it is truly creditable that there are many success stories of spouses as professionals, musicians, dancers, painters and writers.

Diplomacy demands strength of character and physical stamina like very few other professions do. An immense culture shock every three years, the need to be an instant expert on current affairs and local customs in new locations, the very pressure of locating schools, doctors and dentists frequently and the simple physical labour of moving belongings from place to place take a toll on diplomats and their families. Once I met an American tourist at a swimming pool in the salubrious weather of Addis Ababa, who told me that he was taking a holiday to relieve himself of the stress of having moved from Brooklyn to Manhattan after twenty years. I thought to myself that by that standard, I shall have to spend the rest of my life near a swimming pool to relieve the stress of thirty-seven years. But I would rather spend my energies spreading the gospel of diplomacy and urging younger people to brave the challenges of a diplomatic career to enjoy its many charms.

2

DREAMS FOR THE WORLD

'We have to work and work hard to give reality to our dreams. Those dreams are for India, but they are also for the world,' said Pandit Jawaharlal Nehru as India woke to life and freedom at the stroke of the midnight hour on 15 August 1947. For India, it was important to 'attain her rightful place in the world and make her full and willing contribution to world peace and the welfare of mankind', even as India was grappling with the problems of building a new nation. India's global fortunes may have fluctuated in the sixty-seven years of independence, but it has never wavered from its commitment to its global responsibilities.

Foreign policy had been in the public consciousness even before independence and its evolution was dictated by India's geography and history. With his deep knowledge of India and the world, Nehru shaped foreign policy and became its main architect. But just as democracy was the only option for India after independence, the policy of not aligning with either of the two blocs came naturally to India. After years of Western domination, India could not have embraced the West. Nor did the Soviet bloc hold any attraction. India refused to be drawn into the Cold War also because of its reluctance to spend scarce resources on an arms race. Freedom of judgment and independence of action became the hallmark of Indian foreign policy, whether it was called non-alignment in the Cold War days or strategic autonomy today. The establishment of the Non-Aligned Movement and its growth as a major force in the world were essentially inspired by India.

The objective of foreign policy, like that of domestic policy, is economic development of the nation. It aims to create a congenial international environment, free of external threat, interference, terrorism, intimidation and protectionism. It also aims to secure economic cooperation for resources and technology on the basis of equity. In its approach to the United Nations, having learnt a bitter lesson when it took Kashmir to the Security Council in 1948, India seeks to contribute to the global commons rather than to look for unilateral advantages. Interest in world affairs and global issues has been a dominant factor in Indian foreign policy.

India's 'golden era' in foreign policy was, ironically, long before the information revolution, social media and public diplomacy. The prestige of India was at its highest in the world from 1947 to 1962. India, having won independence 'without firing a shot', became a model for those under colonial rule, and moulded itself as a champion of decolonisation, disarmament and a new international economic order. Initiatives in nuclear disarmament, particularly the Nuclear Test Ban Treaty, helped the world focus on the dangers of nuclear war. By raising the issue of apartheid and opposing the division of Palestine, India gave lead to the struggle against the remnants of imperialism.

India's prestige was further enhanced by its participation in the International Control Commission in Vietnam (in 1954), together with Canada and Poland and later, the peacekeeping operation in Congo. The US and the Soviet Union did not appreciate the Indian posture of non-alignment. India's efforts at building a nation of extreme diversity drew some admiration and the prophets of doom of Indian democracy began to rethink their assessments of India. The experiments with a mixed economy and the growth rate, though moderate, were considered hopeful. India has been a candidate for permanent membership for more than twenty years, but there is no enthusiasm for it.

The gross miscalculation of this idealistic phase in Indian foreign policy was the hope and expectation that India and China would work in unison to build a united Asia and pave the way for Afro-Asian solidarity. India's championship of the move to install the People's Republic of China in the United Nations and the Security Council was rooted in this expectation. India was thoroughly unprepared for the Chinese aggression of 1962. The disarmament rhetoric lulled India into thinking that massive infusion of money into defence was neither necessary, nor desirable. The Chinese aggression to 'teach India a lesson' was not unrelated to the rising prestige and importance of India. China had calculated that the dominance of India in Asia would be detrimental to its own quest for leadership in Asia and the world. Nehru's dreams crumbled in front of his own eyes.

India's fall from grace began after the Chinese aggression, when a bewildered India rushed to the US for military aid. If the Chinese had not withdrawn unilaterally from much of the Indian territory and declared a ceasefire, India would have been in a tight US embrace in the sixties. No other factor has influenced India's worldview more than the 1962 defeat at the hands of the Chinese. The realistic phase was bitter to begin with, but India learnt soon enough to take pragmatic decisions, even while maintaining continuity in non-alignment. The Chinese nuclear tests confounded the situation in 1964, but India did not react with its own tests, which could have been possible in a short time, given the scientific and technological base which India had already developed. Instead, India opted for an intensified effort to develop fissile capability. Military modernisation became imperative and India was on the lookout for weapons and technology to defend itself.

A combination of several factors drove India closer to the Soviet Union during this period, largely because the US began getting drawn to Pakistan as its ally in South Asia. The Soviet Union made a dramatic entry into South Asia by forging the Tashkent Agreement between India and Pakistan. While Pakistan moved away to China and the United States, India found merit in leaning towards the Soviet Union to meet the challenges of the time. Many positions that India had taken in the Non-Aligned Movement on Palestine, apartheid etc. coincided with the Soviet view and NAM itself came to be seen as a natural ally of the Soviet Union. Moreover, the Soviet Union offered better terms to build India's infrastructure and defence industry through barter arrangements, manufacturing license etc. Thus, India came to be seen as leaning towards the Soviet Union.

The Indian decision to break up Pakistan, taking advantage of the freedom movement in East Pakistan, received very little global support. The virtual isolation on this issue led to the signing of a Treaty of Peace, Friendship and Cooperation between India and the Soviet Union, which amounted to a military pact. India's non-alignment itself was challenged, but the treaty helped in keeping the US and China at bay during the war. The liberation of Bangladesh in 1971 and the Shimla Agreement with Pakistan won some grudging admiration for India, but the assassination of Sheikh Mujibur Rahman in 1975 and developments in Bangladesh cast a shadow on the Indian victory.

The negotiations on the Nuclear Non-Proliferation Treaty (NPT) marked another setback for India during this period. The NPT itself was an Indian idea, and India offered to sign the NPT in 1966 in return for a nuclear guarantee from the United States and the Soviet Union, but having been rebuffed, decided not to sign the NPT. The Peaceful Nuclear Explosion in 1974 and the declaration of Emergency soon after marked a new low in India's image abroad.

The Janata experiment (political party rule) from 1977 to 1980 did not bring in any significant change in foreign policy. The declared policy of 'genuine' non-alignment was meant to make India distant from the Soviet Union and to build bridges with the West, but nothing significant was accomplished. India's involvement with the Soviet Union continued, but overtures were made towards China, Pakistan and the United States. Continuity, rather than change, marked the Janata interregnum and India, with its poor economic record, continued to be on the margins of the global order.

The return of the Indira Gandhi government coincided with the Soviet invasion of Afghanistan and led to Indian acquiescence in the occupation, placing India squarely in opposition to the United States and other Western powers. Pakistan made use of the opportunity to forge an alliance with the US and received a massive aid package. Pakistan's acquisition of nuclear weapons came to light at this time. Both in Afghanistan and Cambodia, India was with the minority in the international community led by the Soviet Union. Indian foreign policy was virtually at a standstill and India was branded as a Soviet ally. The initial efforts at improvement of relations with China, the United States and Pakistan made no headway.

The collapse of the Soviet Union in 1991 and the end of the Cold War dictated drastic and sudden changes in the economic and foreign policies of India. India lost its ideological platform of non-alignment. A fiscal crisis arising out of the first Gulf War (1990-91) had a disastrous effect on the Indian economy. Repatriation of Indian workers from Kuwait and the resultant drop in remittances made the foreign exchange situation precarious. Faced with an acute economic crisis, PV Narasimha Rao and Manmohan Singh dismantled the license raj, abandoned the socialist flavour of the economy and joined the international trend towards globalisation and liberalisation. Simultaneously, even as India repeated the mantra of non-alignment as the expression of freedom even in a unipolar world, it readjusted policies to befriend the sole super power. Following the signing of the Oslo Accord on Palestine in 1992, India upgraded its diplomatic relations with Israel and scaled down its support to Palestine. India diluted its position of opposition to external powers in the Indian Ocean, initiated the Look East Policy (LEP) to befriend the Association of South East Asian Nations (ASEAN) and generally became soft towards the West.

The extension of the NPT and pressure to sign the Comprehensive (Nuclear) Test Ban Treaty (CTBT), however, made the process of improvement of relations with the United States difficult. The increase of insurgency in Kashmir, fuelled by Pakistan's terrorism and infiltration, engaged the attention of the government on the domestic front. The second Clinton administration (1997-2001) had begun warming up to India and Clinton was contemplating a visit to India at the invitation of Inder Gujral, when the Atal Bihari Vajpayee government, acting on the perception that there was a serious threat from China, decided to exercise the nuclear option in May 1998, bringing India–US relations to rock bottom. The confidential explanation given to the United States that the tests were aimed at China and not Pakistan found its way to the *New York Times*! Clinton demanded that India sign the CTBT immediately as a compromise, and imposed Glenn Amendment sanctions against India when India refused.

The Jaswant Singh–Strobe Talbott dialogue over the next two years, the first of its kind in the history of India–US relations, led to a grudging acknowledgement of India's de facto status as a nuclear weapon state, though no formal decision was taken. The Kargil war in 1999 and the 2001 attack on the Indian Parliament did not result in a full-scale war with Pakistan, partly as a result of US intervention. For once, the United States sided with India and demanded withdrawal of Pakistan from the Indian side of the Line of Control (LoC). The Glenn Amendment sanctions withered away. Clinton's visit to India and Vajpayee's visit to the United States marked a major change in India's relations with the United States.

Indian foreign policy veered towards the United States even more under Manmohan Singh, when it signed the agreement on civilian nuclear cooperation, which turned India from a target of non-proliferation to a partner. For India, it marked the end of its nuclear isolation and for the US, it opened a new chapter in relations with India. The nuclear deal raised expectations of opening up the huge Indian market, including the market for nuclear fuel supplies and reactors. A strong India was also seen by the US as a potential ally in a possible confrontation with China. Though the Civil Liability Act hindered the full implementation of the nuclear deal, the change in US–India relations became irreversible. Today, the cooperation between the two countries ranges from agriculture to space, education to anti-terrorism. The relationship has assumed the nature of a strategic partnership.

The partnership is now believed to have plateaued, with little possibility of moving the roller coaster any higher. In fact, there has been a setback, with the 'despicable and barbarian' arrest and mistreatment of an Indian consular officer in New York in 2013, which has been seen as a national insult by India. But the setback is likely to be temporary, given the stake that each country has in the other.

The latest phase in Indian foreign policy, dubbed as 'NonAlignment 2.0' or strategic autonomy makes India open to select alliances with various countries on the basis of enlightened national interests. India is as much at home in the Non-Aligned Movement as in BRICS, IBSA (with Brazil, China and Russia, and with South Africa), the Shanghai Cooperation Organisation or ASEAN. The approach is to secure the maximum space possible for its own economic growth in order for the country to become reasonably prosperous and equitable. India has strategic dialogues with several countries and joint exercises with the United States, China, Japan and Australia, and it imports defence equipment from the US, Russia and Israel. In the context of the rivalry between the US and China in the Asia-Pacific Region, India has not identified with either and promotes cooperation with the regional and outside powers. A new spring is visible in India's relations with Japan, following Japan's own proactive foreign policy. Relations with Russia remain robust.

The challenges of Indian foreign policy in the future remain serious and complex. The rise of China and its increasing assertiveness in international relations will remain India's preoccupation for the foreseeable future. India has to contend with the problem of border demarcation, including China's occupation of Indian territory and its territorial claims in Arunachal Pradesh, China's all-weather friendship with Pakistan, including nuclear cooperation, China's possible re-engineering of the flow of water from rivers like the Brahmaputra to India and its unfair trade practices. India has adopted a strategy of being firm on these issues, along with extending areas of cooperation with the Chinese in fields of common interest. The incursions in 2013 and 2014 into Indian territory in the Chumar sector in Ladakh and reassertion of claims do not augur well.

With Pakistan, India has been willing to walk the extra mile to normalise relations. But the pattern of appearing reasonable in negotiations and rejecting any forward movement continues, regardless of the changes in leadership in Pakistan. The army, which calls the shots in Pakistan, does not appear to be ready for any change in the posture of hostility it has adopted towards India. The internal situation in Pakistan, the developments in Afghanistan and the fluctuating relations between the United States and Pakistan also militate against the solution of problems with India. Ceasefire violations are frequent on the LoC. Pakistan is no more a dominant threat to India, but it will demand considerable attention. Cross-border terrorism is on top of the Indian agenda in dealing with Pakistan.

India's neighbourhood has been in turmoil because of internal problems. A conscious effort by China to wean them away from the sphere of influence of India has had its effect in these countries. They are increasingly attracted by the Chinese economic and military assistance. The South Asian Association for Regional Cooperation (SAARC) has failed to take off as an effective regional body and India has to deal with the individual countries with a mix of firmness and flexibility. Regional integration in South Asia is more distant now than ever before.

Indian foreign policy has also been engaged in grappling with issues of environment, human rights, nuclear power and trade. India maintains its position, adopted since 1972, that the main responsibility for making the necessary investments in saving the planet belongs to the developed world, which had recklessly endangered environment by conspicuous consumption of the world's resources. But the whittling down of the decisions in the Rio Earth conference of 1992 and increasing pressure on India to accept mandatory cuts in greenhouse gas emissions have posed new challenges. A new consensus on the environment is a priority for India.

India is a signatory to most of the human rights conventions and is faithful in their implementation. The pressure from human rights organisations on law and order issues in Jammu and Kashmir has diminished. India changed its position of not politicising human rights situations by supporting a human rights resolution against Sri Lanka.

A new trend in foreign policy is for it to be influenced by state leaders, particularly of border states. Apart from the policy on Sri Lanka, there have been decisive interventions by West Bengal, Gujarat, Odisha and Kerala in foreign policy matters. While the views of the border states should be taken into account, the hijacking of policy by the regional satraps is dangerous. A price of coalition politics, this tendency should be resisted by the central government.

Nuclear policy relating to weapons and on civilian use has always been an integral part of Indian foreign policy, right from the time of independence. Nehru was as much an architect of nuclear policy as he was of foreign policy. As a pacifist, he had renounced nuclear weapons, but promoted nuclear technology as part of the energy mix for the future. But there is no doubt that a robust nuclear policy, combined with the pursuit of nuclear disarmament has served the country well over the years.

One general criticism against Indian foreign policy is that India does not have a strategic culture and that India is more reactive than proactive. But considering that even those who made mammoth investments in Kremlinology did not predict the collapse of the Soviet Union, there is a case for prompt, consistent and thoughtful response rather than for long-term policy planning, which is likely to be thwarted by events such as the collapse of the Berlin Wall or the 9/11 attacks (the 2001 attack in USA). In answer to the criticism that India has no strategic culture, India's national security adviser, Shivshankar Menon has said, 'I think, what most of them mean is that they do not see the long-term thinking and patient planning that is often (rightly or wrongly) ascribed to other cultures.... India has shown remarkable consistency in the manner of her engagement with the world, across different stages of her development, under governments of divergent political persuasions and in very varied international circumstances. The record has been remarkably consistent.' India has been not only consistent, but also dynamic in its foreign policy, which has served its global interests effectively. As it gains greater economic and military strength, India should be able to attain its desired goal of being an important pole in a multipolar world.

3

THE PRICE OF RETICENCE

President Roosevelt's foreign policy dictum, 'Speak softly and carry a big stick,' has found new followers in New Delhi. Whether they carry a big stick or not, they speak softly to the point that they appear to be not speaking. This is a departure from the past. Even in the old days, when there was a consensus on foreign policy and South Block had the monopoly over foreign policymaking, prime ministers and foreign ministers explained every important decision to the public. To their foreign interlocutors, Indian negotiators were often forthright. By keeping the public informed, they ensured general acceptance of the tough positions they took. Indian positions were always 'principled', or were made to appear so by the spokespersons.

The trend today, to conceal more than reveal the substance of important negotiations and conversations, may stem from the fact that the international situation is in a state of flux and we need to hedge issues to keep our options open. Many of our postures cannot be characterised as 'principled' any more. The communication revolution has also made it difficult to 'lie abroad' or even lie about what happens abroad. The prime minister himself has set the tone and it is followed down the line. Demands for explanations on foreign policy have dwindled because of the prominence that domestic issues have acquired in a pre-election year (2013-14).

One aspect of speaking softly is playing down tricky situations in public. The most eloquent example was characterising the Chinese incursion into the Indian side of the Line of Actual Control as an 'acne' that could be treated with a little ointment. This had no credibility because it was well-known that the Chinese had penetrated deep into our territory and were setting conditions of good behaviour for us in our own land. The sharp criticism against the Chinese action in other quarters was blunted by the official position. As a result, the solution of the issue, when it came, appeared effortless and the details of the concessions, if any, made by India were not fully revealed. The truth of the settlement terms still remains a mystery.

The meeting of the special representatives on the India–China border and the defence minister's visit to China seemed to have gone well, but there again, economy in words was the law. An incident on 17 June, in which Chinese soldiers took away cameras from an Indian post, was hushed up so as not to vitiate the atmosphere of the two visits. On the eve of the Indian defence minister's visit in 2013, a Chinese general wrote, 'The Indian side should not provoke new problems and increase military deployment in the border areas and stir up new trouble.' No Indian reaction to this untimely admonition was seen. Instead, the overwhelming sense after the two visits was that Sino-Indian relations were on the upswing, that the border issue would be resolved sooner rather than later. The reported progress on an agreement to maintain peace and tranquillity on the border, nothing but old wine in a new bottle, gave the impression that there would be rapid movement towards a settlement of the border. The defence minister was at his characteristic best in reporting progress without details. Progress there may well have been, but speaking softly on all these issues is likely to boomerang if the Chinese were to embark on their teaching-lessons policy once again. A reality check on Sino-Indian relations appears imperative.

The India–US strategic dialogue, by all accounts, accomplished little, but the new policy of reticence did not permit even a whimper of disappointment. Both sides said in private that the dialogue made no difference to the relationship, which had reached a plateau. Even the revelation that India was the fifth most-watched nation on the US intelligence list did not make waves during US Secretary of State John Kerry's visit in June 2013. Those who had anticipated that such a serious breach of faith, involving the direct surveillance of the Indian embassy in Washington, would lead to a strong protest were disappointed. Whatever may have happened behind closed doors, the public Indian pronouncement on the issue virtually condoned the incident as nothing out of the ordinary. Against the backdrop of cyber surveillance and cyberattacks assuming dangerous proportions, the softness of the Indian position was shocking. Turning down Edward Snowden's asylum request in July 2013 was appropriate. It was obviously a circular request sent to all democracies. But in the existing atmosphere of reticence, no elaborate explanation was given of the action.

The danger of speaking softly and playing down actual events can help create an atmosphere conducive to patient diplomacy, away from the glare of publicity. It also enables the government to pursue various options without pressure from public opinion. But the gap between perception and reality will widen, and in the process, the possibility of grave disillusionment will increase. Facts emanating from other sources may also embarrass the government, if the truth is not told. If speaking softly becomes a habit, without the accompanying big stick, it may be seen as weakness. At a time of shifting power equations, tough positions arising from strong convictions may be of greater advantage.

4

SELECTIVE ALIGNMENTS, NOT NON-ALIGNMENT

NonAlignment 2.0 was not born in the fertile minds of Khilnani, Kumar, Mehta, Menon, Nilekani, Raghavan, Saran and Varadarajan, the authors of a Centre for Policy Research (CPR) paper, but in a conference room in Accra, Ghana in 1991. At a Ministerial Conference of NAM there, the movement abandoned rejection of blocs as its central pillar and embraced development, human rights and environment as its testaments of faith. Politics, it was decided, would not be the preoccupation of NAM.

The Egyptian Foreign Minister Amre Moussa formally proposed that NAM be merged with G-77 as imperialism and colonialism were not the evils to fight against anymore. Finally, it was agreed that the new generation of non-alignment should focus on equity and justice in the economic order, human rights and the environment.

The reaction to the Accra rebirth of non-alignment was

rather negative among Indian writers, including, perhaps, some of the authors of the CPR paper. The argument that NAM was still relevant even in a unipolar configuration and that it should remain the voice of the developing world had no takers, but it was allowed to remain dormant except when Cuba, Venezuela or Iran revived it for US bashing purposes. India's own involvement with NAM became ritualistic and we pursued our own interests with no ideological obsessions or historical loyalties. While keeping away from its rhetorical assertions on non-proliferation, we associated ourselves with its declarations of one summit after another. NAM summits became non-events in the Indian calendar. G-20, IBSA, BRICS and ASEAN took precedence over NAM and even SAARC. Non-alignment became part of our political heritage, partly glorious, partly embarrassing, not in play in our big game for global status.

Now, many years later, the Centre for Policy Research has christened their paper on search for strategic autonomy 'NonAlignment 2.0', much to the consternation of the rest of the strategic community. A thoughtful and important policy paper has consequently got embroiled in controversy over its title. How could India embrace the very word that the Americans had just used in describing India's attitudes in the UN Security Council? A commentator called it Failure 2.0. The apparent blessings that the exercise received from Shivshankar Menon and his deputies added more mystery to the rebirth of non-alignment as the instrument of Indian foreign policy in the near term of ten to fifteen years, which the report says, is the 'narrow window' for India to succeed. The authors are hard at work to disown their own title and therefore, it should be set aside. They assert that strategic autonomy was the defining value and continuous goal of non-alignment and that they are merely renovating it.

The report is descriptive in its political sections and prescriptive, when it comes to economic issues. In politics, there is an eagerness to have continuity, but in the more successful area of economic policy, much remains to be done. The reason for this anomaly is not far to seek. The economic writers have been more distant from policymaking than the contributors of the political sections. The former have asserted right from the beginning that India's global goals are limitless if it can maintain high growth and maintain democratic institutions. Diplomacy is secondary in their calculations, but deficiencies in minor things too should be avoided. That the kingdom can be lost for want of a horseshoe nail is not just a nursery rhyme, it is a parable about the nature of power they assert.

Surprisingly, the report concedes, for the first time in Indian strategic writing, that China is already a superpower together with the US. When did the reality of G-2 hit our thinkers? When have we begun considering ourselves one of the 'other centres and hubs of power that will be relevant, particularly in regional context'? It looks as though the quest for a multipolar world, in which India plays a global role that K Subrahmanyam and others dreamt of, has been abandoned.

Having thus scaled down our ambition for a role in the world, the report claims that India is not seen as a threatening power except in our neighbourhood and that the rest of the world wants India to succeed. Indeed, Sweden, Argentina and Ghana are quite comfortable with us even if Pakistan, Nepal and Sri Lanka are not. In the same breath, the writers tell us that India is viewed as passive. In other words, India can neither hurt nor help anyone, not a particularly happy situation for a potentially powerful nation.

The threat from China is covered in subdued terms, but its power differential with India, the unlikelihood of the border issue being resolved swiftly, the asymmetry of our capabilities and deployments on the border, the projection of Chinese power in the Indian Ocean, the complex and ambiguous economic relations, the growing trade surplus etc. figure prominently in the report, but with inadequate analysis of these developments. Characterising Sino-Indian relations as the single most important challenge for Indian strategy in the years ahead, the only suggestion made is that India's China strategy should strike a balance between cooperation and competition, economic and political interests, bilateral and regional contexts. It is left to the imagination as to what can be done if such a balance cannot be achieved, a very likely scenario.

India's challenges in South Asia are described in starker terms in the report. The nature of politics and perceptions of India in our immediate neighbourhood not only make it hard for the countries in the region to act on policies of mutual benefit, but also place fetters on India's global ambitions. The report echoes the Gujral doctrine of giving unilateral concessions to its neighbours. Deepening economic engagement is the answer, even to counter the threat of Chinese engagement in the region. The Indian dilemmas in the neighbourhood cannot be resolved with any amount of strategic autonomy. Opportunities abound, but the challenges are equally formidable.

With Pakistan, the report rules out a historical breakthrough and expects incremental improvement as a result of constructive engagement. The US cannot persuade Pakistan to abandon terrorism and the Chinese shield to Pakistan is likely to be reinforced. A number of negative and positive levers have been suggested, but none of them is new and they can be applied only if opportunities present themselves. Restoring the strategic unity of South Asia remains a distant goal.

In West Asia, the suggestion is that India should engage with both, the lawfully constituted authority and the democratic forces, with a view to finding a political settlement. This easier said than done. How much can strategic autonomy help India to prevent external intervention? Equally hard will be for India to avoid sharp choices, like steering clear of the rivalry between Iran and Saudi Arabia.

The elaborate treatment in the report of the international institutions, hard power, internal security, non-conventional security issues, knowledge and information etc. must be studied separately. They are indeed weighty sections. The clarion call to India to rise with our clear values intact and not to fritter away India's enormous legitimacy, when seeking power. We should set new standards for what the most powerful must do.

The passion for strategic autonomy or a new generation of non-alignment, however, should not be the priority of the powerful. They hire and fire allies to suit their strategic objectives. India has already moved away from a pathological attachment to non-alignment and opted for selective alignments on the basis of mutual benefit, giving birth to alignments across geographical and ideological divides. To harp on the primacy of autonomy, to the exclusion of finding common cause with others is a sign of weakness and lack of self-confidence. The authors of the CPR report themselves have not been able to link every solution they suggest to strategic autonomy. Strategic autonomy comes automatically to the powerful. In the pursuit of power, selective alignments are more crucial than non-alignment.

5

FEDERALISM AND FOREIGN POLICY

Some years ago, I worked with a foreign secretary who believed that no Punjabi should deal with Pakistan and no Tamil should deal with Sri Lanka. In fact, when I offered to be posted to Sri Lanka, he told me that I should not go there because of my Tamil sounding name. I pleaded that the name was not uncommon in Kerala, but he said that it was not possible to convince every Tamil Tiger (LTTE cadre) and Sinhala extremist that I was not a Tamil. Today, he might say that no Bengali should deal with Bangladesh, no Bihari should deal with Nepal or Mauritius, nobody from the North-East should deal with China and no Malayalee should deal with the Gulf. Such are the interlinkages that have developed between our border states and our neighbours. The Indian states' concerns about our relations with these countries are so real that foreign policy can no longer be framed or practised without taking into account these state interests.

The constitutional position on foreign policy is crystal clear.

It is within the jurisdiction of the Centre and there is no mechanism to consult the states.

In his letters to the chief ministers, Pandit Nehru often took the regional leaders into confidence on some aspects of foreign policy, more to educate them than to consult them. Foreign policy advocacy by certain states was not uncommon even then. But with the advent of coalitions, in which the regional parties had the power to make and unmake governments, state leaders began to play a decisive role in foreign policy. With globalisation and economic reforms, ethnic, immigration and economic issues and even simple prejudices of regional leaders began to play a role. The most dramatic instances were of Mamata Banerjee holding up the Teesta water-sharing agreement with Bangladesh and Jayalalithaa and Karunanidhi pushing India to vote in favour of a US sponsored human rights resolution on Sri Lanka. Less dramatically, Maharashtra and Tamil Nadu slowed down the Jaitapur and Kudankulam nuclear projects, Odisha forced a revision of a South Korean project and Kerala made it hard for the Centre to deal with the Italian marines, who killed two fishermen off the cost of the state in February 2012.

The only way to deal with the situation is for the Centre to subsume the interests of the states. Coalition politics cannot be permitted to sway foreign policy beyond a point. Trade agreements are particularly important when products, which are special to different states, are covered in such agreements. The virtual veto given to the states on the issue of FDI in retail is a case in point.

Kashmir is, of course, a special case when it comes to foreign policy. The state leaders have always been consulted on our policy towards Pakistan. Moreover, the state has used our differences with Pakistan to push for its own autonomy in various ways. The special privileges that Kashmir enjoys are a consequence of our foreign policy preoccupations. The role that Hurriyat plays in relations with

Pakistan is significant. The All Parties Hurriyat Conference leaders meeting Pakistani leaders in India has almost become routine. In the name of Pakistani sensitivities, the state adopts positions, which the other states will not be permitted to do.

Of late, chief ministers and others have begun to visit foreign countries to canvass investments, to seek changes in immigration policies and to smoothen trade regulations. Increasingly, foreign dignitaries too have begun to visit the states to win potentially powerful regional leaders. Hillary Clinton chose to visit Mamata Banerjee and Jayalalithaa. She made a policy statement on the US rebalancing in the Pacific not from Delhi, but from Chennai. The consulates have stepped up their activities in several states. Requests for appointment of honorary consuls have multiplied. The states have also begun to push for internationalisation of education to gain benefits abroad.

Turning to Kerala, where I have lived for nearly ten years after leaving the Foreign Service, there has been sustained interest in foreign affairs, but it was confined to sending some Menons, Nairs and Panikkars to the South Block and trusting them to take care of Kerala's interests. Even today, Kerala pressurises the Centre to send Malayalee envoys to the Gulf, in the expectation that they would look after the labour from Kerala in those countries better. The possibility of the forced return of Kerala workers from the Gulf creates tremors and Kerala ministers rush to the Gulf even when the issues are dealt with by two central ministers from Kerala. At the time of the nuclear deal, the Left government in Kerala campaigned strongly against the deal and even adopted a resolution in the legislature against it. The same government raised alarm when a trade agreement between India and ASEAN came up. Kerala insisted that the bilateral relations between India and Italy should not be dragged into the legal case against the Italian marines. Even the United Front government, dominated by the Congress Party, felt deceived when its jurisdiction in the case was questioned. Kerala was confident that a settlement could be reached with the Italians with the help of the church, if the Centre had not intervened.

Intensive and continuous interaction between the Centre and the states is important to allay the fears of the states regarding foreign policy being made in Delhi. The Centre should be more sensitive to the needs and concerns of the states. Serving officers of the Ministry of External Affairs should brief think tanks and other groups, who are interested in foreign policy, through outreach programmes and provide provision of support to them for sustaining themselves. More courses should be started in international relations in the universities to enthuse youngsters. State media take interest in foreign affairs only when something of their immediate interest happens, and they tend to be negative about them. The successes in foreign policy elsewhere go unnoticed in the process.

Foreign policymaking cannot be shifted out of Delhi and the regional satraps should not be allowed to dominate foreign policy without the national perspective. But regional inputs should be integral to foreign policymaking at every step of the way.

6

THE BUSINESS OF EXPELLING EXCELLENCIES

We are not unfamiliar with stories of punishment being meted out to the messenger for the message that he has brought. Duryodhana ordered imprisonment of Krishna for the message that the Kauravas would be destroyed in the Kurukshetra war if they did not do justice to the Pandavas. Ravana ordered the lighting of Hanuman's tail for bringing the message that Lanka would be burnt down if Sita was not returned with honour. If they did not have supernatural powers, both these envoys extraordinary would have perished for no other crime than performing their duties. The messages would have, however, outlived the messengers.

The tradition of diplomats not engaging in public debate about sensitive subjects has been built over the years for the protection of the diplomats themselves, as they have nothing but the goodwill of the hosts to remain operational. But occasionally, they may need to express their governments' views in public in order to influence local public opinion. As long as we know that those views are not different from the views of their governments, chastising them on grounds of diplomatic impropriety is not a sign of maturity or strength. Action becomes legitimate only if such statements either distort the policy of their governments or incite apathy or violence in the host country.

The pattern of expulsion of diplomats around the globe reveals that it is often the weaker partner in a bilateral relationship that resorts to expulsion of diplomats to make a point. Expulsions on evidence of spying are another matter and cannot be challenged. When a country feels powerless to change the opinion of a foreign country, it feels tempted to use its prerogative to expel diplomats. Eventually the bilateral relationship gets repaired, but the diplomats concerned and their families get affected by the sudden dislocation and the adverse publicity. One consequence of such expulsions is that those declared persona non grata, even for technical reasons, are unable to get back to those countries. In the case of specialists, the expertise lost is regrettable to both the countries concerned.

In the case of the US Ambassador David Mulford, there is a virtual consensus that he should have shown greater sensitivity to public opinion in India. Clearly, he said things that Indians did not want to hear, even if he was speaking of the realities of the Washington power game. Unlike in India, actions of the government do not always receive the support even of the ruling party in the US Congress. The Congress not only approves policy, but also shapes it in significant ways.

The initial report appeared to suggest that Mulford was dictating Indian policy, how India should vote on the Iran nuclear issues. The text released by the US embassy, however, had none of the sting that was attributed to the scholarly ambassador. He clearly said that the September vote on Iran was not cast by India to please the United States. 'It was a vote that was based on India's judgment of its own national interest,' he said. He even quoted Indian interlocutors as telling him that India did not need another neighbour with nuclear weapons. As for the vote in February, India's decision, he said, 'can be left firmly in the hands of the Indian government to determine.'

Mulford spoke the truth, which was demonstrated earlier, that India's vote on Iran would have a bearing on the consideration of the civil nuclear agreement in the Congress. The unfortunate connotation of the word 'die' in the Congress must have been unintended as this is a phrase commonly used on the Hill, when no action is taken on a particular legislation. What he said about the impact of the vote on the Nuclear Suppliers Group (NSG) was also nothing but the truth.

That such truths need not have been uttered by the ambassador at a time public opinion in India was agitated over alleged aberrations in Indian foreign policy is preliminary. He also did not give any new information to the public as these were being written about widely in the Indian press. He simply provided fresh ammunition to the critics of the government, who directed some of the fire at the ambassador himself. Such indiscretions lead to a quiet and smooth transfer after the passions die down rather than in expulsions and withdrawals. Since he reflected Washington policy, no harm would come to Mulford even if he did not remain in Delhi.

In our own diplomatic service, we have had several instances of quiet transfers and even expulsions in similar circumstances. Since these are not always publicised, statistics are not available in one place. There have been the highly publicised reciprocal expulsions by India and Pakistan at lower levels. Reciprocal expulsions with friendly countries are done most discreetly and sometimes diplomats under orders of transfer are technically expelled to complete the quota. The expulsion of two of our diplomats from China during the Cultural Revolution was deliberately publicised by the Chinese. One of them left the Foreign Service as a result of the trauma, while the other rose to the highest level in the Service, though his expertise on China could not be fully utilised. Quiet advice by host governments and financial irregularities have brought back diplomats with little or no publicity. They will figure in the whispers in the South Block corridors for a time and then die out.

My own expulsion from Fiji in 1989 was a demonstration of Fiji's sense of insecurity vis-à-vis India. The reason given for my expulsion did not convince anyone because the speech I made on the occasion of the destruction of a gurdwara was designed not to incite communal passions. I had said that it was the result of racial disharmony rather than religious antipathy. By expelling me and by closing down the whole Indian mission later, Fiji lost considerable sympathy abroad. It was after repeated pleas that India agreed to reopen the mission after democracy was restored.

Diplomatic life has never been a bed of roses. Diplomats are exposed to slander, arrest, expulsion, physical attack and even assassination for no reason other than being the accredited representative of a country. The expulsion and counter-expulsion by the US and India of their diplomats may be linked in some way to their actions, but often the expulsion is a bolt from the blue. A classic case of expulsion was the ordering out of the Australian high commissioner in tiny Nauru for claiming the expenditure incurred by the Australians in erecting a lamp outside the high commissioner's residence as aid to Nauru. Nauru prides itself on never receiving any foreign assistance, and the Australian action was seen as a national insult, even though it is dependent on Australia for its very existence.

In the case of Devyani Khobragade, the expulsion came as a solution rather than as a provocation. A quiet withdrawal of the officer would have been a better solution than the series of events that rocked bilateral relations. The reciprocal expulsion of the US diplomat, it turns out, was more than deserved, as he had not only conspired to evacuate Indian nationals to the US on a false pretext, but had made no secret of his hatred of India and Indians.

If there is any truth in the reports that the American ire was more against India than against Khobragade, the tragedy of her treatment and expulsion become all the more sad. The bilateral relationship will recover, while she will be deprived of the opportunity to live in the US with her husband and children even after retirement.

Nobody senior from the Ministry of External Affairs showed up at the airport to receive her on her return. She must have also been advised not to speak to the media to avoid contradictory pieces of information coming out.

The distinction sought to be made between official and private activities with regard to consular immunity is patently unfair. A diplomat lives abroad simply because she is assigned there and her life cannot be divided into private and public. Immunity and compensation should cover all activities, regardless of the venue and nature of the event involved.

Lack of public sympathy for diplomats, who are seen as privileged and spoiled, is universal. Even those who enjoy multiple supporting staff at public expense in India sneer at one domestic assistant that diplomats are permitted. Drivers and cars are provided only to the heads and posts abroad, while civil servants in India take such facilities for granted even at junior levels. Diplomats with no support systems abroad should be treated with the same concern as soldiers in the frontline.

India has had its share of martyr diplomats, some murdered, some brutally attacked, some insulted and expelled and some quietly whisked away. India has reacted differently to different cases, without a formula to nurse the survivors back to normalcy or to ensure that their careers are not affected adversely.

There is no grievance mechanism to deal with the trauma, or to compensate the diplomats for their pain and suffering. Each finds her own way to contend with problems arising out of armed attacks or expulsions. No record is available in the public domain of the concessions or compensation given to the affected members of the service. Such information may be of some comfort for those who face danger in the line of duty.

The time has come to ensure that we reduce the number of diplomatic martyrs and have a formula to treat those affected with sympathy and magnanimity.

7

IFS AS A CAREER FOR THE NEXT GENERATION

A bewildering array of opportunities beckons the young people of India today. Making the right choice of discipline in the university, choosing a career in the public or the private sector and deciding to live in India or abroad are options they face. Ability, aptitude and inclination are crucial factors in making these choices. Equally important is the awareness of the merits and demerits of each option.

Even after the advent of immense possibilities in the private sector, the fascination for serving the government has not abated. A fair and transparent method of selection, the sense of security, the assurance of equal opportunity and the prestige of authority attract young people to the Civil Services. There too, they face a difficult choice of services, particularly those who secure high ranks in the examination.

As someone who spent thirty-seven years in the IFS and is still following developments in diplomacy, I have become an evangelist for the IFS and I have no hesitation to say that for a young person with talent and a spirit of adventure, the Foreign Service can be an exciting career. When I see the diminishing enthusiasm for the IFS, I remember a story of my days in the Soviet Union.

If you asked anyone in the Soviet Union what he thought of Pasternak's *Dr Zhivago*, he would say it was a horrible novel. If asked whether he had read the book, he would say no. In other words, he simply parroted an opinion fed to him without checking it himself.

The same thing happens when I ask young aspirants to the Civil Services as to why they do not opt for the Indian Foreign Service. They admit that they do not know much about the IFS, but they know it is not for them. They like the authority and glamour of what they have seen of the IAS and the IPS, but do not realise that greater opportunities await them in a diplomatic career.

As a result, the top service of the country has no takers among those who are on the top of the Civil Services list. From a time when those below the twentieth position could not aspire to the IFS, we have come to a stage when even those below rank 200 can get in. A lack of awareness and the fear of the unknown are responsible for this sad state of affairs at a time when foreign policy has become more complex and we need our best brains to run our diplomacy.

The greatest charm of the IFS is the opportunity it affords to represent our nation in the chancelleries of the world, at the United Nations and other multilateral organisations. No one can aspire to a finer moment than the one when you get to speak for India at the General Assembly or the Security Council. Your individual identity merges with the identity of a nation and your voice becomes the voice of a billion people.

A diplomat, they say, is an honest gentleman, who lies abroad for his country, but after the information revolution, one can hardly lie. But living abroad in different countries, getting exposed to different civilisations, learning the nuances of languages, customs and manners and savouring the flavours of multiple cuisines are delights that only a Foreign Service career can offer. One has to live in rich and poor countries and different climatic conditions, but they average out to comfortable living in mean temperatures.

To drive past the imperial palace in Tokyo, the Dzong in Thimphu, the Kremlin in Moscow, the Empire State Building in New York, the White House in Washington, the Hoffburg Palace in Vienna, the Golden Pagodas of Yangon, the lion sanctuary in Nairobi and the lovely beaches of Fiji every day to work, as I have done, is exciting. People spend their earnings of a lifetime to have a glimpse of these attractions, but you are paid to live in their vicinity. You dine with kings, queens, presidents, prime ministers and foreign ministers and do business with the high and the mighty on a daily basis. You get to play golf in Scotland, tennis in Queens and soccer in Brazil. Everyone will agree that this is a life that dreams are made on.

But the questions that haunt our young people are more mundane. Are we paid enough to live in such exotic places? Will we have savings? How will we cope with the culture shock and stresses and strains of moving from country to country? What about family life and children's education? What about the threat of terrorism and other dangers? What about the temptations of various kinds in Western societies? Is there enough important work to do in our missions? Will we be alienated from India and lose our roots?

The one answer to all these questions is that none of these are a matter of concern. IFS officers are paid a foreign allowance and an entertainment allowance calculated on the basis of the living index of each city fixed by the United Nations, in addition to free and furnished accommodation and totally free medical assistance.

Reasonable savings are possible from the emoluments. Strength of character is essential as much in the IFS as in other areas to withstand the strains and to resist temptations. Facilities for families are provided, except at a very few non-family stations and the government bears the cost of educating children in the best schools in every city. Diplomats are as much exposed to terrorism and other dangers as their counterparts in India.

As for the nature of work, it is true that professional achievements are more nebulous in the IFS than in domestic services. Diplomats cannot point to a bridge or road that he got built or an institution he created. But every input that an IFS officer provides through his study, conversations and analyses goes into policymaking. Most diplomats live abroad in Indian homes with Indian décor and cuisine, thanks to the Indian domestic help provided free of cost. Moreover, they have opportunities to come to India between postings and once during the three-year term. In other words, most diplomats maintain strong links with home and invariably return to India and even to their hometowns. They are much sought-after for their exposure and expertise to write on global issues, and to provide advice to global operations.

On balance, the challenges in the Foreign Service are no more than those in other walks of life and the charms are many more. The more you know about the Foreign Service, the more comfortable you feel about choosing it as a vocation. Ultimately, it is a matter of taste and talent. If you are looking for a glamorous, exciting and meaningful life with infinite variety; if you are willing to learn languages, history and civilisations all your life; if the trappings of power do not fascinate you, IFS should be your choice. You may have reasons not to choose it, but it should be an educated and informed choice. I must confess that my choice forty years ago was not well-informed. I went by a role model, an IFS officer, who did well, but fell victim to the bullets of a deranged person at the prime of his career. But if I am faced with the same choices as I did in 1966, I shall have no hesitation in choosing the Foreign Service. The charms far outweigh the challenges and very often, the very challenges turn out to be the charms of the diplomatic service.

Vibheeshana

India in a Tough Neighbourhood

Vibheeshana, the noble half-brother of the ignoble Ravana, was a principled, benign and brave hero, a 'deva' among the asuras. The battleground of the seventy-five-day war between Rama and Ravana witnessed Vibheeshana's rise to immortality through his pursuit of righteousness. Several commentators of the epic have concluded that Vibheeshana is the most meritorious and sublime character in the *Ramayana*. After Rama's victory, Vibheeshana was ordained the king of Lanka. India's nationhood borne on dharma, righteousness and non-violence reflects the nobility and devotion towards truth that Vibheeshana stood for. In the Yudhakanda of *Ramayana*, a conversation with Hanuman has an anguished Vibheeshana grieving that he is like a tongue surrounded by sharp teeth on all sides, implying that he is the sole individual surrounded by wicked rakshasas in his family and neighbourhood. India's geostrategic woes appear to be similar, with India being the peace-loving nation in the midst of a number of small states, which are paranoid about India's strength and growth. Hanuman's reply to the grouse is quite buoyant though. He says that the tongue came first, the teething took place gradually afterwards; and the teeth are bound to fall in due course, whereas the tongue is there to stay!

The unequivocal fact that India is the world's largest functioning democracy, despite all the tumult and trauma it has been subjected to from within and without, speaks volumes of the strength of its soul as a nation. India has displayed a great deal of resilience in the face of calamities and withstood all temptations to eschew values, as is evident in her crucial decisions to maintain dialogue even with the more recalcitrant neighbours.

Caught in the clutches of internal security concerns, gripped by the claws of scheming neighbours, it has been a bumpy ride for India for the past six decades. With its rapid economic and military rise and dictatorial political climate, China's aggressive pursuit of global dominance contrasts with India's peace-loving posture and democracy.

This section brings a range of articles on India's challenges in dealing with its tough neighbourhood, her geostrategic importance in the new multipolar world and the Asia-Pacific, its various successes and failures and the way forward. TP Sreenivasan, who has served in Bhutan and Burma and also in the foreign secretary's office, has a deep insight into India's complex relations with its neighbours.

***

1

INDIA AND HER NEIGHBOURS

May 1998 was, to borrow TS Eliot's famous phrase, 'the cruellest month' in India–US relations. The news of the birth of a nuclear India came like 'lilacs out of the dead land', but it brought about the bitterest phase in India–US relations. Perhaps, for the first time in history, diplomats of two democracies sat across the table with nothing to say. President Clinton used the exact words about India, which President Obama used later in the context of Iran's nuclear programme, 'We will come down on them like a ton of bricks.' Long-term friends of India turned against us and the Glenn Amendment sanctions kicked in with unpredictable consequences. It was then that the sane words of Henry Kissinger, no great friend of India, broke the eerie silence. 'India lives in a tough neighbourhood,' he said. Those words opened the eyes of India's friends and foes in the US and the dialogue began. The rest is history.

'Tough neighbourhood' is an evocative American expression, which describes a phenomenon present in many American cities. Just a few blocks from the prosperous cities with gleaming skyscrapers and charming fountains, you find settlements with dilapidated homes and listless youth roaming the streets. The limos drive past these streets fast, but they rarely stop and if others have to go to these neighbourhoods, they never go without a weapon to defend themselves. In one phrase, Kissinger aptly described India's situation and justified its acquisition of nuclear weapons. The question he asked was how tough India should be to deal with its tough neighbourhood.

Kissinger was not referring to an unnecessary fear psychosis. He was referring to two of our neighbours, China and Pakistan, who were already in nuclear collusion, had fought wars with India and had not shown any sign of giving up their aggressive pursuit of their claims on Indian territory. A nuclear deterrent was more than justified. But the nuclear capability alone has not ended the enormous challenges India faces even today in its neighbourhood. It is not the threat of aggression in various forms alone that demand vigilance, strength, imagination and diplomacy on the part of India.

In an old Polish joke, students ask the teacher who are the friends of Poland. The teacher promptly replies, 'India, the US, France etc.' The students are intrigued and ask, 'How about the Soviet Union?' 'Oh the Soviet Union, that is a brother, not a friend. Friends, we can choose, brothers we cannot.' The same is true of our neighbours. You cannot choose them. Nor can you abandon them even if they turn against you. This is a reality we must acknowledge.

Contradictions, disparities and paradoxes characterise our neighbourhood. It is a world of shared legacies, historical links and common interests over the centuries. But, at the same time, all the curses of the modern world are present here, including interstate and internal wars, nuclear rivalry, military coups, insurgencies, terrorism and drug trafficking. India is the only stable state in South Asia, an uninterrupted democracy, with borders with every neighbour. The others do not share borders, except Pakistan and Afghanistan.

India's enhanced economic strength should logically benefit its neighbours. The global Indian brand should benefit them as seen in Pakistani, Bangladeshi and Sri Lankan restaurants abroad, parading their delicacies as Indian cuisine. But paradoxically, all of them, even Bhutan, pride themselves in their independence from India and constantly create issues that require urgent solutions.

Paradoxically again, it is fashionable for commentators in India and abroad to observe that India has neglected its backyard. Neither Indira Gandhi's insistence on reciprocity, nor Inder Gujral's doctrine of unilateral concessions has been applauded. The entire spectrum of our relationships, with Pakistan at one end and Bhutan at the other, is attributed to India's inept and insensitive handling of its neighbours.

But the truth is that India has an impeccable record in dealing with the complex issues in its neighbourhood at considerable cost to itself, with a policy of constructive engagement at all times and non-interference in their internal affairs, except when dictated by the possibility of their actions impinging on our national interests. None of the conflicts with Pakistan or China was India's creation and Indian bloodshed in Bangladesh and Sri Lanka was not on account of any expansionist design. A long list of Indian concessions can be cited from the Indus Waters Treaty to Pakistan, Kachativu Island to Sri Lanka, Teen Bigha corridor to Bangladesh and others. Historical treaties have been amended to accommodate the nationalistic aspirations of our neighbours. We have consistently supported their initiatives in the United Nations like those dealing with the rights of landlocked countries and small island states. Even with Pakistan and China, India has been willing to go the extra mile to be reasonable, logical and fair. No hand of cooperation, extended bilaterally or in SAARC with regard to trade, environment and human rights has been turned away. We have sought joint exploration of the economic potential of the region. India has not hesitated to deal with any regime in our neighbourhood, whether it is democracy, dictatorship, military rule or others even when the advent of these regimes meant extreme hardship to India, like it happened in Burma in 1962, when we had to rehabilitate thousands of Indians, who were forced out, leaving their belongings behind. We have been generous in economic assistance without strings to several of our neighbours. Investments have contributed to regional integration.

History is replete with India's goodwill gestures to every country in the region, in the alphabetical order, from Afghanistan to Sri Lanka. India is the largest investor in Afghanistan, regardless of its uncertain political future. Twenty million illegal immigrants from Bangladesh have found their homes in India. The Treaty with Bhutan was revised to reaffirm its independence, sovereignty and territorial integrity. Tibet was recognised as part of China in 2003, thus giving up the Dalai Lama card, which we could have played. In an agreement with Maldives in 2011, India has taken over the responsibility of the maritime surveillance of the islands. India has not only recognised the military regime in Myanmar, but has also extended assistance to its armed forces. Nepal enjoys major concessions on trade and transit without concomitant commitments from our Himalayan neighbour. The peace process, which began with Pakistan in 2003 after the Kargil war was itself a major gesture, which was, unfortunately jeopardised by the Mumbai attacks. Even after the civil war in Sri Lanka, which decimated the Tamils, we are committed to rebuilding the war-torn regions. The list is endless. India has been not only tolerant, but also benevolent towards its neighbours.

But peace and good relations cannot be built by India alone. Much depends on the mindset of our neighbours and the role that external forces play in the region. The legacy left by Britain of a divided South Asia, with seeds of conflict is a major factor. Except for

China, all our neighbours are minuscule, compared with India, with a built-in fear psychosis in them, which projects India as a regional hegemony. In the case of Pakistan, disputes with India give it an existential anchor, an illusion of equality with India and serve as an excuse for securing military and financial support from the US and China. For China, India is a rival for the global dominance it seeks. For Sri Lanka, India is a hindrance to its plans of suppressing the Tamil minority. Just because these problems are not creations of India, we cannot resolve them, even with the best of intentions. We can only manage our neighbourhood with deftness, creativity, compassion and firmness. Indian foreign policy cannot resolve the multifarious internal contradictions within our neighbours, which motivate their actions. What we can hope for is a region free of conflicts and tensions, which will not adversely affect our development.

By inviting the heads of state of the SAARC countries and Mauritius to his swearing-in in 2014, the Indian Prime Minister Narendra Modi not only asserted India's role in the region and extended a hand of friendship, he essentially conveyed his readiness and willingness to contribute to regional cooperation if our neighbours abandon past animosities and turn over a new leaf with India. This was well-begun, but only half-done. India cannot unilaterally impose friendship on its neighbours.

The big question is whether the economic compulsions of the region can remove deep-rooted political tensions. We cannot pin much hope on this seemingly logical question, as developments thereafter do not give reason for optimism. India's phenomenal economic growth in the nineties roused only envy and renewed fear in our neighbours. China's economic growth has made it only more assertive. With India, China is pursuing economic cooperation without an iota of political concession. Its invitation to attend the APEC meeting or the establishment of the BRICS Bank appears friendly, but they seem to have no political meaning in terms of bilateral relations. India has taken many economic initiatives like the offer of trade agreements with Sri Lanka, Bangladesh and Pakistan and involvement in Nepal's economic recovery. Regardless of immediate success of these initiatives, India realises, as pointed out by a Chatham House paper, that, 'India's long-term prosperity hinges to some degree on a conflict free neighbourhood and an economically integrated region is in India's overall interest.' This can happen only on the day India's neighbours begin to perceive their own stake in India's strength and prosperity. That day, unfortunately, is on the distant horizon.

2

MORE CONTINUITY THAN CHANGE

As India moves towards the formation of a new government, there is much speculation about the shape of its foreign policy. Many ideas are in the air to revamp policy, reshape institutions, including the Indian Foreign Service, and to open new chapters in relations with the neighbours and major powers. They will invent catchy phrases and innovative concepts to be flaunted at press conferences. But once the initial euphoria is over and the new government settles down to business, there is likely to be continuity rather than change. It would be old wine, even if it is in a new bottle.

No government makes foreign policy in solitary splendour. In fact, the concept of independent foreign policy itself is misleading, as it should suit not only the originator, but also its 'consumers', who are independent countries themselves, with their own strategic priorities. Constant changes will be needed in foreign policy to resonate with others. Totally unexpected events may overturn carefully crafted policies overnight. The broad policies and strategy, outlined by any government will not be different from the traditional foreign policy, which has enjoyed general consensus. Here, the insights, judgments and instincts of professional diplomats will prevail, as has been seen at the time of changes in the past.

The announcement by the Morarji government of 'genuine non-alignment' and the Vajpayee government of nuclear weapon status for the country are being pointed out as instances of fundamental changes brought about by new governments in their initial stages. But neither of these were fundamental or unanticipated. 'Genuine non-alignment' simply meant distancing the country from the Soviet Union, but the government soon discovered the true extent of our involvement with the Soviet Union and quietly went about its business with the Soviet Union as usual. Morarji went to Moscow to dilute the relationship with Moscow, but came back even without disowning the 1971 Treaty of Friendship and Cooperation.

The nuclear tests of 1998 were not made in a day. Successive governments, right from the days of Pandit Nehru, had maintained the nuclear option and made heavy investments in explosive technology. The experiment in 1974 was nothing short of a step towards weaponisation. It is very well-known that PV Narasimha Rao had scheduled tests and pulled back for fear of economic sanctions. The timing of the tests in 1998 was determined more by the international situation arising out of the provisions of the CTBT than by any ideology. India chose to face sanctions after testing rather than face them for not signing the CTBT. The main proponents of the test were Brajesh Mishra and K Subrahmanyam, who were strategists, not politicians. The fact that the subsequent governments endorsed the tests is enough proof of continuity in nuclear policy. Rumours about the possibility of a new government reviewing India's non-first use doctrine provoked widespread reaction from strategists. The proposal appears to have been dropped.

Practical matters, rather than ideology, have determined our relations with our neighbours, including Pakistan. Changes in policy were triggered by negative reaction from our neighbours. Every possibility has been explored in different shades of our policy ranging from the tough Indira doctrine to the soft Gujral doctrine. No government has advocated war as an option against Pakistan. The Kargil war came after the biggest peace offensive by the Vajpayee government and with all its tough talk, the Indian side refrained from crossing the Line of Control. A new government may criticise Manmohan Singh's 'extra mile' policy, but it will not go beyond reciprocity, as war is not an option between the two nuclear-armed neighbours.

Changes in nuances in Sri Lanka policy will depend on where the two Kazhagams will stand in the new dispensation. But even if a prime minister emerges from those two parties, there will only be war of words, not intervention on behalf of the Tamils. India has tried every trick in the book from equipping the LTTE to fighting it. New initiatives are hard to find when the Sri Lankan government believes that it has solved the Tamil issue. The case is not dissimilar with the other neighbours. The more concessions we give, the more will be asked for; the more we deny, the more blackmailing will be resorted to. We shall see more of the same pressures and pulls under any government in Delhi.

The Vajpayee cabinet had at least one member, who characterised China as 'enemy number one'. Vajpayee himself took Bill Clinton into confidence about the threat from China. But the same government sought a strategic dialogue with China. Manmohan Singh has dealt with China with restraint despite provocations on the logic that China is too big to threaten India. The dragon may well have become vegetarian to make its rise peaceful. No political party has an alternate formula for China. A new government may give defence preparedness more stress, but it will not be more assertive with China than its predecessor.

The relations with the US will be high priority for any government. It will look urgently into the points of irritation, but it will soon find that the issues are intractable. The grievances that the US has against India, like the nuclear liability act, the fighter aircraft issue and liberalisation of the economy to protect the US interests are not easy to deal with. But friendly gestures in Asia-Pacific, such as joint exercises with the US, Japan and Australia will offer sufficient compensation for the US. A new government will have the advantage of being able to distance itself from the Khobragade fiasco and begin relations afresh. But any government, even with participation of the Left, will work hard to improve relations with the only superpower.

Indications of institutional changes, hinted by some political parties, betray lack of insight. Diplomats have been handling economic and trade issues for years, but merging the External Affairs Ministry with the Trade Ministry will have adverse implications for both. Long-term policy planning and strategic thinking, which, according to some American scholars, are lacking in India, will be tried, but soon routine issues will once again dominate foreign relations. No one disputes assigning a greater role for military leaders in policy and doctrines, but equally important is the civilian control of defence. Regional satraps may become prominent if we get a multiparty coalition, but they will not be allowed to dabble in foreign policy beyond a point.

Change will be part of the agenda of any government that comes to power in India later this month. A dream foreign policy that enhances India's power and prestige will be part of it. But, as Barrack Obama found out in the US, the power to change is not limitless, especially in foreign policy. Moreover, the wish lists that they will have to deal with domestically will be enormous and pressing. After the initial declarations of innovative policies potential policymakers will be hatching now, the new government will reconcile themselves to the realities. It is likely to focus on the primary purpose of foreign policy, which is to ensure peaceful domestic development. The devil in the detail may change colours, but the framework will be hard to change.

3

THE NOBEL PRIZE SYNDROME

When politicians grow into eminent statesmen, they develop an intense desire for immortality. Their place in history becomes more important than solution of the mundane issues of the day. Their world expands to embrace universal objectives that transcend national aspirations. Some of them step on to the world stage and make outlandish proposals at the United Nations for international peace, disarmament and development. Proposals for bringing celestial bodies and even Unidentified Flying Objects (UFOs) within the purview of the United Nations have originated from the seekers of global fame. The more ambitious among them go on a quest for the Holy Grail, the Nobel Peace Prize.

India–Pakistan relations are so complex that anyone who can assist in normalising them is likely to be honoured by the Norwegian Academy. The acquisition of the nuclear dimension to the quagmire has made peace imperative between them, in the eyes of the world. Many consider Kashmir a global hotspot, which deserves a global solution. Even President Bill Clinton had eyed Kashmir as a potential road to the Nobel. In India, Morarji Desai (He even tried to dilute India's opposition to the NPT), Inder Gujral and Atal Bihari Vajpayee had developed such ambitions. What held them back was the pressure of public opinion. Their efforts were also thwarted by the duplicity of Pakistan, which gained benefits, but refused to accept matching obligations.

The signs of the Nobel Prize syndrome gripping Prime Minister Manmohan Singh have been visible since the Havana Declaration, which, for the first time, conceded that Pakistan too was a victim of terrorism. Sharm-el-Sheikh statement remains the only document in which Baluchistan came within the purview of bilateral relations. India gradually relaxed the conditions it imposed on Pakistan to deal with the schemers and perpetrators of the Mumbai attack. The tough line on terrorism withered away as the peace process gained momentum. The invitation extended to Pakistan Home Minister Rehman Malik and resumption of sports and cultural contacts were also part of 'the extra mile' theory. But none can point to a single matching initiative on the part of Pakistan. They appeared to respond to the friendly moves of India but plotted at the same time to undermine the Indian state, covertly and overtly. The most blatant was the intrusion in Kargil, coming as it did close on the heels of the Lahore bus yatra. Making the border soft resulted only in more intrusions and arrival of more terrorists.

The desire to build on the gains of the peace process was the sentiment that determined initial Indian reaction to the events of 8 January 2013. The tame response at the official level left the field open for the opposition to claim to know the pulse of the people and to project public opinion. If only the prime minister had spoken of 'no business as usual' within hours of the report on killing of two soldiers, he would have retained the initiative in his own hand. If he had promised firm action, the baying for 'ten heads for one' by opposition leader Sushma Swaraj would not have resonated so well within the nation. She would have sounded irrational if the peace process was halted on the first day. Each day lost added fuel to the fire of public opinion and Pakistan exulted in its denial, without any fear of retribution. They knew well that the image-makers of the prime minister would turn the other cheek. When he finally spoke up, Pakistan had no choice but to budge and agree to commit itself to observe the ceasefire.

The 'peace industry' in India has done more damage than good to India–Pakistan relations. South Block is constantly at pains to satisfy the peaceniks and many fall prey to the attractions of the industry, like fully paid trips not just to Pakistan but also to more attractive destinations. Since the army is recognised as the real source of power in Pakistan, it has become fashionable to invite former generals to these parleys. Many former generals masquerade as civil society in Pakistan, but make no impact on public opinion within Pakistan. On our side, however, the pressure mounts for a soft approach towards Pakistan each time a Track II exercise throws up solutions. The shrill clamour for finding solutions to issues like Siachen and Sir Creek is raised from time to time, raising false hopes that these can be resolved. Siachen has been described as the only substantial military gain that India has made and the call is to throw it away unilaterally. Shimla's lessons have not been learnt.

The truth that Pakistan's existence itself is conditional to its differences with India should be remembered every time we deal with Pakistan. It has no compulsions to make peace with India. By paying a small price, Pakistan has acquired equal status with India in the minds of people across the globe. The peace process gives Pakistan a benign image even as it schemes to undermine the Indian state through infiltration and terrorism. Even when blatant violations of ceasefire take place, the peace industry is willing to ask whether, after all, India had pulled the trigger first. It is willing to close its eyes to the fact that the beheading incident was not just a case of ceasefire violation, but a highly humiliating act that demoralised our fighting forces.

The call on India is often to do everything possible to strengthen democracy in Pakistan. Even if the theory that a strong and prosperous Pakistan is in the interest of India is accepted, India can do little to strengthen democracy in Pakistan. Looking for democracy in Pakistan is like looking for the proverbial non-existent black cat in a dark room. Successive democratic governments in Pakistan have either been facades or apologists for the army. Pakistan has only denigrated Indian democracy and not tried to learn from it.

The lessons of the past dictate that our Pakistan policy should be based strictly on reciprocity. Unilateral concessions have never yielded benefits in the past and will not in the future. If we relax on past crimes, new crimes will follow. As in the case of beheading, Pakistan is guilty of a multitude of crimes, which should be accounted for. Any misguided forgiveness will only encourage the Pakistan Army to commit worse atrocities.

India's reluctance to call a spade a spade is not on account of fear of a nuclear war. We have always believed that the most inextricable of issues can be resolved through negotiations. But, in case of Pakistan, final solutions may not be possible for any of the problems that bedevil our relations for another generation. Our best hope is to manage the relations in such a way that our vital interests are protected. Strict reciprocity is the only strategy that will work with Pakistan.

4

SINO-INDIAN RELATIONS: INSCRUTABILITY, THY NAME IS CHINA

When I wrote about China in December 2010, soon after the visit of the Chinese prime minister to India, it unexpectedly provoked a response from the *Global Times*, the voice of China. I had then said, 'We have assurances from those who know China well that1962 will not happen again. They contend that China is no more an isolated dragon.... As it has grown large and powerful, it has become domesticated and would like to tango with the elephant. The elephant can relax in the thought that the dragon will not step on its toes or its fiery breath will not incinerate it.' I went on to say, however, that there was clear evidence to show that there were more contentious issues between the two countries in 2010 than in 1962. I made a list of the issues that provoked a war in 1962 and a list of issues that plagued the relationship in 2010, and drew the obvious conclusion that the second list was longer. In addition to the land occupied by China in

Ladakh and Kashmir, their claim of Arunachal Pradesh, the stapled visa, more nuclear stations for Pakistan and the disappearance of 1,600 km of border between India and China in Chinese maps. The only silver lining was that India and China were cooperating at the international fora. 'Otherwise, those who know China would not be complacent enough to think that the Chinese threat is an illusion,' I concluded. In a sharp reaction to my article, the *Global Times* said, 'Some people in India continue to make provocative statements with regard to China–India relations. A few days ago, former Indian ambassador, Mr TP Sreenivasan made an irresponsible assertion that the future of China–India relations is bound to result in conflict. He also said that "the current state of China–India relations is even worse than 1962."' The *Global Times* did not deny the points raised by me, but quoted the then Foreign Secretary Nirupama Rao and our president to the effect that the friendly relations between the two peoples would last for generations.

One of the many occasions when India and China worked together in the twenty-first century was at the Durban conference on climate change. The Chinese delegate was the first to support our environment minister when she said that India would not surrender the principle of burden sharing between rich and poor. 'We should maintain the principle of common, but differentiated responsibility,' said the Chinese delegate. But a close examination of the Chinese position since the Rio summit of 1992 will show that China has been hiding behind India in the climate talks, while increasing its CO_2 emissions, reaching a higher level of emissions than the US. China's share in emissions is 23 per cent, while the US has 18.11 per cent and India's share is only 5.78 per cent. Our argument of per capita emissions suited China and it argued for equity, but it worked closely with the developed countries before and during the 2009 Copenhagen conference for a new consensus on climate, which eventually resulted in the virtual rejection of the 1997 emission trading Kyoto Protocol. Faced with the possibility of being subjected to mandatory cuts in emissions, China decided to let the US off the hook. It was the shift in the Chinese position that resulted in a Copenhagen package, which was rejected by most developing countries. China hides behind India in the environment debate, but works with the developed world to protect its own interests.

The situation is not very dissimilar in the case of trade, another area in which India and China cooperate in the multilateral system. Both India and China are committed to an open, fair, equitable, transparent and rule-based multilateral trading system, in cooperation with other developing countries. We demand measures to eliminate trade distortions and to open their markets. At the same time, China has itself imposed trade restrictions on certain items in India and built up a trade imbalance with us. Even while professing solidarity with the developing countries, China has been making deals with the developed countries to develop its own trade.

In fact, the fundamental posture that China adopts in the UN is that it is uncompromisingly on the side of the developing countries. The joke is that a Chinese representative said that 'China is a developing country and it shall always remain one.' China sees itself as a developing country and identifies itself with the G-77 without becoming a member. Even when it is vying for the position of world's number one with the US and hobnobbing with the other permanent members, it finds it convenient to have the developing country image. The celebrated Chinese veto against Waldheim over and over again, when he sought a third term as the UN Secretary General, endeared China to the developing world. There are other examples of this kind. But China rarely confronts the Western P-3 and has developed the practice of abstention, which, in effect, is a positive vote. The Security Council Charter prescribes that concurring votes of the five permanent members are necessary to adopt a resolution, but many crucial resolutions, including the last one on Libya, were adopted with Chinese abstentions. The double face of China in the UN needs no further elaboration.

As members of the Asian Group, India and China often come face to face for posts in which both are interested, and in the name of cooperation, we make adjustments and let China retain positions for years together. In 2011, however, India decided to challenge China's effort to retain a position on the Joint Inspection Unit, after serving on it for ten years continuously. India had not served on it since 1977 and was fully entitled to it on the basis of rotation. Even though the Chinese candidate happened to be the Chinese Ambassador to India, we decided to contest and won it with a clear majority. I am sure that China must have played its solidarity card to persuade India to withdraw. Our victory in the first ever direct contest between India and China was indeed a landmark for us in the UN. The presumption that a permanent member can win any election was proved wrong several times in the case of the US because it often takes positions against developing countries, but this is the first time that another developing country confronted China and defeated it, showing that the world at large has begun to question China's profession of being a champion of the developing world.

China's position on the expansion of the Security Council is a classic case of double talk. China professes that it supports the interests of the developing countries, most of whom wish to see an expansion. In the case of India, China maintains that it wants India to play a bigger role in the Security Council. But China has not even gone as far as the US in support of the Indian aspiration. China hides behind the US in its opposition to the expansion of the Security Council and it will not hesitate to use the veto if the situation warrants it. China is firm in its position as a permanent member and acts in that spirit even when giving lip service to G-77 solidarity.

As I contemplate upon the aforesaid instances of conflicts

and cooperation between India and China, there is one phrase that comes to my mind as tailor-made for China—Inscrutability, Thy Name Is China!

The world has long recognised that China behaves in enigmatic ways and has accepted that we do not know enough about its history, language and temperament to explain its actions. Such a reputation gives China the freedom to do what it wants internally and externally, without having to explain its actions. The onus is on others to fathom the true intentions of China and rationalise its actions. China merely carries on in its own inimitable ways, asserting its rights as the Middle Kingdom, trampling upon the rights of its own citizens and of other countries and peoples. The world breathlessly awaits a handshake here, a smile there or an aphorism here to figure out the real meaning of China's words and deeds.

The Sinology industry has assumed the dimensions of Kremlinology industry of the past. The constant refrain from this exalted group is that there should be more Confucius Centres, Chinese language institutes and China chairs to learn about China. The secret of Chinese actions, they say, lies in the unravelling of its history, language and philosophy. While the Chinese are busy learning English to compete for world leadership, we are being exhorted to learn Chinese to understand Chinese actions.

Many years of Chinese studies have not made us any wiser, though. We have still not analysed fully what the purport was of the Chinese claim that it was merely teaching India a lesson in 1962, at a time when India was helping it secure a rightful place in the world. The phrase came up again when the Dalai Lama was about to visit Arunachal Pradesh. Does it mean that India has not yet learnt the Chinese lesson? If so, we need to fathom the lesson before hoping to have normal relations with China. The lesson was administered to us at a time when India was at the forefront of the struggle to secure for China its rightful place in the world. Our vision of Afro-Asian solidarity, anchored on close Sino-Indian cooperation was very much in evidence at that time. Whether China intended it or not, the lesson we should have learnt was that China's pursuit of domination is not tempered by any atmosphere of friendliness that we create.

Many more events in Sino-Indian relations remain unexplained and we do accept that the Chinese will never explain them. Our response is generally bewilderment first, self-accusation second and then finding a temporary solution that fits the Chinese agenda. Nothing is resolved finally, but we pursue our friendship moves in the expectation that an atmosphere of trust will prevent unfriendly moves in the future. We find common cause with the Chinese at the United Nations, not on our priority of reform of the Security Council, but on trade and environment, in which China gains by its partnership with India. We open up our markets for their consumer goods, intrusive IT tools and boast of $100 billion trade figures all in favour of the Chinese. Our comfort zone is not disturbed till we come across another unfriendly act, much to our surprise.

We do not know why China invaded Vietnam when the Indian external affairs minister was on Chinese soil. That Atal Bihari Vajpayee (Minister in 1979) had to leave suddenly made no impact on the Chinese and no explanation was offered for the lesson taught to Vietnam. We do not know why China decided to take off nearly 2000 km from the length of its border with India or why residents of Kashmir, including a general of the Indian Army, were discriminated against in matters of visa. We still wonder why there was much sabre-rattling when the Indian prime minister visited Arunachal Pradesh or when the Indian envoy decided to attend Nobel Prize ceremonies for a Chinese dissident. No explanation was offered for violating NSG guidelines to supply nuclear reactors to Pakistan. Nor is there any guidance as to why China is undermining Indian influence in South

Asia by showering favours on Sri Lanka and Maldives. On our part, we anticipate Chinese sensitivities and do everything possible not to provoke.

We seem to have accepted the Chinese proclivity to see issues not in terms of months or years but centuries, when it comes to the border question. The principles of negotiation took long to settle and we are nowhere near tackling the real issues. We do not rush them in the pious hope that the Chinese have their own ways of dealing with such important issues left behind by the colonialists. Another century is a drop in the ocean in Chinese thought and we might as well accept the time frame. The fact that an unsettled border is a sure recipe for trouble whenever the Chinese are inclined to teach us a lesson does not seem to trouble us. The deafening Chinese silence on the Brahmaputra issue at the Durban summit did not seem to disturb us. We ought to be patient, we tell ourselves, and wait for the right signals, the right moment to strike a deal. Our patience is proverbial; our acceptance of the Chinese mystery is incredible.

When the Chinese army decided in April 2013 to move deep into the Indian side of the Line of Actual Control and set up tents after many years of comparative inactivity in the area, we sought no explanation and the Chinese gave none. We went on to give them the benefit of the doubt as though we had unwittingly provoked them by building bunkers in our own territory. We characterised it as a localised incident, with no implications for Sino-Indian relations, mere acne to be healed by an ointment. The media noise was drowned out by soft words of perfect understanding on the part of the government. Finally, victory was declared when we withdrew from our own side in return for the Chinese withdrawing from our side. The easiest way was to attribute the whole episode to the 'inscrutability' of the Chinese.

Some analysts even celebrated the episode as a welcome change in China's approach to the border question. The 'non-threatening, but provocative military action' was apparently a benign signal of new activism on the border issue, which should be resolved as soon as possible, as set out in the new Panchsheel unveiled by the new president of China. The Chinese spokespersons have been speaking in generalities, but we see the Chinese action as a response to our own activities to strengthen our own defences on the volatile border on our side. We even concede that the action may well have been taken to prevent India from becoming a pivot for the United States in the Asia-Pacific. China 'acts' and we find 'explanations' for their actions.

The Chinese reputation for inscrutability, which has been developed over centuries, is its greatest asset. A bewildered world, including India, spends more time deciphering its motives and intentions, rather than in responding to them.

5

JAPAN–INDIA HONEYMOON

The star attraction in the Indian pavilion at the Osaka Expo '70 was a white tiger. There were, of course, handicrafts and sari-clad women serving Darjeeling tea. The Japanese, having reached the pinnacle of fame as the electronic capital of the world, politely praised the wonders of India, recalled Buddhist bonds, reminisced over Netaji Subhas Chandra Bose, who dreamt of conquering the world under Japanese leadership and Judge Radha Binod Pal, who defended the Japanese after the war and earned a monument for himself in the Yasukuni Shrine, talked of Asian solidarity and moved on.

Prime Minister Indira Gandhi had just visited Japan a few months earlier and relations appeared cordial, with no issues to be resolved. Agreements to continue the modest Yen credit for projects were signed. Some Japanese wanted the ashes, believed to be of Netaji Subhas Chandra Bose, kept at the Rinkoji temple, to be returned to India and Indira Gandhi promised to look into it, knowing well the intensity of the feelings among people in West Bengal, if the ashes of a man they still believed alive were to be brought there. Not much later, Justice GD Khosla arrived to ascertain the authenticity of the ashes, made a thorough investigation and established that the ashes were indeed those of Netaji. The ashes still remain there.

India and Japan were never indifferent to each other. But both had different preoccupations. In the 1970s, even when Japan was basking in its fame as the master manufacturer of the world, it was embarrassed by the ceremonial suicide of its young poet, Yukio Mishima, exhorting Japan to resume a militaristic posture. Ichiro Kawasaki, a Japanese diplomat and rising author, unmasked Japanese weaknesses and asserted that, without a huge landmass, sizable population and abundant resources, Japan would never be a significant world power. Japan had outsourced its foreign policy to the US. India, a leader of the Non-Aligned Movement, was a nuisance to US cold warriors, who wanted to contain the Soviet menace. Japan shared that sentiment. Moreover, India's defiance of the NPT was unfolding and Japan, sitting in the shade of an American nuclear umbrella, looked askance at Indian nuclear policy. The closed Indian economy had no great attraction for the export-hungry Japanese. The period of benign neglect stretched on for years.

Now that the rain has begun, it pours. Prime Minister Manmohan Singh's visit to Tokyo in 2013 within a week of Prime Minister Li's visit to India was a coincidence, but it turned out to be a Kautilyan masterstroke. The handshake across the Himalayas, as Li characterised his visit, was aimed at creating a facade of friendliness, without any fundamental change in China's quest for global domination. The agenda was Chinese, happily gobbled up by India for its own reasons. The visit to Tokyo was marked by a new strategic consensus between Japan and India, following a rediscovery of common interests. For Japan, it also marked the new politics and economics of Prime Minister Shinzo Abe.

The Japanese saw the possibility of nuclear trade with India, which is committed to expand its nuclear power generation, even while Japan was reducing its dependence on nuclear power after the 2011 Fukushima radiation leakage following an earthquake and tsunami. Though the agreement was not signed, the machinery was laid out for strategic cooperation. An unprecedented visit of the emperor and empress of Japan followed, and Japanese prime minister squeezed in a visit to India to be the chief guest at the Republic Day parade. India showed sensitivity to Japanese sentiments by not displaying its latest lethal acquisitions. The comfort level in relations reached such proportions that Japan was prepared to begin negotiations for the sale of sea planes, which Japan had never sold before.

China undoubtedly is the unwitting Cupid, which brought about the India–Japan honeymoon, which it denounces. Japan is open about its strategy of befriending India with an eye on China, while India remains the bashful bride. Prime Minister Abe wrote in his book, *Towards a Beautiful Country* (2007), that India–Japan relations would overtake Japan–US and Japan–China relations in a decade. India is right in asserting that it had never been unwilling to cultivate Japan and that the latter developments are the culmination of an ancient relationship, rooted in history and culture. The PM's Japan visit was a befitting sequel to the euphoria about a new phase in Sino-Indian relations, which came close on the heels of the despondency in Ladakh. The Japan card was well played. Together with our refusal to reiterate the One China policy and the PM's assertion that settlement of the border issue is essential for normalising relations, it gave the right signal to the Chinese. It was India's turn to teach the Chinese a lesson or two.

India declines the offer of the status of the pivot in Asia-Pacific, whether it is of the US or Japan. But it merrily joins military exercises with both and also hobnobs with the Chinese Navy. Strategic autonomy remains in place even in the face of Chinese provocations.

Similarities between Arunachal Pradesh and Japan's contested Senkaku Islands remain the unspoken narrative of the configuration.

India does not seem to doubt Japanese motivations in pursuing a 'friendship offensive' with India, and does not doubt its logic. The weakening of the global influence of the US and increased assertiveness of China seem to dictate only an intensification of the Japan–India interaction. But the Japanese doggedness in pursuing national objectives and its ruthlessness in taking tough positions should not be forgotten. The stiff position on non-proliferation is one example. The other example is the long history of our partnership with Japan in seeking reform of the United Nations Security Council. Japan has been a comrade in arms in that struggle from 1979, when India sought to expand the non-permanent membership of the Security Council. But whenever there was likelihood of Japan getting an entry by itself or with Germany, it had abandoned the partnership with India, in pursuit of its own agenda. When South Korea snatched the South Asian slot for membership of the Security Council by striking a deal with Sri Lanka in 1995, and India sought to contest the East Asian slot in 1996, Japan was adamant to the extent of being hostile in its contest with us. Japan would not even consider the various formulas India advanced, and chose to fight a bitter election with no holds barred. Talking to Japan was like talking to a wall at the time.

Japan and India look like natural allies today, but today's alliance was brought about not by tradition or culture, but by the propitious configuration of stars that guide international relations. Trust and confidence may develop to prolong the productive alliance, but what will prevail is self-interest, which Japan is quick to grasp and act upon with vigour.

6

THE EMPTY GESTURE

British diplomats joke that the inelegant acronym, CHOGM, stands for 'Chaps on Holiday on Government Money'. Some also say that wealth is the only thing which is not common in the Commonwealth. In fact, after the days of colonialism and apartheid, the Commonwealth has been an organisation in search of an agenda. It duplicates the work of the United Nations in various ways, but since it has no unifying thread other than memories, the Commonwealth does not even endeavour to take a position of its own in the UN. It tried to identify certain issues in which the Commonwealth had a special talent, such as problems of small and island states. But these have not particularly benefited from the Commonwealth.

India, therefore, had nothing to lose from the prime minister skipping the Commonwealth Heads of Government Meet (CHOGM) in Colombo in November 2013, and it was not for the first time that an Indian prime minister has missed such an event. Charan Singh did not find it worthwhile to attend the Lusaka CHOGM either. Nobody, except the Indian delegation, shed tears for the absence of the Indian prime minister. Even the minister of external affairs could have spent his time more productively in neighbouring Maldives.

On the bilateral front, it was not even certain that President Rajapaksa would have time for the prime minister of the biggest democracy in the world. Intoxicated by liberation from the threat of Prabhakaran and his LTTE, the president spoke of one Sinhala nation with no minorities. In his vision of Sri Lanka, neither the Rajiv Gandhi–Jayawardene agreement nor the Thirteenth Amendment found any place. To him, India was only a destination for Buddhist pilgrimage. In his eyes, India's only role in Sri Lanka was to moderate the belligerence of the LTTE. With the LTTE gone, India has no teeth and Rajapaksa would rather deal directly with the Lankan Tamils than with their patrons in India.

The irony is that even though the Indian prime minister's attending the CHOGM was not important and he may not have been welcome to pay a bilateral visit to Colombo at this juncture, the decision to cancel a multilateral engagement for a bilateral reason betrayed several weaknesses in foreign policy decision-making. First of all, the Centre underestimated the depth of feeling that the approaching elections (General elections 2014) had forced Tamil politicians to demonstrate. The link to the elections is evident because the same politicians were silent during the war, when Tamils faced brutalities in Sri Lanka. India's opinion was very relevant to the choice of Colombo as the venue for the CHOGM. Having had to shift its position in Geneva several times, New Delhi should have anticipated another embarrassment and seen to it that the CHOGM was moved out of Colombo. With the Commonwealth's focus on democracy and human rights, we could have gathered enough support to shift the venue.

The unseemly fact of Tamil Nadu holding the nation's foreign policy hostage does India no credit internationally. Multilateral diplomacy has enough precedent of treating the venue of a conference as neutral ground, which should have been explained to the Tamils. When Fidel Castro or Yasser Arafat travelled to New York to attend the UN sessions, even the most vociferous of their followers did not object to it as reflective of fraternisation with the US. To accept the argument that by boycotting the CHOGM, India is registering some kind of displeasure with the Sri Lankan government is to disregard the conventions of multilateral behaviour. In foreign policy, the Centre should be the final arbiter, even if the border states are consulted on certain matters that concern them.

We have short memories, but the archives in Delhi must have details of what Prime Minister Rajiv Gandhi accomplished at Melbourne CHOGM, soon after the military coup against Fiji Indians. For the Fijian chiefs, who had masterminded the coup, their link with the Commonwealth was vital and it was that very link that Rajiv Gandhi severed. He met the heads of many of the delegations in Melbourne and stressed that Fiji should be expelled from the Commonwealth on account of its racist constitution, imposed by a military government. India's success helped democracy return to Fiji within a very short time. In the case of Sri Lanka, we could have accomplished something similar.

International public opinion is already agitated over Sri Lanka's war crimes, and initiatives within the Commonwealth would have served the Tamil cause better. Before the meet, Commonwealth Secretary General Kamalesh Sharma had hinted that the international body would 'assist' Sri Lanka in setting up a national inquiry on torture to investigate all charges, starting from 2009. This was a proposal with immense possibilities. The Indian prime minister could have strengthened the proposal and gained more for Tamils in Sri Lanka and India, than the empty gesture of his absence accomplished. Electoral exigencies should not blind us to the potential of diplomacy, which India has exploited fully in the past.

7

AUNG SAN SUU KYI'S LONG ROAD TO DEMOCRACY

Aung San Suu Kyi's long journey to democracy brought her to the country that shaped her personality and inspired her to fight for freedom for her people. Rising to deliver the Nehru Memorial Lecture in New Delhi in November 2012 was one of the finest moments of her life, perhaps next only to receiving the Nobel Prize for Peace. It was also a poignant moment, as she had to come to terms with India's policy of befriending the very military junta, which kept her in a cage for more than twenty years.

'I was saddened,' she said, 'by the fact that India had drawn away in our most difficult days but always had faith in our lasting relationship.' Even more significantly, she observed, 'Friendship should be based between people and not governments: Governments come and go.' This was a masterstroke on her part. In a way, she justified the Indian action by attributing it to compulsions of governments or realpolitik from time to time. If there were to be an opinion poll in India during the period of her incarceration, she would have been voted more popular than any of the other military leaders in Myanmar. The people of India were with her throughout, while the government had to deal with the people in power. India's position has always been that it recognises states, not governments and that it deals with every government that has control over territory.

At no time in history has an authoritarian regime permitted a democratic leader to campaign for democracy abroad, even before democracy becomes a reality in that country. Nor has an American president ever visited a country in which the US has sought, but not accomplished a regime change. The military leadership, Suu Kyi and Barack Obama are taking calculated risks with implicit and explicit motives, which are not mutually complementary. The military, which has penetrated every sector of the society of Myanmar, has much to lose if full democracy is restored, and it will struggle hard before conceding any ground to democracy. At the same time, the army needs to get the sanctions lifted and foreign investments facilitated. Suu Kyi has to watch her steps and words carefully to ensure that the army is not offended, and the pro-democracy movements in Myanmar and outside are not disillusioned. Obama must have satisfied himself that the democratic reforms in progress will not be reversed, even while enjoying the hospitality of the junta. All three have a stake in the future course of Myanmarese history.

Suu Kyi has been impeccable in her pronouncements on democracy abroad. In Delhi, she said, 'We have not achieved the goal of democracy. We are still trying and we hope that in this last—I hope—and most difficult phase, the people of India will stand by us and walk by us as we proceed along the path that they were able to proceed many years before us.' She is not unaware that the path ahead is different from the path India took, but she clearly hinted that the path ahead was hard and unpredictable.

In 1971, Suu Kyi arrived in Bhutan as the young bride of Michael Aris and was mistaken initially in the social circles as one of the Bhutanese princesses. She was friendly with us in the Indian embassy in Bhutan because of her long association with India, which she narrated with exquisite charm and nostalgia, this time in Delhi. She gave a subtle hint of her father's path being different from that of Gandhi and that Netaji Subhas Chandra Bose was a greater hero than Pandit Nehru in the eyes of the Burmese. The generosity that Pandit Nehru showed to Aung San's family after the latter's death was particularly significant against that backdrop.

India's policy towards Burma, under the long reign of Ne Win and his successors, took several twists and turns. Ne Win, who once took over power by invitation and later by a military coup, had an ambivalent attitude to India. While he was ruthless in depriving the fleeing Indians of their wealth, he maintained good relations with the Nehru family and the Indian leadership. His isolationist policy kept us away from Burma, except for cultural contacts, though we tried to open up trade contacts by importing rice from Burma. But among all our neighbours, Burma made the least demands of us and caused us no embarrassment internationally. When Indira Gandhi was assassinated, Ne Win flew to an unnamed destination to meditate in grief. I accompanied him to Delhi when he went on a condolence visit and saw for myself the love he showered on Rajiv Gandhi as the 'uncle', who came calling at the time of grief. India was a sentimental link even for Ne Win, but it never translated into a meaningful relationship.

Right through the elections, the bloodshed and the consolidation of the junta, India remained committed to democracy and showed our attachment to Suu Kyi. We blocked the return of Myanmar to the Non-Aligned Movement at a ministerial meeting in Bali. The subsequent decision to do business with the military regime in Yangon was an effort by India to wean Myanmar away from China, and to seek some economic benefits for us at a time when Western sanctions were in effect. Myanmarese saw in our overtures an opportunity to diversify their external relationships and to gain respectability. As for the benefits, which accrued to us, these have not been significant, essentially because we ourselves have been negligent of follow-up action to many proposals for cooperation.

One welcome indication out of the visit of Suu Kyi even, before the advent of democracy is that she carries no grudge against India for its proximity to the military government. But how soon will she become the leader of a democratic government and pursue policies friendly to India is a matter of speculation. In fact, she will be beholden, first and foremost, to those who stood by her and brought her back to the reckoning and that is the signal that she is giving to China by not going there before her trips to the US and India. We too will have to take our turn to benefit from the opening up of Myanmar.

The limited agenda of seeking cooperation in dealing with the insurgents on the India–Myanmar border, sharing some of the energy resources of Myanmar and establishing the base for a beneficial trade relationship can be pursued even during the transition to democracy. But whether democracy will eventually give us immense benefits is a matter to be seen. China and the United States are likely to call the shots even in a democratic structure.

Suu Kyi's pursuit of democracy could be long and arduous, but she has shown remarkable skills in managing the military so far. She has the potential to get on with governance, whatever role she assumes in the years to come. She has refused to take sides in the conflict between the Buddhists and the ethnic Muslim Rohingyas, on the plea that her role would be to bring about reconciliation rather than to take sides. The same spirit may prevail in Myanmar if she succeeds in sending the military back to the barracks.

Ashwatthama
The United States

The illustrious son of Dronacharya, Ashwatthama, is believed to be a Chiranjeevi with a curse on his head. During the Kurukshetra war, while the enemy camp was in slumber, Ashwatthama stealthily entered their tents and murdered them in cold-blood, including the five young sons of the Pandavas. Clutching at the final straw, he was to demonstrate his prowess and use the ultimate weapon of mass destruction—*Brahmastra*—the technique of which was known to him alone. The heavens, devas and rishis, seethed around him like dark clouds and reproached his reprehensible act. Sage Vyasa and others advised withdrawal of the *astra*, lest it should cause the destruction of the entire human race and life on earth. Not knowing how to withdraw the *Brahmastra*, Ashwatthama redirected it to one single target; the last and only offspring of Pandavas—Uttara's unborn child. At this final instance, the Lord cursed him that he would live a painfully long life and would roam about the earth as a Chiranjeevi. Legend has it that Ashwatthama's wound on his forehead festers till date, as a bitter reminder to every human being, every society and every country that wounds borne out of unethical code of conduct never heal.

The United States of America, the reigning superpower since the end of the USSR, brings to mind the story of Ashwatthama. Power can contaminate, if the minds that wield it do not have compassion; weapons can exterminate if the hands that wield them do not have caution. Just as absolute power corrupted Ashwatthama, the United States is blinded by its unique position and goes about the world changing regimes and trampling upon the rights of other nations. India–US relations have been like a roller coaster ride because of the pride and arrogance of the US. The following section comprises of ten insightful articles on USA with particular reference to Indo-US relations. TP Sreenivasan spent a good part of his official career in the US and acquired deep knowledge of the country and its policies. Following his retirement from the service, he was also a visiting fellow on foreign policy at the Brookings Institution, Washington in 2009. He is also associated with think tanks and universities such as the CSIS, CEIP and Columbia University.

1

BARACK OBAMA: BUILDING A LEGACY

Barack Obama has done it all. He spoke his way up the Democratic hierarchy, won the nomination against Hillary Clinton, became the first African American to occupy the White House, won the Nobel Peace Prize, secured a second term with ease and made no great mistakes as president. Now is the time for him to start thinking of building the Obama Library and moulding his legacy and his possible role in his post-White House years.

Obama's obvious choice is the image of a fighter for justice for the black population rather than of a man of change, a man of peace, a conciliator or a nation builder. He can claim a little bit of the legacy of each, but he realises that nothing is more enduring than the image of a liberator a la Martin Luther King. Many presidents have come and gone, but King (never a president) remains a beacon of hope not just for the black people of America, but also for the underprivileged around the globe. History might judge his presidency harshly, but might readily accept a black messiah image, if carefully cultivated. The death of a young black man in Florida in February 2012 gave Obama an opening to start the process.

'Trayvon Martin could have been me, thirty-five years ago,' said Obama in an unscheduled appearance at a press briefing on the acquittal of a white man, who shot the African American boy. 'There are very few African American men in this country who haven't had the experience of being followed when they were shopping in a department store. That includes me. There are very few African American men who haven't had the experience of walking across the street and hearing the locks click on the doors of cars. That happens to me—at least before I was a senator. There are very few African Americans who haven't had the experience of getting on an elevator and a woman clutching her purse nervously and holding her breath until she had a chance to get off. That happens often.'

He had spoken earlier about the Florida events in the 'presidential' mode, how unfortunate the shooting was, how the justice system had dealt with the case fairly and how Martin's kin had reacted to the tragedy with courage. But his tone and tenor were entirely different after the acquittal. He spoke reflectively and forcefully with more than a touch of anger. He said, 'That all contributes, I think, to a sense that if a white male teen was involved in the same kind of scenario, that from top to bottom, both the outcome and the aftermath might have been different.' The frustration and bitterness in the words of a black president in his second term were striking.

Obama is literally an African American, unlike others in the US who use the term as a euphemism, with no recent links to Africa. But it was by a biological accident that he was born looking more like his father than his white mother. His identification with the black community was a masterstroke that brought Obama to the White House, breaking the glass ceiling. His incessant call for change went beyond his race and the expectation around the globe was that he would be a very different president, one who would change the world. Some visualised Air Force One flying to Teheran and Havana, not to speak of Beijing and Moscow to usher in a new world of friendship and cooperation. But it became clear that the most powerful man on earth had no power to change even the most glaring inequities in the US itself. It did not take long for Obama to realise this truth and to abandon his slogan of change. He found himself entangled in the multiplicity of checks and balances, which constrained him in every direction.

The other choice he had was of building the image of a man of peace. The Nobel Committee literally embarrassed him with the Peace Award very early in his presidency. The explanation given by the Committee was that the Prize was given for raising expectations rather than for accomplishing anything. The chairman of the Norwegian Nobel Committee said, 'We cannot get the world on a safer track without political leadership. And time is short. Many have argued that the Prize comes too early. But history can tell us a great deal about lost opportunities. It is now, today, that we have the opportunity to support President Obama's ideas. This year's Prize is indeed a call to action to all of us.'

Obama was on the point of apology when, accepting the Prize, he referred to the controversy about the Prize and the fact that it came at the beginning and not at the end of his labours on the world stage. He said, 'Perhaps the most profound issue surrounding my receipt of this Prize is the fact that I am the commander-in-chief of a nation in the midst of two wars. One of these wars is winding down. The other is a conflict that America did not seek; one in which we are joined by forty-three other countries—including Norway—in an effort to defend ourselves and all nations from further attacks. Still, we are at war and I am responsible for the deployment of thousands of young Americans to battle in a distant land. Some will kill. Some will be killed. And so I come here with an acute sense of the cost of armed conflict—filled with difficult questions about the relationship between war and peace, and our effort to replace one with the other.' The wars are far from over and Obama has been as steadfast in the wars as his predecessor was. He has no hope of being known as a great peacemaker.

Obama's third option was to be the builder of reconciliation among his people, not only between the Democrats and the Republicans, but also between races and the rich and poor. No one grasped the hand of reconciliation he extended and the economic problems persisted well into his second term. His economic formula, which helped him to win the first election proved elusive and he was elected a second time, not as a saviour, but as one who muddled through the crises the country faced. The European economic crisis and the looming Chinese rise do not augur well for him to turn the situation to earn the legacy of an economic wizard.

No wonder then, that Obama, or his image-makers, are veering towards building his legacy as an African American hero, who not only captured power, but also fought relentlessly for the downtrodden. That will enable him to escape the criticism that he did not end racism as president and to fight racism and racial discrimination till the end of his life. Obama's remarks on Trayvon Martin echoed King's dream speech and the promise he held out to overcome oppression. Obama may well be on his way to inherit the mantle of King and to claim kinship with Gandhi.

2

US IN ASIA-PACIFIC: AN INDIAN PERSPECTIVE

The distant drums of an approaching new Cold War were audible at the 2012 Asia-Pacific Roundtable on Asian Security Governance and Order in Kuala Lumpur. The increasing influence and assertiveness of China in the region seemed to invite a matching response from the United States.

The striking point about the rise of China was the perception in the region, at least among some countries, that the Chinese presence was benign. Prime Minister Razak of Malaysia, for instance, said that he would not belittle 'the positive transformational effects China's ascendancy has and will continue to have on Asia and beyond'.

Mahathir Mohammed, the elder statesman of Malaysia, sought to allay the fears about China by saying that the Chinese, who had contacts with the region for centuries, had never colonised any country, while the Portuguese and other Europeans merrily built empires in Asia. He said that Malaysia should fear the Europeans more. He revealed his admiration for the Chinese when he said that the Chinese were cleverer than the Russians. The Soviet Union collapsed because it tried to reform both the economic and political systems at the same time. The Chinese survived as a nation because they only reformed the economic system.

Malaysians were not the only ones to praise China or to predict that China would determine the future of the Asia-Pacific Region. The assessments of China were always positive and there was never even a hint of human rights violations or curtailment of press freedom. Mahathir favoured a certain amount of authoritarianism in government and was as tolerant of 'some killings' by the Chinese as of American atrocities against terrorists.

China's own perceptions about security in Asia and the Pacific were quite patronising, bordering on arrogance. The Chinese ambassador to ASEAN spelt out the Chinese position on the South China Sea, making light of the repercussions of the Chinese assertiveness on this matter. Other Chinese scholars openly admitted that confrontation with the United States was inevitable, as the US 'Back to Asia' security policy was targeting China. But even while admitting strategic distrust, they said that shared interests made the two countries cautious and pragmatic in managing tensions.

According to the Chinese, China's increasing importance and influence were making the countries of the region perform the feat of 'putting legs on two boats'. Even though China continued to play a positive role in managing the new complex relations and challenges, the situation gave rise to nationalism and a 'new victim feeling', a strange concept of fear, which led, ironically, to greater assertiveness. China clearly sees a competition between the old US-dominated military alliances and the new structures in which China plays a central role. It realises that the key to political dominance is economic penetration, and the Chinese make no secret of their strategy.

It is not surprising, therefore, that the US has identified the arc extending from the Western Pacific and East Asia into the Indian Ocean region and South Asia as the region which needs to receive greater attention. The rebalancing means shifting the US concentration from the Middle East to Asia and a broader reach in Asia itself with more flexible deployments and rotation of troops. President Obama was candid about the US strategic objective in Asia. He said, 'I am determined that we meet the challenges of the moment responsibly and that we emerge even stronger in a manner that preserves American global leadership and maintains our military superiority.' The real debate today is not about the importance of Asia, but what methods should be used to increase the US engagement in the region.

The US interests in the region should be seen against China's growing military capabilities and its asserting of claims, which has implications for freedom of navigation. Although the president is committed to reducing the defence budget, the disengagement in Afghanistan and Iraq may release enough resources for Asia-Pacific. In November 2011, Secretary Hillary Clinton recalled that the stability and security in Asia was guaranteed for long by the US military. The US could not afford not to strengthen its presence in Asia at a time when the region is likely to shape global security itself, she said.

The new strategy appears to be to reduce ground forces and focus on nuclear forces and the navy, in which the US has clear superiority over China. Old alliances in the region need to be strengthened and new friends need to be found. Since the region straddles two oceans, the Pacific and the Indian, shipping and strategy have to take the interlinkages into account.

Although the US has maintained that its rebalancing of forces in Asia is not directed against any country, China has repeatedly accused the US of pointing at a Chinese threat to perpetuate its hegemony in Asia. It has said that a de facto empire on borrowed money is flexing its muscles, while its creditors are at the door. China believes that it is all a matter of Cold War mentality and that nobody will believe that the US actions are not directed against China. If anything, China will be more assertive of its claims on the South China Sea and other disputes, as became evident at the ASEAN summit.

India–US relations have undoubtedly benefitted from the change of scene in the Asia-Pacific Region. When the then External Affairs Minister SM Krishna and Secretary of State Hillary Clinton met in June 2012, there was spring in the air, not blowing in from the Potomac, but from the distant Pacific and Indian Oceans. The issues that had bedevilled the bilateral relationship in the previous two years were all there, but there was certain urgency about putting them behind and moving forward to larger objectives. The ripples that grew into waves in the South China Sea and the changing equations in Asia-Pacific gave their parleys new content and a sense of purpose.

No doubt, after initial hesitations, the US has begun to see India as the 'lynchpin' of its new security architecture and India became a doorway to the Pacific. Defence Secretary Leon Panetta made it clear that he was on a mission to recruit India as a partner in Asia-Pacific, whatever may have been the irritants in the past.

The elaborate Joint Statement issued at the end of the strategic dialogue makes the context very clear. 'The US and India have a shared vision of peace, stability and prosperity in Asia, the Indian Ocean region and the Pacific region and are committed to work together, and with others in the region, for the evolution of an open, balanced and inclusive architecture.' Such a firm assertion of the role of the two countries in the region is rare in India–US statements. What is more, Secretary Clinton welcomed India's growing engagement in the Asia-Pacific. The Indian Ocean Rim Association for Regional Cooperation (IOR-ARC), an old Indian initiative, which had lost momentum, received a boost when the US sought to become a dialogue partner of the Association.

The US, once wary of Indian activism in Afghanistan for fear of Pakistan's displeasure, has declared its intention to seek new opportunities to intensify the efforts of the two countries for consultation, coordination and cooperation to promote a stable, democratic, united, sovereign and prosperous Afghanistan. India, in turn, has welcomed the announcement of the Chicago Summit of NATO of progress in the security transition process, acknowledging the legitimacy of NATO operations in Afghanistan. The statement also favoured the elimination of safe havens and infrastructure for terrorism and violent extremism in Afghanistan and Pakistan. No better evidence was necessary of the disillusionment of the US with the role of Pakistan as an ally in Afghanistan and its desire to work with India.

The reference to defence relations was of particular importance. Instead of harping over the disappointment over the fighter aircraft contract, the statement celebrated the fact that India had awarded defence contracts worth US $9 billion to US companies. It noted the many military exercises and exchanges in the last six years and reaffirmed their desire to strengthen defence cooperation through increased technology transfer. Defence Minister AK Antony had stressed to Secretary Panetta the need to transform the buyer–seller relationship into a partnership in technology and strategy. In New Delhi, earlier the US had conceded that India's unwillingness to sign a couple of basic agreements relating to defence cooperation should not stand in the way of new defence deals.

Among the differences, which were pushed under the carpet was the nuclear liability issue, which had prevented nuclear trade between India and the United States so far. No mention was made of the obstacles to the licensing and site development work associated with construction of the new Westinghouse reactors in Gujarat, but they welcomed progress towards the full implementation of the nuclear deal. The need of the hour was to highlight points of convergence, not of divergence.

An endless list of issues of agreement in diverse fields such as counterterrorism, intelligence, homeland security, cyber security, energy, climate change, education, development, trade, agriculture, science and technology, health and innovation and people-to-people ties found place in the Joint Statement.

The spring in India–US relations, evident after the third round of the strategic dialogue, comes from the anxiety of the two countries to rebalance them in the face of Chinese assertiveness. Compulsions of security in Asia-Pacific may well bring the two democracies closer together in the future.

The Indonesian foreign minister at the Kuala Lumpur meet expressed the dilemma of the countries of the region in these words, 'What worries us is having to choose; we do not want to be put into that position. The Pacific is sufficiently accommodating to provide not only the role of China and the US, but of emerging powers too.' A spokesperson of ASEAN said that ASEAN would not like to dictate the roles of different powers in the region. It would rather act like a flight controller at an airport, making sure that all arrivals and departures are smooth and there is no collision.

But sooner or later, the countries in the region will have to develop a cohesive Asian strategy to deal with the challenge of Chinese assertiveness. Chinese domination of the sea lanes of Indian and Pacific Oceans will be a major concern for India. Assertion of its claims in the South China Sea, if it succeeds, will encourage China to press its territorial claims on India. India considers its strategic autonomy sacrosanct and India's engagement with the US will become stronger and more productive in the light of the evolving situation in Asia-Pacific.

India has a stake in working with the US, China and other countries in the region to rearrange the regional security system, which accommodates rather than collide with India's security interests. India's efforts have been to identify issues, particularly multilateral issues, such as global trade, the financial system and the environment in which cooperation with China can be enhanced. But three major issues still divide India and China, with the potential for an adversarial relationship. The unsettled border between the two countries, the Chinese propping up of Pakistan against India and the possibility of China diverting the water, which flows into India are intractable. Some scholars have suggested an India–China diplomatic structure to monitor these issues and to find temporary, if not final solutions to these issues. But given the continuing assertiveness of China, it is not likely to help matters. India will have to search for its own security in the larger context of the evolving situation rather than bilaterally with China.

3

THE AUTUMN THAW

US And Iran

The salubrious early autumn in New York offers the ideal setting for the United Nations General Assembly, which takes place in the third week of September every year. War clouds were visible in the Syrian firmament as delegates packed their bags in 2013 to head to the General Assembly. Money, it was opined, was no problem, as the oil-rich Arabs would finance the war.

The experts were obviously wrong. The American, British and French people were in no mood for war, even if their leaders were. Mohammed Morsi's removal from presidential office in Egypt and the cold-blooded murder of the American ambassador to Libya, who had also been the architect of the new Libyan regime, had dampened the enthusiasm for change. Assad still seemed strong and fundamentalist elements had crept into the dissident movement.

The beginning of the thaw in US–Iran relations was all the more dramatic, as the two countries had not spoken to each other since 1979. The first feeble signs of change, after Iranian President

Hassan Rouhani took over, were dismissed as unreal. But the announcement of direct contact between the two country leaders, via a telephone call from Obama to Rouhani, shook the foundations of the theory that war was inevitable. What was more, Obama said that it was not merely a goodwill call. Iran's nuclear programme was discussed and the US president was even persuaded that there was basis for an agreement. Obama called the discussion 'an important breakthrough'. He also suggested that it could serve as the starting point for an eventual deal on Iran's nuclear programme and for the renewal of relations between the two countries, which once were close allies. 'The test will be meaningful, transparent and verifiable actions, which can also bring relief from the comprehensive international sanctions that are currently in place,' added Obama.

India at the UN

India also contributed to this autumn of hope with Prime Minister Manmohan Singh's visit to the White House. An agreement was signed to begin work on the installation of a Westinghouse reactor in Gujarat.

One exception to the general mood of change for the better was the disastrous India–Pakistan meeting in New York. Indian and Pakistani leaders did not even have the courage to announce the meeting beforehand. Prime Minister Nawaz Sharif did not even have the courtesy to avoid referring to Kashmir in his speech at the General Assembly. Whether he referred to Manmohan Singh as a 'dehati aurat' or simply narrated the story of a village woman who constantly complained about her neighbour, Sharif's body language did not show any warmth. The meeting did more harm than good, because it highlighted that the two leaders were hostages—Sharif to his army and Singh to Indian public opinion. The claim that nothing was lost is untenable. We lost at least a dozen lives to terror attacks on the eve of the meeting. Though the meeting failed to take things forward, in the eyes of international observers, it fitted into the general trend of relaxation of tensions.

4

INDIA–US: THE LIMITS OF ENGAGEMENT

Unsavoury incidents involving diplomats and their families are not rare in friendly countries at the best of times. The issues are dealt with in terms of diplomatic protocol and reciprocity, without even the press getting wind of it. When reciprocal expulsions become necessary occasionally, care is taken to order home those diplomats who have completed their terms so that breaches of diplomatic civility do not cloud bilateral relations. But the US and India have been showing increasing irritability in dealing with such issues. Some harsh US actions have elicited uncharacteristically sharp responses from the South Block. The US is even holding up clearance for a new Indian consulate in Seattle, Washington, according to press reports.

India–US relations are far too important, diverse and complex to be affected by thoughtless actions of law enforcement agencies or even diplomats. But the oversensitivity, demonstrated of late, appears symptomatic of a deeper malady. The creeping disillusionment in major areas seems to spill over to the diplomatic level. Hillary Clinton's 2011 visit was seen as a rescue mission. Many areas in the strategic partnership still require immediate and focussed attention.

Of course, both sides will vehemently deny this proposition, as they did to me in Washington and New Delhi a couple of years ago. Both will point to the umpteen working groups, quietly working away to fulfil the promises of the Obama visit and the latest round of strategic dialogue, not to speak of high-level visits from both sides. They will quote trade figures and speak of the intensity of economic dialogue to demonstrate the robustness of the relationship. They will even attribute any gloomy assessments to ignorance. But ask them about civil nuclear cooperation, balance of trade, India's candidature to be a permanent member of the UN Security Council, the record of cooperation in the Security Council on West Asia and non-proliferation and then you will hear from both sides the tales of unfulfilled promises and unchanging mindsets. The grievances on both sides are so well-balanced that it is difficult to determine who should or can make the first move. The nuclear deal had raised the highest hopes for a sea change in the relationship and had accomplished most; the disillusionment is also most acute in that area. Our perception is that President Bush signed the deal for his own selfish reasons, but the official line and popular thinking in America has been that it was a price paid to win India as an ally. A senior American official repeated the question we had heard from 2005 as to what India has done in return for the nuclear deal, which dramatically changed India's profile. The give and take within the deal itself is not at issue here, but the transformation of the relationship from a friend to an ally. The US feels that while India has derived immense benefits from the deal, it has made no readjustments in policy, worthy of a natural ally of the United States. The unchanged voting pattern in India and echoes of Cold War rhetoric continue to make them uneasy.

To make matters worse, the promise of nuclear trade worth billions of dollars has remained unfulfilled on account of the Liability Law and we have done little to help President Obama reduce his unemployment burden, which has reached unbearable proportions. No American president has won a re-election if the unemployment rate is 7 per cent or above. There is no sign that President Obama can bring the unemployment down to safe levels by 2012. The 'fighter aircraft shock' has worsened the situation. In the American view, India opted for the purchase of an aircraft from Europe, while the US was offering a friendship package. India, on the other hand, believes that we adopted the Liability Law in our own interests and chose the fighter that suited our functional requirements. These are done deals, which have little scope for changes at this stage.

India maintains that the US should find ways to accept the suppliers' responsibility and also fulfil the promise of full civilian nuclear cooperation, including transfer of enrichment and reprocessing (ENR) technology for enrichment and reprocessing of spent fuel, in accordance with the 'clean' NSG waiver for India. India would also like the US to push harder for India to be admitted to the NSG and the MTCR, a promise held out by President Obama during his visit. More than the practicality of these measures, the truth of the matter is that the Obama administration would rather have no nuclear trade with India than dilute its non-proliferation commitments. I was told two years ago that the US would not be unduly concerned if there was no nuclear trade at all, provided it was compensated in other ways. Moreover, the increasing scepticism regarding nuclear power after Fukushima has also become a factor in nuclear cooperation. Steering around the nuclear irritant is still a major challenge.

On the Indian side, the lack of any forward movement on the reform of the Security Council after the promise held out by President Obama in the Indian Parliament is another instance of disillusionment. India continues its heroic efforts at the UN to move the proposal forward, but without any tangible support from the US. The latest G-4 move, masterminded by India, to seek an endorsement of the principle of expansion in both categories has elicited no US response. The US stakes in the expansion puzzle go beyond bilateral considerations.

If anything, India's performance as a non-permanent member of the Security Council has only enhanced concerns in the US over revival of Indian 'non-alignment'. On Iran, Libya and Syria, congruence of policies is hard to accomplish even with the best of intentions. The emerging contours of policy on both sides cause concern.

When Strobe Talbott, chosen by *India Abroad* for the Friend of India award, said bluntly that 'India and the US are not now and may never be allies,' he was pointing to the fundamental contradiction in expecting a fiercely independent India to serve US interests in the region and the world. The public opinion in India is such that the assertion of a certain distance from the US policies is essential for any government in New Delhi. The limits of engagement with the US, breached during the first term of the Manmohan Singh government, have come into play once again. The US too has learnt its lessons on the extent of the strategic relationship possible with India.

The Hillary visit certainly made progress on a number of vital issues of cooperation, the logic of which is beyond question. But an alliance of minds, which is essential to elevate a strategic partnership to a higher level, appears hard to accomplish. A new sense of realism, rather than undue optimism, will prevail in India–US relations in the future. As long as expectations are curtailed and mutuality is established, there will be neither recrimination nor disillusionment. In the end, it may not be a defining relationship of the new century, but a mutually beneficial partnership.

5

THE US MAY HAVE NO NUCLEAR TRADE WITH INDIA

Lucrative nuclear trade with India, including supplies of reactors, was among the obvious reasons for the Bush administration to think in terms of offering India a special dispensation for full civilian nuclear cooperation.

Varying assessments of the massive increase in jobs in the United States on account of the expected trade in equipment were made. These projections went a long way in vetting the appetite of the industrial sector in the United States and in aggravating suspicions in the non-proliferation lobbies.

The enthusiasm for the nuclear deal by US–India Business Council (USIBC), consisting of the big players in India–US trade was attributed to the lure of nuclear trade with India. The USIBC engaged professional lobbyists in Washington to promote the deal on the Hill and elsewhere and there was considerable jubilation in it when the deal was signed.

In India too, the presumption was that significant nuclear trade with the US would follow the deal. Although experts knew that the US had no ready reactors to sell, it was believed that the US industry had already begun to fabricate reactors, using old technology to capture the Indian market.

The US insistence on strict regulations on nuclear trade and its reluctance to give assurances of perpetuity of supplies were seen as mere ploys to get the best business terms for nuclear trade. The argument was that the US would not sacrifice business opportunities for the sake of non-proliferation objectives.

Why should the US work so hard to secure Nuclear Suppliers Group (NSG) waiver for India merely to facilitate supply of reactors by Russia and France to India?

There were whispers in India during the negotiations that we should be Machiavellian in our approach to the United States. Some suggested that India should go along with the US conditions till we obtained the necessary clearances and then not place any orders with the US if the conditions of supply were not favourable to us.

The natural reaction of the US side was to extract a Memorandum of Understanding from India that we would seek to secure a significant percentage of our nuclear supplies from the US. It was also insisted that India should earmark two locations for the installation of US reactors in India.

The Obama administration has maintained this position and one of the trophies that US Secretary of State Hillary Clinton carried back from India was an assurance on locations for American reactors.

But the latest indication from Washington is that the US may not be interested in supplying nuclear material and reactors to India under the new dispensation. This is emerging as a matter of policy as well as a practical measure. President Obama does not want to stand in the way of the implementation of the 123 Agreement, but he is sensitive to the criticism that he is willing to dilute his commitment to non-proliferation for the sake of commercial advantages.

He has, therefore, embarked on a path to do the minimum necessary to let the deal run its course without the US itself contributing to the growth of the nuclear strength of India. He wishes to remain committed to the universalisation of the NPT, while pursuing the vision of a nuclear weapon free world in the long-term.

The Washington move in G-8 on enrichment and reprocessing should be seen in this context. While the discussions on reprocessing, as provided for in the 123 Agreement, will proceed, supply of equipment and technology in the sensitive areas will be ruled out. The US will also work for a gradual revision of the NSG consensus to put sensitive technology beyond the reach of India and others.

Nor will there be ironclad guarantees of perpetuity of supplies. The US understands that an inevitable consequence of this strategy is that the US will not be able to supply any nuclear material to India at any time. This fact is being accepted as a reality and as a virtue. It will demonstrate to the world that the US is serious about its non-proliferation protestations.

The new men and women in charge of non-proliferation in Washington do believe that the nuclear deal is not in the interest of non-proliferation and they want to curb it to the extent possible without appearing to back off from it.

The US is also reconciled to Russia and France supplying fuel and equipment under the terms of the NSG waiver. It may not be averse to indirect participation in the French deals if such opportunities arise, but it is gradually preparing the industry to close their options to open nuclear trade with India.

The compensation that the US expects is in terms of defence deals with India, which have as much potential, if not more, for job creation and overall growth in trade. The US has, therefore, been diligent about pursuing the end user agreement, without which defence deals would not be possible under the US laws.

The US had no doubt that this would be clinched as India had agreed to have similar agreements in the past. Compared to the legal rigmarole that the industry would face in the case of nuclear supplies, the defence formalities are not difficult to complete.

Defence supplies will meet the needs of a vibrant industrial complex, which cannot sustain without exports, while nuclear trade regulations in the US are too complicated to be tackled. The choice, therefore, is clear for the US policymakers.

As for India, no tears will be shed for loss of unreliable supplies from the US as long as the other suppliers keep their commitments.

The new strategy in the US will mean the emergence of tough choices for India in the years ahead. Once the US not obsessed with the attractions of nuclear trade with India, it will be more direct in pursuing its non-proliferation objectives with India.

When the Comprehensive Test Ban Treaty (CTBT) and the Fissile Material Cut-off Treaty (FMCT) are mature for ratification by India, the pressure on us will be very great indeed. There will be no industrial lobby to shield India at that time.

If the US is willing to give up its nuclear trade with India and the China factor is diminishing, what other factors will make it possible for the United States to sustain the deal?

Two theories have surfaced over time. One is a cynical view that the deal was just a lollipop offered to India to compensate for the massive supply of arms to Pakistan, which was already on the anvil during the Bush era.

India could hardly complain as the beneficiary of a waiver on nuclear matters when the US stepped up military cooperation with Pakistan. This theory assumes that President Bush had the foresight to anticipate the Af-Pak crisis.

Another theory is that the real reason for the deal was that the US wanted a massive infusion of Indian nuclear technicians into the country in the next few years, when the US unveils its own plan to reduce dependence on foreign oil. By offering India the deal, the Bush administration was simply setting up a nursery of nuclear scientists, who could be transplanted to the US at the appropriate time. This may be far-fetched, but the theory exists.

(The Nuclear Liability Law, which blocked nuclear trade subsequently, was not anticipated at the time this article was written)

6

INDIA AFTER THE INDIA–US NUCLEAR DEAL

I have been a witness to and a part of several defining moments in Indian foreign policy during my thirty-seven years in the Foreign Service. These moments transformed the way Indian leaders and diplomats looked at the world and dealt with international issues, even though there were no announcements of any change of policy. They coloured our thinking and determined our judgments and clearly marked a break from our past habits and attitudes. Attaining self-sufficiency in food grains, the victory in the Bangladesh war, the PNE of 1974, the declaration of the Emergency and the subsequent change of government, the suppression of the coup in Maldives, economic liberalisation and the nuclear tests of 1998 were some of these moments. That India did not have to depend on food imports to feed its millions sharpened the independent edge of Indian foreign policy. The victory in Bangladesh destroyed the notion that religion should determine nationhood. The PNE of 1974 made us proud of our scientific prowess. The Emergency made us hang our heads in shame, but the subsequent elections, free and fair beyond doubt, strengthened our democratic foundations. The liberalisation of the economy unleashed India's economic strength. The tests of 1998 removed the last vestiges of insecurity from Indian minds.

The India–US nuclear deal of July 2005 marked yet another defining moment. It broke the barriers of NPT and CTBT to transform itself from a non-nuclear weapon state in possession of nuclear weapons to a responsible state with advanced nuclear technology with the rights and obligations similar to those of other such states, 'such as the United States'. India overcame its half-a-century-old paranoia about US domination and felt confident about reaching an accommodation with it. It struck a balance between its need for technology and equipment and its fierce desire for autonomy in nuclear maters. It was a major event, as spectacular as the others, which dictated a new mindset for Indian diplomatic practitioners. But, unlike the other major events, the nuclear deal became a bone of contention within India and opened up an unprecedented foreign policy debate. The nuclear deal was still a blueprint when it was revealed and there were issues to be resolved before it became an accomplished fact. Both its promoters and detractors went to work and new issues emerged. No other bilateral agreement has been the subject of so much analysis before it came into effect. But if such an interregnum were available, many agreements would have been in jeopardy. Even after the end of the Cold War, there is no change in the basic perception that the US has its own agenda in dealing with India. This is particularly grave when it comes to nuclear matters. Before the tests of 1998, even discussing nuclear issues with the United States was considered hazardous. The reaction to the tentative movements made by Morarji Desai and Narasimha Rao in this area was negative. But the Indian public became comfortable after May 1998 in seeking an understanding with the US, short of rolling and eliminating our nuclear capability. But the suspicion became deeper after the United States acknowledged Pakistan as a frontline state in its fight against terrorism. In the Indian mind, Pakistan was not just the initiator and promoter of terrorism but also a global supporter of it as an instrument of freedom struggle. So the repeated declarations by the United States that it wished to see India as a great power had not made much of an impact on public opinion in India. It has been pointed out that no state can make another a great power, this being dependent on various inherent strengths such as economic and military strength, political resilience and a country's own greatness. No power would want to build up another to compete with it. At best, the mood is to keep an open mind. The Iran crisis: First the pipeline and then the nuclear waltz in Vienna had further muddled the perception.

The question as to why the Bush administration moved beyond the Jaswant Singh–Talbott exchanges and even next step in strategic partnership (NSSP) to legitimise the Indian nuclear capability has not been answered fully yet. The official Indian explanation is that India had become such an important factor in global issues of interest to it that the US wanted to build a partnership with it. The interest shown by the EU and others to build partnerships with India supports this view. The more popular understanding is that the US wished to build a relationship with India to counter the spectacular economic, military and political power of China. Sufficient evidence exists to reinforce this theory, even though India itself does not endorse it. At the same time, it is obvious that the India card is only one among the many tools that the US has in dealing with the emergence of China and, therefore, this factor should not be exaggerated beyond a point. At least one group of strategic thinkers believes that China is no threat to India or the United States. One theory is that the US motivation was to get a hold over the Indian nuclear capability by enticing India into the non-proliferation regime by making illusory concessions. Those who subscribe to this theory see in the deal a Machiavellian strategy to circumscribe the Indian nuclear capability.

A section of the Indian public does not seem to be convinced as yet that India needs the nuclear deal for its civilian or military needs. The Gandhian insistence on 'swadeshi' or indigenous effort is deeply embedded in the Indian psyche and it has been nursed by occasional reports from our scientific establishments that the necessity of denial has become the mother of crucial inventions. The Indian nuclear programme has not been transparent and even the demand for transparency is muted by the awareness of national security considerations. There are half-baked notions about India using its plentiful thorium resources to replace uranium. The wastefulness of reinventing the wheel does not seem to impress the 'swadeshi' fraternity. Since the dire need for nuclear fuel—if not for modern technology and equipment—for energy generation has been a well-kept secret, many in India do not see why India should go out of its way to secure nuclear cooperation.

The global debate about nuclear versus conventional energy for development is also present among the Indian intelligentsia. Many believe that India's quest for electricity on the nuclear route is neither necessary nor desirable. The existing low share of nuclear energy in the Indian energy mix and the fear of accidents generated by Chernobyl have impacted Indian thinking. Some do not even accept that nuclear energy is the cleanest form of energy. While it is free of greenhouse gas emissions, it has other hazards that make it unattractive.

Even those who understand the imperatives of joining the global nuclear mainstream think that India has made too many concessions in the deal. According to them, the total freedom that India had professed for many years had been sacrificed for the sake of minor benefits. The separation of military and civilian establishments, voluntary placement of the civilian establishments under IAEA safeguards and the signing of an Additional Protocol are seen as violative of our nuclear sovereignty. The scepticism in India has further increased by the suggestion that the separation of facilities might not be entirely at India's discretion. The danger of reopening of issues already negotiated and settled stares the deal in the face.

The votaries of non-alignment too are uncomfortable with signs of abdication of freedom of action. This is based more on ideology rather than on the fact that India was never a part of the consensus on non-proliferation within the Non-Aligned Movement because of its position as a non-NPT country. The Non-Aligned declarations on non-proliferation were attributed only to NPT member states. If anything, the deal will only bring India closer to the Non-Aligned position on non-proliferation. More than the terms of the nuclear deal, what provoked the Left and the Non-Aligned were the coincidental developments with regard to Iran. For many years, India had walked the tight rope in Vienna, striving to balance Iran's rights and obligations with regard to its nuclear activities. Neither the United States nor Iran was displeased with the natural Indian position that Iran should live up to its obligations under the NPT and that Iran should allay the fears of the international community by providing answers to the questions raised within the IAEA. Referral to the UN Security Council is an action required of the Board of Governors under the statute in the event of a determination of non-compliance. India and the Non-Aligned Chapter in Vienna had never ruled out such a referral and indeed used it as a pressure point on Iran. It is clearly understood that a referral to the Security Council does not mean sanctions or war automatically. But in the wake of the nuclear deal, India's position on Iran in Vienna became a litmus test of its commitment to non-proliferation. In a situation where Russia and

China, two nuclear weapon states and Pakistan, a US ally, abstained, India was pressurised to support a resolution, which it virtually disavowed in its explanation of vote. The Indian vote was cast to save the nuclear deal, not to castigate Iran. The Indian assertion that its vote was to get Iran more time to resolve the remaining issues carried no conviction.

The fact that India had never acted against US interests in Vienna, even before, was not highlighted. In the IAEA itself, India gained on account of the vote as it moved from the sidelines of the Iran debate to the centre stage.

Another unfortunate twist of fate was that the deal came at the very moment when India's quest for a permanent membership of the Security Council was at its most intense phase. In Indian popular perception, permanent membership is synonymous with global status and its denial is seen as contradicting the declared intentions of the United States. Another anomaly that baffles Indians is the exclusion of India from APEC. Praise of India's liberalisation, economic performance and democracy does not jell with India's exclusion from a group to which it rightfully belongs in every way.

The way the Indian public reacted to the mention of the then Minister of External Affairs and former diplomat Natwar Singh and the ruling Congress Party in an annex to the Volcker report was not unrelated to the nuclear deal and the Vienna vote (This was a report by an American economist on the food-for-oil programme that implicated Indian foreign service officials, diplomats and politicians.—ed.) The first to play up the Volcker report were the Left on the assumption that the implicated minister was the architect of the new relationship with the United States. When the minister sought to distance himself from the new posture in Indian foreign policy, the Left became his supporters and the opposition his detractors, leaving very little option for the prime minister other than divesting him of the crucial external affairs portfolio due to uninvestigated accusations. The nuclear deal claimed its first victim. Normally, the uninvestigated reference to the minister and his party would not have raised such a storm in India. It simply merited an investigation and the minister could have continued till the charges were proved. It is the height of irony that those whom Volcker had indicted remained in high places while India lost a minister who happened to figure in an uninvestigated allegation.

Opinions on the nuclear deal continue to be divided both in India and the United States. The non-proliferation concerns of the United States were essentially over horizontal proliferation; and vertical proliferation in India is constrained by India's own policy of minimum deterrence and the moratorium on testing. The constraints imposed by the deal itself, such as inspections under an Additional Protocol will also guarantee that India does not engage in an arms race. The fear of the deal setting a bad example for others is unfounded as the case of India is sui generis. There is no other country with the same attributes and circumstances as India. Above all, smooth implementation of the nuclear deal and a sound global impact of the same will finally remove the apprehensions from the Indian mind about the motivation of the United States.

7

IMPLEMENTATION IS IMPERATIVE

Implementation of existing agreements, rather than negotiating new ones, has turned out to be harder in international relations, as in private lives. Reaching of agreements often happens out of idealism and optimism or even romance, but when it comes to implementation, imponderable impediments spring up and implementation often falls short of expectations. The test lies in the ability of the partners to stick as much as possible to the sentiments that originally engendered the agreements and implement them in good faith.

However, the story has another side. Agreements have a certain historical context and compulsion and it may not be possible or even desirable to implement them in letter. It may become necessary to implement them in spirit and set aside some elements of the written word to suit the new context and compulsion. History is full of agreements, which served a purpose at the time they were signed and approved, but much imagination and flexibility became necessary to sidetrack some details and proceed with the purposes and principles of the original document. Bringing the agreements in line with the implementation may be so hazardous that it is better to let the anomalies lie. This is demonstrated in the mother of all agreements, the UN Charter itself. Nobody asks for the implementation of the 'enemy clause' or the original composition of the permanent members of the Security Council, as recorded in the Charter.

Coming to the specifics of the agreements between the US and India, the general situation I just laid out holds good in diverse ways. The bottom lines of the two countries were so diametrically opposite that a meeting of minds was unlikely. I am referring to India's rocky determination not to sign the NPT, and the abiding faith of the US in NPT as a cornerstone of its global non-proliferation policy. It was such irreconcilable positions that the Indo-US nuclear deal sought to bridge. What enabled the two nations to reach an agreement was the willingness of the two to keep their own respective understandings to themselves.

In their effort to convince their own constituencies, both sides issued declarations and passed legislations to show that they had not reneged on the fundamental positions they held. But each of these steps made the implementation complicated. The most celebrated of these was the declaration of the Indian side that there was nothing in the deal that would prohibit India from testing again and the declaration on the side of the US that the deal could be annulled if a test took place. The provisions in the deal itself were ambiguous on the issue, but both had their respective interpretations. Similarly, many provisions of the Hyde Act were anathema to India, but it was explained that these were unilateral US assumptions to which India was not party. The US side clarified time and again that the Act was part of the deal and was binding. Even the meaning of 'full nuclear cooperation' and the 'clean waiver' given by the NSG left many loose ends. But the agreement was signed because of political compulsions, rather than practical considerations. The fact that it has not been fully implemented should not detract from its significance as a milestone in US–India relationship.

I wrote an article in 2009, when I was a fellow at Brookings, entitled, 'The US may have no nuclear trade with India', which sent shock waves among strategic thinkers and the nuclear industry in the US and in India. I received phone calls from major US companies. My logic was that the US, while it had enabled India to enter the nuclear mainstream, had no intention of contributing even remotely to India's nuclear capability. This was not my own surmise, it was someone else's logic. First of all, the US had no significant new technology to share with India. The political purpose of the deal was fulfilled when the NSG clearance was given. US nuclear trade could not be resumed just with the 123 Agreement (Sections of the 1954 US Atomic Energy Act that deal with cooperation in this respect with other nations). There were more conditions built into the system. I concluded that the US would find it hard to provide nuclear technology or material to India. Many people had opposed the deal in India because it was being signed with the US. My US interlocutor told me that India's wish would be fulfilled and it should rejoice at the outcome.

The liability issue and the controversy over enrichment and reprocessing technology, which arose subsequently, have delayed the full implementation of the deal. A sentimental debate on the Bhopal tragedy gave the opposition an opportunity to amend the liability bill, knowing fully well that it would block nuclear trade with the United States, which involves private companies. What they could not accomplish during the debates on the deal was achieved through the mechanism of the Nuclear Liability Act. The French and Russian positions on the Liability Law were not different, but since the companies involved were state entities, the law did not affect the supplies, which were already in the pipeline. Both, US and India were engaged in finding a way to remove the legal impediments imposed by the Liability Law and an MoU was signed between NPCIL and Westinghouse in June 2012. But both sides may not be unhappy by the turn of events, if my contention in my 2009 article turns out to be right.

The reiteration in 2011 by the major suppliers that ENR technology would not be available to India, should not have come as a surprise to India. But India insists on the principle of 'full nuclear cooperation' and the 'clean waiver', knowing full well that India will not get it. India has the necessary technology and the agreement is specifically about the establishment of reprocessing facilities, not technology. No tears need be shed on account of restrictions on ENR technology, though it has become a Holy Grail for India, when the implementation of the deal is considered. Though the government is determined to pursue the path of developing nuclear power for its energy needs, there is sizeable popular opposition to the establishment of new nuclear reactors, as was demonstrated in Kudankulam.

After all is said and done, what matters is the political will. The Obama administration, and for that matter, the second UPA government, have been ambivalent about the strategic partnership between the two countries. The promises made at the time of the presidential visit have not been fulfilled as of yet. The proposal for India to be admitted to the NSG, MTCR, the Australis Group and the Wassenar arrangement has been sacrificed at the altar of the NPT. The search for strategic autonomy resulted in its non-permanent positions in the Security Council, not purchasing fighters from the US and not being helpful on Iran.

The winds, however, seem to change, with the US decision to rebalance its forces in Asia-Pacific and defence cooperation with India becoming the linchpin in this context. Several issues, which had remained dormant, came up for favourable consideration, including some relating to the nuclear deal.

Suffice it to say today that we can expect a greater degree of implementation of the agreements and understandings as the new realities of the global situation unfold. But implementation should be measured against the context of the agreements and the changing perceptions of their current relevance, rather than on the implementation of every clause. It is the spirit that should be implemented and not the letter.

Parasurama
Weapons of War and Peace

Parasurama is believed to be the sixth incarnation of Lord Vishnu, named after the deadly weapon '*Parasu*'. He is said to have killed several successive generations of corrupt rulers of a specific clan and filled up five lakes of blood. Parasurama was born a Brahmin as the son of Sage Jamadagni and Renuka Devi who had a Kshatriya lineage. Moreover, though he was born in the priestly class, he lived and fought as the ultimate warrior, defeating all sinful Kshatriyas. Thus, he is a *Brahmakshatriya*, comparable to India, essentially a peaceful and non-violent nation, which acquired nuclear weapons as a deterrent. For many years, India developed nuclear technology solely for peaceful purposes. India's acquisition of nuclear weapons against use of nuclear weapons and nuclear blackmail, have been characterised as weapons of peace. Parasurama's raising of the axe was never without provocation, much like India's no first-use policy. Parasurama beheaded his own mother at the command of his father, but obtained a boon from the latter to bring her back to life, which shows that when absolutely necessary, one might be compelled to do the undesirable. But the modern comity of nations should realise that we are bereft of any divine boons to undo the mistakes committed in a fit of rage. His incarnation is depicted in great detail in both the epics *Ramayana* and *Mahabharata*; and the impact of his weapons is said to have lasted through the ages of several further incarnations of Lord Vishnu himself. In the same way, nuclear arms and ammunition will have their effects, reverberating through generations even after they cease to be deployed actively. India continues to remain committed to a nuclear weapon free world and spreads the message of peace and non-violence across the globe. Nuclear disarmament is a process and a goal in itself. The peace dividend of complete nuclear disarmament is enormous. When Parasurama finally flung his axe into the ocean, there arose the fertile land, which became God's own country.

The following section throws light on India's nuclear policy, ranging from peaceful uses, deterrence, non-first use and commitment to Global Zero, based on the author's wide experience in the First Committee of the United Nations and the International Atomic Energy Agency. His change from being a votary of nuclear power to a nuclear sceptic, following the Fukushima disaster is also traced in this section. He has been advocating a gradual reduction of India's dependence on nuclear power and development of alternate energy sources so that nuclear power can be phased out over the years.

***

1

DOES NUCLEAR POWER HAVE A FUTURE IN INDIA?

The development of nuclear power in India is driven as much by fantasy and romance as by scientific and strategic calculations. Like its foreign policy, planning and scientific temperament, Pandit Nehru bequeathed nuclear policy to India, on which there has always been a national consensus. Homi Bhabha is a national hero and his tragic death in an air crash is considered part of a conspiracy against India. Extreme secrecy surrounds nuclear policy and programmes in a country, which is brutally open about other matters of national importance. Even when prophecies and projections are proved wrong and official actions become inexplicable, no system exists to explain unforeseen developments. Sanctity is attributed to policies formulated and projects launched many years ago and course correction, even when it is made, is projected as business as usual. Much has, meanwhile, happened in the nuclear arena and India is committed to its nuclear future. Nuclear power in India will certainly grow despite dire predictions to the contrary and the fact that public opposition is growing both on account of safety considerations and new scientific information, which calls into question the feasibility, the cost effectiveness and the wisdom of long-term reliance on nuclear power. The way India has dealt with the issues arising out of the India–US nuclear deal, Kudankulam and Fukushima confirms that its faith in nuclear power still abides. The three-stage nuclear power development programme, adopted more than half-a-century ago, is alive and well, though the pace of progress from the second to the third stage has been slow and the envisaged use of thorium has not become viable as yet.

The bewildering twists and turns in the negotiations and the political storm the India–US nuclear deal created in both countries are evidence of its complexity. The steadfast pursuit of the deal on the part of President Bush and Prime Minister Manmohan Singh was admirable. For diplomats like me, who worked at the IAEA, with just Pakistan and partly Israel for company, it was a dream come true. India emerged out of its isolation in the nuclear community and it became possible for India to import nuclear fuel and other materials for its nuclear power industry. We paid a heavy price for it, but it was considered small in the context of ushering in a brave new world of international nuclear cooperation. But as of today, no new imported reactor has been commissioned, no dramatic increase has been achieved in power generation and our non-signatory status in NPT and CTBT regimes is still an impediment, when it comes to bilateral agreements or membership of bodies like the NSG. Some frontiers of nuclear science are still closed to us. The villain is made out to be the Indian Liability Law, which makes the supplier liable to damages in the event of an accident, in contravention of the existing international practice. I suspect that there may be other reasons for the nuclear deal not being able to deliver the deliverables. Today, neither side has disavowed nuclear trade, but no way has been found to get around the Liability Law and other issues.

The story of Kudankulam has demonstrated the perils of setting up an imported nuclear power plant. The signing of the Kudankulam agreement in 1988 with the Soviet Union, barely two years after Chernobyl power plant accident in 1986, had raised eyebrows and finding a location for it was not easy. Subsequent developments, particularly after the 2011 Fukushima disaster, have added fuel to the fire. The Supreme Court of India has termed the operationalisation of Kudankulam nuclear power plant as necessary for the country's growth. The court stressed that development of nuclear energy is important for India. While the government is committed to commission and expand the plant further, it is imperative at this point in time that the trust deficit is tackled in some way or the other. Apart from an international inspection of the safety features of the plant, adequate provision should be made for medical facilities, evacuation areas and disaster management. The situation will be replicated in other locations of new nuclear power plants and delays will be inevitable in the nuclear programme.

The crippling effect of the Fukushima disaster on the future of nuclear power has not been fully comprehended in India. Fukushima has dealt a severe blow to the nuclear renaissance envisaged in the IAEA 2020 report. The responses have ranged from outright rejection of nuclear power to uneasiness and delays. Reduction of reliance on nuclear power has been felt globally and even countries which swear by nuclear power do not remain unaffected and India is no exception.

According to the *Nuclear Intelligence Weekly* of May 2013, the renewables programme is rapidly overtaking nuclear power generation in India, with renewables generating 72 per cent more electricity than nuclear plants. The weekly avers that India is unlikely to attain the goals set out in 2005. Nuclear power still accounts for just 2 per cent of India's total installed power generation capacity. The data covering April-August 2012 shows nuclear power at 13.72 billion Kilowatt-hours, compared to 23.6 billion Kilowatt-hours for renewables. The slow growth in nuclear power is attributed to the Liability Law, protests and administrative delays. It also makes a big difference, as nuclear power is in the hands of the government, while renewables attract a high level of private investment, lured by tax holidays and other incentives. But renewable energy is still priced higher than nuclear energy in India, as the investments in nuclear energy are not fully taken into account while calculating costs.

Analyst and researcher MV Ramana argues in his significant, but combative book, *The Power of Promise*, 'Projecting nuclear capacity has always been easy. Translating those forecasts into reality, however, proved impossible and the installed capacity in 2000 was only 2720 MW. Understanding the reasons for this enormous gap between achievements and projections is crucial for judging whether the setting up of hundreds of GW of nuclear power capacity by mid-century is feasible.'

India cannot but be affected by the gloomy nuclear energy scenario around the globe. It is becoming increasingly clear that targets cannot be achieved, the anti-nuclear lobby is gaining strength and the cost of nuclear energy will be higher, if all the hidden costs are taken into account. The costs of waste disposal and the clean-up costs in the event of an accident are enormous. Indian public opinion is divided between a majority that has abiding faith in nuclear power and a minority, which opposes it. In my view, which does not seem to have any takers now, is that we should gradually alter our energy mix to reduce our dependence on nuclear power for generation of electricity, with the long-term intention of eliminating it.

As of now, India cannot abandon nuclear power as a means of production of electricity, as the policy followed so far cannot be reversed. But if greater attention is given to research and development of alternate sources, it should be possible for us to make a transition within a time frame. This will mean freezing the use of nuclear power at the existing level and reducing it gradually as we develop alternatives. For the small component of nuclear power that we envisage in our energy mix, we should find viable alternatives, which are already available. More than anything else, such a step will remove the fear that for generations to come India will face the danger of nuclear accidents, a fear that fuels the agitation against nuclear plants in India.

Indeed, the policies of every government that has come to power in India and the popular sentiment in India have coincided in favour of nuclear power being an important part of the energy mix for the foreseeable future. In fact, the global trend against nuclear power has presented opportunities for India in terms of prices and availability of nuclear plant and material. But the nuclear power scene in India cannot but be influenced by new scientific research on nuclear power, including its costs and dangers, as well as on availability of safe and efficient alternatives.

2

FROM HIROSHIMA TO FUKUSHIMA

The long journey of the nuclear genie from Hiroshima to Fukushima and beyond has kept humanity on the edge of a precipice for more than half a century. We have been through many twists and turns, with fear of total annihilation looming large even while rays of hope emerged on the distant horizon from time to time. Sincere efforts were made to put the genie back in the bottle or to put it to productive use, but the nuclear danger has remained with us till today in different manifestations. Sadly, nuclear policies of various countries were determined by their ambition to acquire destructive power in their search for security. But security has eluded the planet, initially by the threat of use of nuclear weapons by design or accident, then by nuclear terrorism by non-state actors and now, by the possibility of accidents in civil nuclear stations. The devastation of Hiroshima and Nagasaki was caused by an act of war, but it set in motion a chain of events that led to the atoms for peace initiative, the creation of the International Atomic Energy Agency (IAEA), the advent of the NPT and related treaties and the dream of a nuclear weapon free world and Global Zero.

Just as Hiroshima marked the beginning of a rethink on the possession of nuclear weapons, Fukushima should mark the beginning of a relook at civilian nuclear power as we know it today.

It is not enough that we audit facilities and satisfy ourselves that we are safe against known risks like earthquakes and tsunamis. Needless to say, we should strengthen safety features and open our facilities for peer review to ensure that we are in tune with the best standards in the world. There should be transparency in the operations of our reactors and the results of studies done in the past on risks should be shared with civil society. But above and beyond these measures, we have to rethink the whole question of civilian nuclear power, generated by the same processes that are employed in the making of weapons. We should not be lulled into the belief that physical protection will save us from the vagaries of nature or simple human errors. We owe it to the future generations to start thinking of alternatives, whether it is fusion, sun, wind or waves. Fukushima must set us thinking on the use of nuclear power as much as Hiroshima prodded us to start thinking of the elimination of nuclear weapons.

The lessons we learnt from the horrors of Hiroshima and Nagasaki are valuable even though a world without nuclear weapons is nowhere near realisation. Nations still consider nuclear weapons indispensable for their security, though 9/11 demonstrated that the power to destroy the world many times over provides no guarantee of security. The world tends to huddle under its nuclear installations and nuclear umbrellas in a futile quest for security. Those outside these false comfort zones find ways and means to acquire dubious nuclear capability from merchants of death like AQ Khan, the Pakistani scientist. The grand bargain of the NPT has not prevented proliferation even among the signatories. The IAEA, which was designed as a mother cow to bestow the benefits of peaceful nuclear energy on developing countries, was transformed into a watchdog without keeping the concomitant promise of nuclear disarmament by nuclear weapon states. The CTBT and the FMCT are still in limbo. The India–US nuclear deal is embroiled in the liability act and the ENR guidelines.

In the distant horizon, however, there is hope because of the lessons we have learned and unlearned after Hiroshima. Today, there is no serious fear that any sovereign nation will use nuclear weapons against another. Four Cold War veterans began trudging along a difficult path of disarmament, which goes beyond arms control and non-proliferation, to reach the top of a mountain from which a new vista of a nuclear weapons free world might come to view. Prime Minister Rajiv Gandhi had visualised that vista long ago and drawn up an action plan to reach there. President Barack Obama started a journey from Prague in the same direction, though he is not sure whether he can complete that journey in his own lifetime. The Global Zero has inched away from the proverbial square one. Hiroshima and Nagasaki had their impact on mankind.

Today, a major challenge is to protect nuclear material from terrorists, whether state-sponsored or non-state. They obviously have no conscience to be touched by Hiroshima or Nagasaki. Much of the nuclear material, which has been reported lost, has not been recovered, but some material has been recovered, which was never reported lost. Sufficient knowledge and material are out there to put together a dirty bomb or even a clean one. A failed nuclear state may even place a sophisticated arsenal in the hands of terrorists. The war on nuclear terrorism is an urgent necessity, a lesson we have learned after 9/11 and other terrorist attacks in different parts of the globe.

A nuclear renaissance emerged at the turn of the century out of a sense of security as the Three Mile Island disaster in 1979 and Chernobyl were caused by human error rather than by systemic deficiencies or natural disasters. The increased awareness of climate change and the role of nuclear power in mitigation of global warming gave nuclear power a new halo. In 2009, the IAEA reported that sixty-five countries had lined up at the IAEA to seek technology to either start or expand nuclear power programmes. While the growth of nuclear power slowed down in the US and European Union, it began to grow exponentially in Asia, notably China and India.

The Fukushima Daiichi plant disaster of March 2011, involving a series of equipment failures, nuclear meltdowns and release of radioactive materials following a 9.0 magnitude earthquake and tsunami, could not have come at a more inopportune time for the nuclear renaissance. It was the biggest industrial catastrophe in the history of mankind. The severity of the nuclear accident was rated seven on the International Nuclear Event Scale, indicating an accident causing widespread contamination with serious health and environmental effects. Fukushima had an instant impact on the use of nuclear power everywhere in the world, ranging from evaluation of the safety situation everywhere to announcement by Germany and Switzerland of complete withdrawal from nuclear power by 2022 and 2034, respectively.

Although many countries, notably India, declared 'business as usual', the nuclear power scene around the world has changed beyond recognition. In any event, it was clear that by 2050, nuclear power would be absent from the US and the European Union. Whether any announcement is made or not, every country has begun to plan quietly for finding viable alternatives to nuclear power. The lesson we learned from Fukushima is that the prospect of dotting our coastline with nuclear reactors is perilous, even if it guarantees much-needed electricity as an engine of growth. Human survival should have a higher priority than human development.

Fukushima has clearly accentuated the divide between those who believe in nuclear power as the panacea for our power shortage and those who believe that nuclear power is fraught with dangers, ranging from accidents to proliferation risks and long-term damage from waste disposal. The former group would have us believe that the risks far outweigh the benefits of nuclear power, while the latter would have us close down reactors instantly and switch to solar, wind and wave energy.

Having been a champion of nuclear energy and its benefits, I would advocate a third way. First and foremost, let us not minimise or hide the impact of Fukushima on mankind by arguing that nobody has died in the Daiichi plant while thousands perished in the tsunami. We do not know how and when the radiation leaks will manifest in disease and death. The reports on the aftermath are alarming. *The Wall Street Journal* reported on 20 July 2011 that Japan has banned all beef exports from the affected areas, and introduced a health review of human beings for thirty years.

'Business as usual' is not an option for nuclear power after Fukushima, just as we learned after Hiroshima that nuclear weapon should not be a legitimate weapon of war. We should begin visualising a world without nuclear power in thirty, forty or fifty years and begin developing alternate sources with the same vigour with which we developed nuclear reactors. Once that vision is recognised, human ingenuity will be channelised into innovation. We do not need to halt production or stop imports of nuclear material and reactors, but let there be a 'sunset clause' for nuclear power in our planning for the future. I am painfully aware that there are no takers for this approach yet and the established camps on both sides of the divide have dismissed it as utopian, foolish and worse, devious. I am no scientist, but someone who argues that the imported reactors are bad, while the indigenous reactors are benign, cannot be credited with much scientific wisdom. If the processes are the same and safety features are similar, how can 'swadeshi' be better than 'videshi'? Nuclear disarmament was also dismissed in the same manner before, but at least the vision of a nuclear weapon free world is now shared by the 'haves' and the 'have-nots'. The lessons of Hiroshima have been learned, but the lessons of Fukushima are wished away.

The nuclear dilemma persists, despite the process of learning and unlearning ever since the atom was unleashed, but some truths must be recognised from experience, regardless of whether one country or the other incorporates them in its policy framework.

First, the devastation from the use of nuclear weapons is so great for the present and future generations of mankind that use of such weapons should not even be contemplated. Nuclear weapons must be declared illegitimate and eliminated. Second, non-proliferation efforts on discriminatory basis will not eliminate the threat. As Mohamed El Baradei says in his book, *The Age of Deception*, 'The threat will persist as long as the international community continues to address only the symptoms of each nuclear proliferation challenge, waging war against one country, making a deal with a second, issuing sanctions in a third, seeking regime change in still another. So long as nuclear weapons remain a security strategy for a limited few possessor countries, with umbrella arrangements that extend that security to a secondary circle of allied countries, so long as others are left out in the cold, the proliferation risk will be with us.' The need for total elimination of nuclear weapons is a lesson that Hiroshima taught, but it took us sixty-six years just to acknowledge it. No one knows how long it will take to eliminate nuclear weapons.

Fukushima, preceded by Three Mile Island and Chernobyl, has also had its lessons. First, nuclear power carries with it a safety risk, which cannot be ignored, whatever be its benefits. As Amarjeet Singh said at this very forum in 2010, 'Safety makes all plants mutual hostages.... A nuclear accident anywhere in the world affects the prospects of nuclear power everywhere.' He was prophetic when he said, 'Nuclear energy is more brittle than other strategies to mitigate climate change as one major future accident could overnight nullify the resources and time invested in nuclear power up to that point.' Fukushima came just eight months after those words were uttered in this very hall.

We have seen political, economic and environmental colonialism and should be aware of 'nuclear power colonialism' in the making. We appear to be eyeing the 'buyer's market' in reactors and fuel as their supply increases because of major countries moving away from nuclear power. We should not forget that President Bush had defended his nuclear deal with India by saying that India's use of nuclear power will reduce pressure on oil. A Japanese minister has just declared that Japan might terminate its Fast Breeder Reactors to eliminate the rationale for reprocessing. When developed countries move away from such technologies, export incentives for such material to developing countries will increase. The reduced demand in some countries makes the market move to other regions. In fact, fear has been expressed that the ironic consequence of Fukushima may be a more dangerous global nuclear landscape.

Hiroshima and Fukushima have brought to light two facets of the danger from the nuclear genie. Man developed nuclear weapons in his quest for security and realised the folly of mutually assured destruction. The quest for energy security has driven him to develop nuclear power, the more benign manifestation of the atom. The time has come for him to pause and ensure that the second quest does not prove as dangerous as the first.

3

NUCLEAR POWER: THE THIRD WAY

The expectation of the nuclear establishments around the globe soon after the Fukushima disaster was that the extreme anxiety about nuclear power would die down sooner or later and that business would be as usual thereafter. The world is not there yet, but time is not far when Fukushima will be just a bad memory except for those who were affected by radiation. Not to learn its lessons from Fukushima is a grave error that humanity can make. By holding future generations hostage to nuclear power, we are doing them a great injustice when we know that no nuclear reactor is absolutely safe. We have every right to jeopardise our own generation, but those unborn should not be victims of our blind faith or lack of innovation or imagination. By dotting our coast with nuclear domes, we are leaving the future generations to live under the hood of a cobra.

Those who insist that nuclear power should be abandoned altogether at this instant and switch to other sources seem to be in a dream world. The investments made in the development of nuclear energy, particularly in the developing world, have paid rich dividends. As of now, the cost of nuclear power production is comparable with other sources and helps reduce greenhouse gas emissions. More than anything else, the current shortages of power cannot be met without expanding nuclear power in the short-term.

When public opinion was divided between pro-nuclear and anti-nuclear technologies, different governments had responded differently to the Fukushima tragedy. Germany and Switzerland were unequivocal in their decision to phase out nuclear power. Others, including Japan, the US, China and India announced investigations and innovations to reduce dangers. Those who were on the threshold of the nuclear age have quietly dropped their plans. Even some of the countries, which have pledged to stay on course, will alter their plans, slow them down and look for alternatives, particularly if the safety reviews reveal inadequacies as in the case of the US. The studies have already concluded that the US reactors cannot withstand multiple natural disasters, as it happened in Japan. China has lost some of its enthusiasm for nuclear power. In India, the mood in the establishment is cool confidence that nothing will go wrong here. Inspections and studies are pro forma as the conclusion is known. India will continue to develop nuclear power to meet its energy needs, even if there is an element of risk in it. The prime minister has ruled out phasing out of nuclear power, regardless of the outcome of the studies. It calls into question the purpose of the studies themselves.

There must be a third way, since committing the world to perpetual use of nuclear power is hazardous and we are in no position to switch to alternatives immediately. India should be able to visualise a world without nuclear power after twenty or thirty years. The optimum average age of a nuclear reactor is thirty years, and it will not be unreasonable to phase out the reactors, including the ones being installed now in a period of thirty years. Once we establish this as an objective, the entire planning of energy in India should be revised to ensure that we have sufficient capacity to develop alternative sources of energy within that period. Scientists speculate that if India had invested its resources and time on other forms of energy, we would not have needed nuclear power at all.

India was the first country to give the world the vision of a world without nuclear weapons. The point that it was an impractical idea did not deter us from sketching the various steps that would lead to Global Zero. After the deadline that we had set for it passed, the world has woken up to the wisdom of it. Why do we not put on our thinking caps again and draw up a plan of phasing out nuclear power in thirty years? Such a time frame will not immediately affect our nuclear programme, including acquisition of reactors from abroad. We can commission French reactors, if the location is acceptable to the people in the area and develop an adequate safety system for a short period, rather than for an indefinite length of time. Inevitably, we need to develop alternatives like solar and wind energy, in addition to traditional sources, which have to be tamed to protect the environment. If fusion technology or any other safe method of using the atom develops in the meantime, we shall be prepared to adopt them in place of fission.

Fukushima has roused the conscience of humanity in a way Three Mile Island and Chernobyl had not done. Faster communications and deeper knowledge of what happened there has dramatically altered the way the world looks at nuclear power. To argue that nobody has died of radiation, while thousands have perished in the raging waves and the falling bricks is to underestimate the impact of Fukushima on the minds of the people.

What India says to the ministerial meetings of the IAEA, and to the world at large is hugely significant. If we merely say that we will undertake inspections and make our inspectors fiercely independent and our processes transparent, we will miss an opportunity to give humanity a way to break away from fear. The choice should not be between fear of radiation and lack of development. A proposal by India to strive towards a nuclear power free world by 2040, with adequate development of alternative sources will be a major contribution to a world without using nuclear technology.

4

IAEA—THE WAY TO GO AFTER FUKUSHIMA

A distressed director general of the International Atomic Energy Agency, who helplessly witnessed a nuclear catastrophe in his own homeland with no authority or capability to help, invited the foreign ministers of member countries to Vienna in June 2011 to devise ways and means to strengthen the safety role of the Agency. Normally, conclaves of the IAEA are gatherings of top nuclear scientists and Vienna-based diplomats who claim monopoly of wisdom on matters nuclear and insist that the greatest danger to the world arises from proliferation of nuclear weapons beyond the designated nuclear weapon powers. But this time, the invitees were policymakers, who were tasked to think out of the box to rid the world of the scourge of nuclear accidents. Safety is too important a subject to be left to those with vested interests.

Now that the horrors of Fukushima have gone off the television screens, comfort is being sought in the thought that no one has died of radiation as against the thousands that perished on account of the earthquakes and tsunami. Like the Three Mile Island and Chernobyl, Fukushima will fade into history as another accident that did not need any more attention than its predecessors. But it will be unconscionable for the concerned authorities to just pay lip service to the safety mantra and move on with the business as usual in the comfort that God is in his heaven and all is well with the world.

The world seems to have long forgotten that the IAEA was created to harness atoms for peace safely, without diverting them for military use. The subsequent emergence of the Nuclear Non-Proliferation Treaty turned the Agency into a proliferation watchdog, with much of its resources devoted to the 'safeguards' aspect of its activities. Rightly did the director general lament that the IAEA was not a safety watchdog and it had no choice but to be on response mode when a meltdown took place in Fukushima. It took several days before the IAEA was given any responsibility. It had no source to tell them about the seriousness of the situation.

Prevention of accidents should be the highest priority for the IAEA. Its role should start from the designing of reactors and continue through installation and operation. Presently, such responsibilities rest with private companies, for whom profitability is paramount. Even state authorities give importance to efficiency and cost, rather than safety. Apart from setting standards, the IAEA should be involved in selecting venues to ensure that the places, which are vulnerable to earthquakes and tsunamis are excluded. It should be mandatory to involve the IAEA at every stage and the IAEA should, in turn, be given the resources necessary to respond to requests immediately and meaningfully. Peer reviews organised under the aegis of the Agency must also be mandatory for member states to accept.

Should an accident occur, the IAEA should be instantly involved in minimising the danger of radiation. Questions of sovereignty should be set aside as in the case of humanitarian intervention in the event of internal conflicts. To equip the IAEA to perform such functions, there should be a team at the disposal of the director general, which can be deployed at short notice, much like the rapid deployment forces maintained by governments.

When a group of eminent persons formulated a vision for the IAEA for 2020, the focus was on a nuclear renaissance. Today, the priority is to restore confidence in the people, particularly in the vicinity of reactors. Governments have little credibility in this matter and the IAEA should fill the gap.

The IAEA should restore the balance originally envisaged between promotion of nuclear energy, safety and safeguards. The overwhelming importance given to safeguards has deprived the Agency of its safety dimension. Only after safety is ensured can the IAEA engage in promotion of nuclear power. The IAEA should become as much a watchdog for safety as it is of non-proliferation. The future of nuclear power will depend on the confidence that the IAEA can eventually instil in humanity.

5

KUDANKULAM: THE JUDGMENT AND BEYOND

No one could fault the Supreme Court of India for its judgment on the diverse issues concerning the Kudankulam nuclear power plant. It was realistic, comprehensive and well-balanced. But neither did the protesters of Kudankulam, nor did the nuclear sceptics around the world find anything in it for comfort. The crisis in our energy scenario, sparked off by the global anxiety about safety, will continue to persist beyond the judgment. Stressing the indispensability of nuclear power for our development and highlighting the need to strike a balance between safety and development may only induce more apprehensions. While the court order has laid out the fundamentals, we have to go beyond it to device a way of operating the plant with adequate safety guarantees for the residents in and around Kudankulam.

Dismissing a petition challenging the Madras High Court's earlier order in favour of the plant, the Supreme Court termed the operationalisation of the Kudankulam nuclear power plant as necessary for the country's growth. The court stressed that development of nuclear energy is important for India and said, 'While setting up a project of this nature, we have to have an overall view of larger public interest rather than smaller violation of right to life guaranteed under Article 21 of the constitution.'

The court dismissed the risk element by stating that we have to balance economic and scientific benefits with that of minor radiological detriments on the touchstone of our national nuclear policy. 'Public money running into crores and crores of rupees has already been spent for the development, control and use of atomic energy for the welfare of the people and hence, we have to put up with such minor inconveniences, minor radiological detriments and minor environmental detriments,' the court said.

Turning to the need for safety, the court said that the regulatory authorities are obliged to perform their duty to ensure that safety measures are adequately taken before the plant commences its operation. 'Safety, security and life would constitute a pyramid within the sanctity of Article 21 and no jettisoning is permissible.' The delicate balance in other spheres may have some allowance, but in the case of establishment of a nuclear plant, the safety measures would not tolerate any lapse. The grammar has to be totally different. The court also said that problems highlighted were not unique to India and that other countries were also grappling with the situation. But it glossed over the measures taken by other countries to reduce dependence on nuclear power after the unfortunate accident at Fukushima.

The court adopted a conciliatory attitude towards the protesters by asking the local authorities to consider withdrawing the hundreds of cases clamped on the protesters, who were accused even of colluding with foreign countries to sabotage the plant. Accusations were made at the highest level that foreign funding was freely available to the agitators. The suggestion that the United States might be behind the agitation did not seem justified, as the US had a greater stake in India's nuclear future than any other country. By withdrawing the cases against them, the court had expected that the concerned people would heave a sigh of relief and quit the scene.

The judgment had not altered the situation on ground. There was indeed no legal bar against commissioning the reactor. Even the protesters were in no position to block the commissioning of the plant. What prevented the prime minister from keeping his promise to President Vladimir Putin were technical glitches related to the completion of the plant. No details of the problem came out till the Russian company, which supplied parts of the reactor, was hauled up in Moscow for supplying substandard components to plants throughout the world. The authorities in Kudankulam were forced to open up several segments of the plant, to inspect them for quality and precision. Some defective components like valves were discovered and they had to be replaced. The Supreme Court judgment was not relevant to those who are struggling day and night to meet the deadline for commissioning the plant.

The protesters announced that the judgment had made no difference to their plight either. They had not sought a court order to prevent the plant from being commissioned. They were more concerned that the several elaborate measures concerning safety steps, which were prescribed by the courts, had not been taken. The reports about the installation of defective components only fuelled their angst. They were still not fully aware of the disaster management plans and details of the emergency measures that would be available in the event of an accident. They see no hospitals coming up in the vicinity or earmarking of area for evacuees in an emergency. Their determination has only hardened after the Supreme Court judgment because they know now that they have no recourse to law on the basis of right to life. The court wants to give them better quality of life with the blessings of nuclear power rather than freedom from fear. As for withdrawal of cases, it does not seem to matter to them whether they live in the prisons or outside. They have pledged to continue their peaceful protests, regardless of the outcome.

Kudankulam reactors may well function normally as the other twenty reactors in our country have done for several years. There may be no serious earthquake or tsunami in the area and India may maintain its impeccable safety record. Power-starved Tamil Nadu and Kerala will find some reprieve and those in the cities will have a better quality of life.

But the question of safety raised after Fukushima will remain a concern as we continue to bank on failing memories and claims that the damage at Fukushima was not as catastrophic as it was projected to be. It is imperative at this point of time that the trust deficit be tackled in some way or the other. Despite the many assurances given by the government that the Atomic Energy Regulatory Board (AERB), the Indian regulatory agency, would be an independent body, it still remains subservient to the Atomic Energy Commission. In the face of lack of credibility of local authorities and even reputed scientists, it would be useful to get the IAEA to carry out a safety inspection of the plant. The IAEA would be only too happy to mount such an inspection. India has been fighting shy of IAEA safety inspections, but an inspection by its Operational Safety Review Team (OSART) of the Rajasthan Atomic Power Station was reassuring.

The ultimate solution, till a technological breakthrough eliminates radiation dangers, is to alter our energy mix, to reduce and discard nuclear energy for generation of power. For the small component of nuclear power that we envisage in our energy mix, we should find viable alternatives which are already available. Even a declaration by the government that we will strive for zero nuclear power in the long-term will give some comfort to the people who worry constantly about future generations.

Regardless of the wisdom contained in the Supreme Court judgment, we need to go beyond commissioning of plants after making sure through an international inspection, that it is safe to create a fool proof disaster management system and make a pledge that India will progressively move towards elimination of nuclear power within a given time frame.

6

NUCLEAR DISARMAMENT: TIMELINE CHALLENGES

Nuclear Base Camp: The Numbers Conundrum

Ever since Robert Oppenheimer invoked the Bhagavad Gita to create the mother of all metaphors, 'the radiance of a thousand suns' and 'the destroyer of worlds', nuclear disarmament efforts have given us many images and metaphors. But they were all images of mutually-assured destruction and inevitability of a nuclear catastrophe. There was even a telling image of the world resting comfortably under the hood of a cobra. But despair has turned into hope with the metaphor of a mountain which, though distant and high, does hold the promise of a panoramic view of a nuclear weapon free and non-violent world if we reach the summit. The world realises that the climb up the mountain will be slow and hazardous, but there appears to be a universal desire to make a determined effort.

The metaphor of the mountain has led to the image of a base camp, which is necessary to equip ourselves and to prepare for the climb. It is indeed a practical and necessary stage and has translated into practical measures; it encourages all nations, whether they possess nuclear weapons or not, to build a staging ground. It means the establishment of intermediate goals towards disarmament on which there could be a consensus.

The proponents of this concept have explained that the idea is to agree to proportional disarmament instead of smaller nuclear countries waiting till the others come down to their levels, before they contemplate disarmament. They would like to craft a treaty, whereby countries, coming from different levels, could agree to work at reciprocal and proportional cuts, which would aim at all countries reaching the same lower number of weapons at a future date. Former Secretary of Defence William Perry characterises the base camp as a place that would be safer than where we are today. It also serves as an organising principle to 'lead, but hedge', in keeping with the US nuclear posture.

While the base camp concept is novel in the new context of optimism, it has been part of every plan that has been put forward in the past. Though the general and complete disarmament is the ultimate objective, giving priority to nuclear disarmament and that too through various intermediate stages is not very different from the base camp idea. The Rajiv Gandhi Action Plan of 1988 and the other practical steps put forward by various powers have contemplated intermediate stages of various descriptions. The proposal for a complete freeze was another logical step, which did not find acceptance by the nuclear weapon states. The proposed FMCT is another interim measure which is desirable and logical.

It is not clear, however, whether we can approach the base camp concept on the basis of numbers. Such an approach has been adopted in the case of the Strategic Arms Reduction Treaty (START), but the world is sceptical about the numbers involved in the negotiations, as all categories of weapons are not included in the numbers game. Transparency is highly desirable, but often absent when it comes to counting weapons. Fixing agreed numbers to reach the base camp is likely to elude us. The idea of proportionate reduction in arsenals regardless of the existing size of the holdings will be anathema to those countries, which have only a minimum deterrent. India, for instance, has not revealed the number of weapons it considers necessary to have a credible minimum deterrent, and the numbers are a matter of speculation. How would India participate in negotiations in reduction without revealing the numbers?

A broader approach, which takes into account the optimism generated by President Obama's Prague speech in 2009, the sighting of the mountain, the encouraging signs at NPT Review Conferences and the Nuclear Security Summit, should move the disarmament effort forward.

India and the United States attempted precisely that at the summit level in their Joint Statement in 2010. The prime minister and the president agreed to join in a 'strong partnership to lead global efforts for non-proliferation and universal and non-discriminatory global disarmament.' Further, they 'affirmed the need for a meaningful dialogue among all states possessing nuclear weapons to build trust and confidence and for reducing the salience of nuclear weapons in international affairs and security doctrines.' The key words here are 'trust and confidence' and 'reducing the salience of nuclear weapons' in strategies. This will be a very good start for our journey to the base camp and beyond, but not easy to do as it requires fundamental rethinking in many capitals of the world. As the Norwegian foreign minister observed, 'Every small demonstration of our willingness to move forward towards abolition make many of the intermediate obstacles more surmountable.'

The nuclear weapon states, sadly, still consider nuclear

weapons important for their security and do not wish to consider a timeline for their elimination. In my view, the base camp will not be meaningful unless there is a collective commitment to a multilateral framework for negotiations within a time frame. Neither the NPT nor the CTBT has succeeded in accomplishing this. The FMCT negotiations remain stalled. An alternate route will be, as India has suggested, working on a global non-first use agreement as the first step towards delegitimisation of nuclear weapons. Hesitation on delegitimisation on the ground that it will outlaw retaliation seems unfounded, as any use of the weapons will be unthinkable if there is delegitimisation. A commitment to negotiating a Nuclear Weapons Convention may also be an appropriate element of the base camp.

Changing of postures, rather than agreeing on nuclear force sizes may be a practical approach to the base camp. In the case of the two countries which possess 95 per cent of the nuclear warheads, numbers are relevant to build mutual confidence, but for the others, the doctrinal commitment to nuclear weapons, regardless of numbers is the greater threat. It is no great comfort for the world to know that the nuclear weapons can now destroy the world only a dozen times, not dozens of times.

The coming to force of the START treaty in February 2011 has been universally welcomed. But further progress may be stalled on account of fears of China's growth. The focus is likely to shift to Asia, where the numbers game will be even more complex. In the Asian context, it will also be difficult to count the numbers considered necessary for minimum deterrent by different countries. Here again, a review of doctrines rather than entering a debate on numbers will have the desired impact.

The optimism that has entered the disarmament debate has not been fully justified by the latest signals from the major nuclear weapon states. The mountain and base camp images raise hope, but do not instil confidence. The urgency for nuclear disarmament going beyond legal obligations has also been sidestepped in the process of setting up long-term and intermediate stages. The time frame to reach Global Zero must be shorter if the world has to be safer.

7

BRINGING INDIA'S DREAM TO FRUITION

Global Zero or a world without nuclear weapons is not just a desirable goal; it is an imperative for the survival of mankind. A nuclear war between nations is unlikely. But the alarming picture of a terrorist holding a particular country or region, or even the whole world, to ransom by threatening to use a nuclear weapon looms large on the horizon. Instability in countries that possess nuclear weapons is a cause of particular concern. Even the most elaborate command and control systems are not immune to viruses or hackers. Today's civilisation can be protected and preserved only if nuclear weapons and other lethal materials are eradicated. Nuclear technology itself must be defanged sooner rather than later to make it benign enough to serve mankind. In other words, Global Zero must have no caveats.

Advocates envisage a phased plan for the verified elimination of nuclear weapons, starting with deep reductions in the Russian and US arsenals, to be followed by multilateral negotiations among all nuclear powers for an agreement to eliminate all nuclear weapons. The commitment of the presidents of Russia and the United States to a nuclear weapons free world represents a historic opportunity. This opportunity is also available to rising powers such as India. The world has a stake in the success of the initiative, and it is essential that New Delhi play a role in finding an effective and efficient path to reach that goal. India not only believes that 'getting to Zero' is possible, but it is the only country that has actually put forth a potential disarmament framework. Even after declaring itself a nuclear weapons state in 1998, India has pursued its disarmament agenda actively. India sees its nuclear arsenal only as a necessary evil in a world in which every major country has nuclear weapons. The general reduction of tensions in the world and the US–India nuclear deal, which has made India a partner rather than a target in non-proliferation and disarmament efforts, augur well for the Indian dream.

The concept of a nuclear weapons free world is attributable to India, where it was articulated with different names by Indian leaders since 1947. The idea of general and complete disarmament goes beyond a nuclear weapons free world; it also seeks a non-violent world envisaged by the Buddha and embraced by Mahatma Gandhi, who (after Hiroshima) said, 'The only moral which can be legitimately drawn from the supreme tragedy of the bomb is that it shall not be destroyed by counter-bombs. Violence cannot be destroyed by counter-violence. Mankind will only emerge out of violence through non-violence.'

India brought the concept to the international political level in 1988 with Rajiv Gandhi's action plan for a 'world order free of nuclear weapons and rooted in non-violence' to the UN General Assembly. There were four essential features of the plan: a. A binding commitment by all nations to eliminate nuclear weapons in intervals by the year 2010 at the latest; b. Participation of all states in the process of nuclear disarmament, whether or not they have nuclear capabilities; c. Demonstration of good faith by all states by making tangible progress at each stage towards the common goal; and d. An ideological change in policies and institutions to sustain a world free of nuclear weapons by undertaking negotiations to establish a comprehensive global security system under the aegis of the UN. The plan also suggested specific negotiations and treaties at different stages until the world reaches Global Zero, but also sustain it without apprehensions. Unfortunately, 2010 is long gone and the goal that India had envisioned to have reached by now is not even close.

But there is hope. In April 2009 in Prague, President Barack Obama declared, 'So today, I state clearly and with conviction America's commitment to seek the peace and security of a world without nuclear weapons.' The trajectory Obama suggested, however, was not new or unfamiliar. He advocated reducing the role that nuclear weapons play in national security strategies, renegotiating START with Russia, ratifying the CTBT, seeking a new fissile material cut-off treaty, strengthening the NPT and preventing terrorists from acquiring nuclear weapons. To strengthen the basic bargain of the NPT, Obama stressed that countries with nuclear weapons should move towards disarmament and countries without nuclear weapons should not try to acquire them, while all should have access to peaceful nuclear power.

The Mistake: Revitalising the NPT Bargain

The major disappointment of the Prague speech was that although the ultimate objective was laudable, the path suggested was the same old NPT track, which is considered discriminatory by non-nuclear weapons states. Although discrimination would end with the attainment of the goal, the world in the long interim period would remain divided, with the 'haves' accumulating more weapons and the 'have-nots' feeling a sense of diminishing security. The NPT, ratified in 1970, originally only had a shelf life of twenty-five years, and the review mechanism left open the possibility of it evolving with the times. No treaty, particularly one that bases itself on scientific knowledge and developments, can be made effective without making the appropriate changes over time. Extending the treaty indefinitely in 1995 was a sure way of making it a historic relic rather than a dynamic instrument to determine international behaviour.

The ultimate irony is that indefinite extension of the NPT prompted the Indian and Pakistani nuclear tests of 1998, adding two more nations to the list of nuclear weapons states. The perpetuation of the NPT, and that too as an unchangeable document for all times to come, removed the last hope that India had of shaping a new non-discriminatory regime by consensus. With the possibility of disarmament by the nuclear weapons states receding further, it had to blast its way into the nuclear club to secure for itself a place among the 'haves'. Pakistan followed suit.

The NPT has become an anachronism today. But there is some opportunity for India with former US Secretary of State Hillary Clinton's declaration in October 2009, 'In India we see a full partner in this effort and we look forward to working with them as we try to come up with the twenty-first century version of the NPT.' Unfortunately, there is no real evidence of such an effort in any of the road maps in Washington. 'The twenty-first century version of the NPT' must necessarily move away from the presumptions of the 1960s and take into account the dictates of the present day, including the energy crisis, the advent of non-state actors and technological advancement. The energy crisis and the threat of climate change would inevitably demand greater use of nuclear energy for peaceful purposes. A new arrangement with international facilities for enrichment and a fuel bank will support the energy development of developing countries.

Programmes for the development of economical and proliferation-resistant reactors do exist in the agenda of the IAEA, but they receive little attention. There should be greater accountability on the part of states to safeguard nuclear material. The existing system has no provision to deal with either the nuclear 'Walmart' of Abdul Qadeer Khan or the leakage of nuclear material from state sources. The new non-proliferation system must address these three key consideration: The grand bargain of the NPT has not led the world to security, essentially because it seeks to perpetuate rather than eliminate nuclear weapons in a discriminatory manner. By condoning vertical proliferation, it permits the further sophistication of nuclear weapons by the nuclear weapons states. The NPT does not impose any restrictions on the designated nuclear weapons states to control their arsenals. It addresses horizontal proliferation by asking the non-nuclear weapons states not to cross the nuclear Rubicon, without any restraint on vertical proliferation. Even the CTBT permits laboratory tests, which only the technologically advanced states can perform.

No less alarming is the fact that the nuclear powers have deliberately violated the NPT provisions not to transfer weapons technology to non-nuclear weapons states. The most celebrated case of such violation is by China, which shared technology with Pakistan and North Korea. Pakistan and North Korea have, in turn, helped others such as Iran and Libya with equipment and technology.

The commitment of the nuclear weapons states, in adherence to Article VI of the NPT, to pursue negotiations in good faith for general and complete disarmament has not materialised. The projection of the NPT, therefore, as an end in itself rather than as the first step in a long journey towards international peace and security has transformed the context and rationale of the grand bargain. Relying on the NPT bargain as the path for the future undermines the credibility of the goal of a truly nuclear free world. A fundamental change from mutual assured destruction to a collective security structure, which encompasses nuclear and non-nuclear states, must take place right now.

Similarly, the CTBT and the projected FMCT will only be partial measures, even if they come into force in the near future. The US Congress is not yet ready to ratify the CTBT. Even if it does, the caveat enshrined in the Treaty that a number of designated countries should ratify it before it comes into force will delay its implementation. There is also criticism that it is neither comprehensive nor is it a ban on testing. An FMCT is still in its infancy in Geneva, and its growth and maturity are not guaranteed. The demand that an FMCT should cover eliminating existing stockpiles may sound its death knell before it even develops. Both these treaties should be linked to disarmament rather than remain the pillars of the NPT edifice, which has begun to crumble.

The first requirement of moving towards a nuclear-free world is for its proponents to recognise the antiquated nature of the NPT. A paradigm shift from relying on the Treaty is a fundamental requirement for the idea of the elimination of nuclear weapons to be universally accepted. Faced as they are with the threat of global warming, many countries are knocking at the IAEA's door to seek technology to use nuclear power in such crucial sectors as power generation, medicine and water. Unless the IAEA has sufficient resources to meet these increasing needs, it cannot play its non-proliferation role effectively.

The vision of a nuclear weapons free world is shared by most countries, but the way forward is far from clear. The START process, delayed though it has been, is reassuring but it should bring in the other nuclear weapons states as part of the move towards Global Zero. Freezing the production of weapons and related materials should add credibility to reduction proposals.

Finally, concerns over evolving requirements for what

countries believe is necessary for minimum deterrence will have to be tackled as countries' nuclear arsenals decline. The number of weapons that each country will insist on keeping until they are certain about their security will change as their perceptions of the external threat evolves. Altogether, these obstacles to achieving a world without nuclear weapons are enormous, but not insurmountable if a step-by-step approach with measures for verification can be devised that does not rely on using the outdated NPT framework.

How to Use the US—India Partnership to Get to Global Zero

India, as stated earlier, had believed in and championed general and complete disarmament, particularly nuclear disarmament. India's nuclear doctrine, to the extent it is known to the world, is based on a minimum deterrent. The development of nuclear weapons by China, which had invaded India in 1962, was a compelling factor in India's decision to test. It was also well-known that Pakistan had developed a clandestine nuclear capability long before the Indian tests of 1998. India has not abandoned its various initiatives for nuclear disarmament at the UN, even after it acquired nuclear weapons, and is committed to eliminating nuclear weapons together with the other nuclear weapons states. Due to the US–India nuclear deal, India assumed the responsibilities of a signatory of the NPT without actually signing the treaty by agreeing to: a. Subject its non-military facilities to IAEA inspections, which included fourteen out of its twenty-two power reactors; b. Sign the Additional Protocol, which will allow for more detailed inspections by the IAEA; c. Commit to halting further nuclear testing; d. Work to strengthen the security of its nuclear arsenals; e. Pledge to negotiate an FMCT with the United States in good faith and to sign it when ready; and f. Ensure that all equipment for nuclear reactors and fuel imported from other countries, including the US, will be for peaceful uses only. In other words, an India-specific dispensation was made in light of the new confidence in US–India relations during the Bush administration. Yet, the Obama administration has begun to hark back to the NPT, the CTBT and an FMCT, essentially setting the clock back.

Once the commitment of the nuclear weapons states to complete disarmament is established, with concomitant changes in security strategies and related global postures, the others, such as India, will feel confident about the intentions of those with abundant nuclear arsenals. The international situation is still characterised by lack of trust and political will, as demonstrated by the total absence of any reference to non-proliferation and disarmament in the 2005 UN World Summit outcome. The first step, therefore, is to seek international consensus in the UN General Assembly through the Conference on Disarmament, which was established in 1979 as the only multilateral disarmament negotiating forum. Unilateral declarations, however sincere, and UN Security Council resolutions, however well-intentioned, will be no substitute for such a global consensus. India will be able to join the United States in the quest for an alternative non-proliferation system once there is a global consensus on complete disarmament.

The action plan presented by Rajiv Gandhi to the Conference on Disarmament in 1988 still remains the most comprehensive initiative on nuclear disarmament, covering issues from nuclear testing and fissile materials trade to a time-bound elimination of stockpiles and eventually of nuclear weapons. Currently, India has five basic priorities in the global dialogue regarding disarmament and non-proliferation: a. To have all nuclear powers reaffirm to completely eliminate their nuclear weapons with a specified framework of time; b. To extract a promise from these states to reduce the salience of nuclear weapons in their national security doctrines; c. To reduce nuclear danger, including the risk of accidental nuclear war, particularly by de-alerting nuclear weapons; d. To negotiate a global agreement among nuclear-weapons states on no-first use against other nuclear powers and the non-use against non-nuclear weapons states; and e. To enable multilateral disarmament bodies such as the UN's Disarmament Commission and the Conference on Disarmament to make effective contributions to the goal of nuclear disarmament process worldwide.

Broadly speaking, the two political aims pursued by India are nuclear disarmament through a process of delegitimisation of nuclear weapons and reducing the immediate nuclear danger. New Delhi has supported a non-discriminatory and verifiable FMCT and shown interest in the Proliferation Security Initiative as well as in regional fuel banks. India would like to have inter national agreements to ban anti-satellite weapons as well as the deployment of weapons in outer space. The so-called Four Horsemen's proposal issued by Henry Kissinger, Sam Nunn, William Perry, and George Schultz in 2008 advocated 'a series of steps that will pull us back from the nuclear precipice'. The first of these steps is changing the Cold War posture of deployed weapons to increase warning time and reduce the danger of accidental or unauthorised use of nuclear weapons. Obama's declarations have transformed the scene, with his emphasis on the need for the United States to take the lead in reducing the strategic significance of nuclear weapons.

Less Words, More Action

Any initiative to move towards a nuclear weapons free world should address the threat or use of nuclear weapons by any state or non-state actor. This would entail a combination of non-proliferation and disarmament because horizontal and vertical proliferations pose grave challenges to humanity. Simultaneously, it should promote peaceful uses of nuclear energy without fear of safety or proliferation. Particular attention should be given to prevent nuclear terrorism, which has become a high priority. Universality of participation is essential for decision-making, so the existing UN mechanisms should be strengthened. In this context, the IAEA presents a ready and available forum to assist the UN General Assembly to shape a consensus.

The UN has been engaged in a quest for a nuclear weapons free world from its very inception. The very first resolution of the UN General Assembly, adopted on 24 January 1946, sought the elimination of nuclear weapons and other weapons of mass destruction. Three special sessions on disarmament made significant contributions to that goal, but a lack of a consensus has prevented the General Assembly from holding another such session.

In a strange turn of history, the threat of global nuclear war has gone down, but the threat of a nuclear attack has gone up. More nations have acquired these weapons. Testing has continued. Black market trade in nuclear secrets and nuclear materials abound. The technology to build a bomb has spread. Terrorists are determined to buy, build or steal one. Our efforts to contain these dangers are centred on a global non-proliferation regime, but as more people and nations break the rules, we could reach the point where the centre cannot hold. Although the diagnosis is perfect, the treatment envisaged is far too inadequate to address the emergency. A fundamental change in perspective, amounting to the delegitimisation of nuclear weapons and the abandonment of the outdated NPT, is required to change the strategic mindset of the nuclear powers.

A nuclear weapons free world is far in the distance, but the time has come to move from pious declarations to concrete action. As a reluctant nuclear weapon power with a minimum deterrent and an active disarmament agenda, India will be in the forefront of the movement for a nuclear weapons free world. It is already ahead of some of the nuclear weapons states by advocating delegitimisation of nuclear weapons and negotiations on a Nuclear Weapons Convention. The world can count on India as a partner in non-proliferation and disarmament, particularly if there is a universal commitment to move towards a verifiable nuclear weapons free world.

Kripacharya
The United Nations

Kripacharya, the venerated *kulguru* of the Pandavas and Kauravas of the Kuru dynasty, and the Yadavas and Vrishnis—the clan to which Lord Krishna was born into—was a wise sage, an iconic teacher, an astute advisor, a pious priest. Kripacharya was an unassailable protector of righteousness and dutifulness. Placed in the middle of a family feud, he remained committed to impartiality and sought solutions for the common good. After the great war of Kurukshetra, the new emperor Yudhishtira insisted that Kripacharya—though he fought on the side of the enemy force obliging duty's call—stayed on and served as an uncontaminated ray of light to illumine the path of integrity and goodwill for several generations to come.

The United Nations Organisation born in the post-war scenario embodies the spirit of Kripacharya, remaining as it does as the sentinel of justice in an unjust and disunited world. Several voices of dissent may have been heard and several wars may have been fought even after the UN came into existence, but it is an undeniable fact that but for the UN, the world might have witnessed a third world war by now. The spirit of Kripacharya's wisdom should live through unbiased, impartial bodies like the UN in order to inculcate reason and rationale at the core of world affairs. Analogous to the role of Kripacharya at Kurukshetra, the UN was established in order to instil an atmosphere of peace and cooperation among the nations, in the aftermath of the WWII. The UN has been serving as the ultimate negotiator for safeguarding peace, human rights and justice ever since.

India, a founding member of the UN, has played a significant role in the UN through its active participation in the discussions, proposing seminal resolutions and acting in the interest of the global commons. India has always had a clear vision and an unbiased take on issues of international concern, especially newer issues like climate change, nuclear disarmament, global economic crisis etc. It is hoped that Chiranjeevi Kripacharya's pearls of wisdom and impartiality will continue to lead the way for India and the UN to ensure a future of peace and harmony. This section consists of a series of essays and talks on the functioning, successes and failures and proposed reforms of the United Nations, with special focus on India.

Few Indian diplomats can claim the kind of vast experience of the UN that TP Sreenivasan has. He has served at the ambassadorial level in three of the four UN headquarters cities: New York, Nairobi and Vienna. He is considered to possess an encyclopaedic mind on negotiating processes in the UN. The pieces here reflect his erudition and wealth of information on the world body.

1

UNITED NATIONS: RELEVANCE IN TODAY'S WORLD

The task set out for me is to cover four sets of issues relating to the United Nations today—the relevance of the United Nations in the emerging world order, the role of the Security Council in the maintenance of international peace and security and the urgent need of its reform, peacekeeping operations and the proposal for a standby force for the UN and the funding mechanism of the UN. I shall deal with them on the basis of my personal experience of the UN in different capacities and locations, during the period 1980 to 2004, updated by studies and reports.

UN is like motherhood—universal, unquestionable and unassailable. It is considered benign, benevolent and even beatific. Against its larger purpose and mission, we gloss over its inadequacies and blemishes. It was a dream-come-true after a devastating global conflagration to save succeeding generations from the scourge of war with a pledge to beat swords into ploughshares. In embracing the UN Charter, the original member states and those who joined later reposed their faith in its principles and endorsed its purposes even if they had lingering doubts about its structure and procedures. At age sixty-eight, the United Nations remains a beacon of hope for humanity. It attracts the mighty and the meek, the strong and the weak, the big and the small and each finds satisfaction, even if it is only in its aspirations finding utterance or in contributing its mite to the UN's growth.

In analysing the relevance of the United Nations in the emerging world order, it should be remembered that the United Nations is only as relevant as its members want it to be. As the first Secretary General Dag Hammarskjold once remarked, 'The UN is not an abstract Picasso, but a drawing made by each of its members.' It was established in the name of 'we the people', but it is essentially an intergovernmental club, in which every member jealously guards its sovereign equality. Writer Alexander Solzhenitsyn said, 'It is not a United Nations Organisation. It is a United Governments Organisation.' Membership of any international organisation entails the surrender of a fraction of the state's sovereignty, but they assert their sovereignty at every point of decision-making. For smaller and weaker states, membership of the UN itself is a guarantee of its sovereignty. The powerful nations constantly endeavour to turn it into an instrument of foreign policy and when they fail, they question its relevance. Governments do not always want the UN to succeed when they refer issues to it. They want to pass the buck. Failure is an essential part of the UN's 'proven capacity to fail'.

The democracy deficit in the United Nations is evident in its structure, which has a one-nation one-vote system in the General Assembly, while the more powerful Security Council has a P-5 oligarchy, which seeks to shape international peace and security according to its own whims and fancies. The Charter has made the United Nations a conservative body, with the provisions for change most stringent. Even the most anachronistic provisions of the Charter remain frozen in time. The unwritten sartorial laws and archaic forms of address bear testimony to the conservative nature of the United Nations.

The relevance of the UN, however, is ensured by its resilience, which has enabled it to move with the times, in response to the specific needs, unanticipated at the time of its inception. Instead of amending the Charter, the UN has readjusted itself by dealing with new areas of concern such as terrorism, environment, HIV/AIDS and piracy and by inventing new concepts such as peacekeeping, peace building, Responsibility to Protect (R2P) etc. The Charter has not stood in the way of expanding the agendas of every organ of the United Nations.

When it comes to the structure of the United Nations, including the size and composition of the Security Council, the resistance has been uncompromising. The reason is not far to seek, because nothing short of a revolution can change the entrenched supremacy of the permanent members. Since the last expansion of the Council in 1963, the membership of the UN has increased dramatically and game changing developments have taken place, but the size and structure of the Council has remained static.

The question today is not whether change is needed, but whether the provisions of the very Charter that established the institution can bring about a real change. If history is any guide, major changes take place when the time is ripe, in unexpected ways, regardless of the strength of those who seek change and those who resist it. The provisions of the law that seek to protect the establishment will be thrown to the winds and the old system will yield place to the new. We have many examples in history to show that those who have conceded changes have lasted longer than those who have resisted the forces of change.

India was among those who lit the first spark of inevitable change back in 1979, at the height of the Cold War, when an item entitled, 'Equitable representation on and increase in the membership of the Security Council', was inscribed on the agenda of the General Assembly. The demand was to add a few more non-permanent members, on the simple logic that the ratio between the strength of the General Assembly and that of the Security Council should be maintained. The exponential increase in the membership of the UN should be reflected in the size of the Security Council. This principle was, in fact, followed in 1963 when the number of non-permanent members was raised from six to ten. The reaction from the permanent members was instant and shocking. In an unprecedented show of solidarity, they opposed the move tooth and nail. They argued that any expansion of the Security Council would undermine its efficiency, integrity and credibility and ensured that the agenda item was postponed year after year, with a nominal and sterile debate. The idea remained alive, but no action was taken till the end of the Cold War.

The game changed in the early nineties, when the idea of adding new permanent members was brought up by Brazil, and India initiated the exercise of ascertaining the views of the members and setting up a mechanism to study the proposals and to reach a consensus. The permanent members, led by the US, offered a 'quick fix' after initial hesitation and proposed the addition of Japan and Germany as permanent members on the ground of their being the highest contributors to the UN budget after the US and a marginal increase in the non-permanent membership. If India and the other Non-Aligned countries had not stopped the quick fix and insisted on comprehensive reform, the door for expansion would have been closed after inducting Japan and Germany at that time. We demolished the payment argument by stating that permanent membership should not be up for sale. If I may be permitted to quote from my own speech at the Working Group in February 1995, 'Contribution to the UN should not be measured in terms of money. We do not agree with the view expressed by a delegation that permanent membership is a privilege that can be purchased. Financial contributions are determined on the basis of "capacity to pay" and those who pay their assessments, however small, are no whit less qualified for privilege than the major contributors.'

As a lethargic debate went on in the Working Group for years, national positions evolved and loyalties changed, but it became clear that the expansion of the Security Council could not be easily accomplished. The formation of an interest group called the 'Coffee Club' and later, 'Uniting for Consensus', which opposed any expansion of the permanent membership made the situation more chaotic. We ourselves advanced our position from seeking to establish criteria, such as population, seminal contribution to the UN, participation in peacekeeping operations etc. to staking a claim and began campaigning bilaterally in capitals. Over the years, our claim has been recognised. One adverse consequence of the debate, however, was that the discussions highlighted that a vast majority of member states had not served even once as non-permanent members on the Security Council, while countries like India, Japan, Pakistan and Egypt had served on the Council several times. This led to our long absence from the Council from 1993 to 2010, after having been elected as a non-permanent member seven times in the earlier period.

Efforts made outside the Working Group were also fruitless. After the deliberations of a High Level Group, Secretary General Kofi Annan proposed two plans: Plan A proposing creation of six permanent and three non-permanent seats and Plan B proposing eight new seats for four years, subject to renewal and one non-permanent seat. The Plan B had greater acceptability in the Group and it was at the insistence of the Indian member of the Group that Plan A was included. Another exercise undertaken by India, Brazil, Germany and Japan (G-4) to get the General Assembly to adopt a resolution on expansion failed to take off because of differences with the African Group.

It, however, resulted in the G-4 conceding for the first time that they would not insist on the veto at least for fifteen years. The General Assembly entered intergovernmental negotiations to suggest a 'timeline perspective' to agree on reform in two stages on the basis of a draft text, but no progress has been reported as yet. A move was initiated by the G-4 to introduce a resolution to decide that both permanent and non-permanent membership will be expanded, but it did not command majority support and was abandoned.

The only silver lining in our quest for a permanent seat on the Security Council is that the need for expansion has been recognised by the entire membership and that there is also recognition that if the permanent membership is ever expanded, India will be the first developing country to find a place in it. For the rest, there are almost as many views as there are members of the UN about the size, composition and rights and responsibilities of the members of the Security Council.

A major development in February 2013 was the emergence of a draft resolution from the Caribbean Community (Caricom), which is nothing but a wish list of the aspirants to permanent membership as well as of those who seek an expansion of the non-permanent membership. The draft envisages a Security Council consisting of eleven permanent members with veto and sixteen non-permanent members. The additional seats will give two permanent seats to Africa, two permanent seats to Asia, one permanent seat to Europe and one permanent seat to Latin America. The G-4 has reason for joy about this formula as it meets its own demand. Africa's demand for two permanent seats has also been met. But the permanent members, the Coffee Club and several countries, which have championed the abolition of the veto, will vigorously oppose the Caricom draft. But if it can secure more than 128 votes in the General Assembly, the pressure will increase on the permanent members to at least offer an alternative formula and enter into serious negotiations in a new forum as the existing intergovernmental negotiations have reached a dead end. But as it has happened in the past, the permanent five will try, by hook or by crook, to stave off a vote on the Caricom draft in the General Assembly.

The US, which had supported Japan and Germany in the early nineties, now favours 'two or so' new permanent members, including Japan, and 'two or three' non-permanent members making an addition of only five more to the Security Council. Such a formula is a non-starter. The support extended to India by President Obama during his visit to India is in the form of a wish without a commitment to bring it about. His words were, 'In the years ahead, I look forward to a reformed Security Council that includes India as a permanent member.' Though this is a significant departure from the previous US position, it is not enough for the US to extend support to India; it should shape a formula which is acceptable to the membership. Its reservation over Germany and Brazil will itself deprive it of being decisive on the issue of expansion.

We did not need WikiLeaks to find the reasons for the reluctance of the US to bring about expansion of the Council. But we now have it in black and white what we knew from the beginning. 'We believe expansion of the Council along the lines of the models currently discussed will dilute US influence in the body.... On most important issues of the day—sanctions, human rights, Middle East etc.—Brazil, India and most African states are currently far less sympathetic to our views than our European allies,' said the US ambassador in a cable in December 2007. The US delegation at the UN seems to have only a watching brief till intervention becomes necessary to prevent an expansion that will not serve US interests. A special report of the Council on Foreign Relations, which has urged the president to do so, makes the expansion contingent on demonstration of the qualifications of permanent membership. The position of the aspirants on non-proliferation, climate change and human rights will be subject to scrutiny.

China is opposed explicitly to Japan and implicitly to India, on the issue of representation of developing countries in the Council. Its position could be decisive, as the permanent members will coordinate their positions before any advance is made. France, UK and Russia are not likely to support the draft, despite their declared support for a modest expansion, including recognition of India's credentials for permanent membership.

It is clear that it will be difficult to accomplish the fundamental change we are seeking by way of the procedure laid down for change. Like it happened in the case of the formation of G-20 when the G-8 could not resolve the unprecedented economic crisis, a situation may arise when the P-5 find it difficult to maintain international peace and security without additional permanent members, and thus, their hands may be forced to accept change. Such an ominous future was predicted by the president of the General Assembly, when he said on 16 May 2011, 'Unless we find the determination to advance on the issue, the UN will lose its credibility. Our organisation will be marginalised and important issues will be discussed in other forums and groupings, which are perceived to be more efficient and more representative of the new realities of the day.' Such a situation may arise sooner than later and that gives us reason for hope.

The Security Council chamber at the UN headquarters in New York, originally a gift from the Norwegian government, was refurbished in 2013 with another grant from the Norwegians, but there was no provision for extra space for the aspirants at the horseshoe table. Shashi Tharoor, who was present, put the UN on notice that the table would have to be extended soon to accommodate new entrants. 'This event is a reminder that institutions and places that looked fresh and relevant in 1952 need extensive repair work to bring them up to date for 2013. What was true of the fixtures, wallpaper and electronics of the Security Council is also true of its composition and working methods,' he said. But the constraint will not be the size of the table, but the mindset of the mighty permanent members.

The effectiveness of the Security Council in the maintenance of international peace and security is contingent upon achieving unanimity of the permanent members. The concept of such unanimity stands diluted, as abstention on a resolution by a permanent member does not amount to the absence of a concurring vote. Unanimity was virtually impossible during the Cold War and the Security Council remained paralysed when wars raged in many parts of the world, leaving it to other initiatives to order ceasefires and to bring about reconciliation. But beginning with the first Gulf War, the Security Council was able to unite in dealing with several hotspots. The largest number of peacekeeping operations was launched during this period. Even the provision of the Charter, which prohibits interference in the internal affairs of member states, did not militate against measured interventions. Principles of such interventions under R2P have been drawn up. But there have been instances of lack of unanimity among the P-5, as in the case of Syria. The balance sheet of the Security Council will show that, as long as the vital interests of the P-5 are not involved, the Security Council is able to act in accordance with the Charter.

The advent of terrorism and the threat to international peace and security from non-state actors is a new phenomenon that the Security Council has to contend with. The lack of a UN definition of terrorism and the theory that one man's freedom fighter is another man's terrorist did not stand in the way of resolute action by the Security Council. A comprehensive convention against terrorism has still eluded the UN, but various ways have been found to take action against terrorist outfits. Declarations of terrorist organisations and sanctions imposed against them have helped the fight against terrorism, including in Jammu and Kashmir.

Taking advantage of the end of the Cold War and the expansion of UN peacekeeping operations, Secretary General Boutros Ghali proposed an Agenda for Peace in the early nineties, with a number of proposals to make peace operations more effective. He used the provisions of Chapter Seven of the Charter to justify military involvement without the consent of the parties. Although the Charter had envisaged enforcement action by an international military force, this had not happened except in the Korean case in 1950. The evolution of peacekeeping operations was haphazard and the procedures for approving, organising forces, equipping them and deploying them were cumbersome and time-consuming. Ghali proposed, therefore, the establishment of a standby force for rapid deployment as soon as the Security Council authorised an operation. This proposal earned him the reputation of trying to be a 'general' rather than a 'secretary general'. The proposal was treated politely by the General Assembly and the Security Council, but sidelined by adopting a series of measures such as notification by member states of specific forces or capabilities, which could be made available with the approval of the national authorities.

The proposal comes up off and on in diplomatic and academic circles, and polls taken in some member states show that support for a standby force has wide support among the public. Sentiment has grown for such force to be used to prevent conflict, to combat terrorism and to enforce non-proliferation. But member states have been wary of the proposal because each peace operation is distinct and complex and a single formula cannot apply to all situations.

A standby force for rapid deployment has merits, as that will enable the Security Council to act quickly to avoid the kind of tragedies that occurred in Rwanda, Darfur and Kosovo. It will be a peacemaker and peace enforcer if it has a strong mandate. But the member states are not yet ready to bestow such sovereign powers either on the Security Council or on the secretary general. The Security Council embodies a necessarily selective approach in deploying forces, depending on the circumstances in each case. The UN is reluctant to involve the Security Council in certain conflicts and selectivity is rooted in caution and prudence. The command structure is distinct in different cases and has to be non-partisan and meritocratic. A UN standing force is generally considered impractical for these reasons.

The number of peacekeeping operations has dropped of late and the UN is able to put together troops at fairly short notice, as there are several countries, which place troops readily at the disposal of the UN. India, Pakistan and Bangladesh have been good troop contributing countries. Peacekeeping training centres have come up in some countries, including India and the frequent consultations with troop contributing countries have facilitated early resolution of routine problems. India lost five soldiers in South Sudan, adding to the considerable Indian casualties in peacekeeping operations. Unlike in the US and other Western countries, where there is a hue and cry when their soldiers lose lives in the service of the UN, India has come to accept casualties in peacekeeping as inevitable price for keeping the peace. The evolution of a command and control system, away from NATO doctrine has also been helpful.

The UN peacekeeping operations had their moments of glory like in Cambodia and Namibia and when it was awarded the Nobel Peace Prize, but their failures have also been glaring. Peacekeepers have been helpless spectators of butchering of innocent lives and even genocide for lack of mandate, equipment or funding. Even worse, peacekeepers have been found guilty of corruption, crimes and exploitation of the very people they were supposed to protect. But, according to Lakhdar Ibrahimi, UN special envoy for Syria, 'No failure did more to damage the standing and credibility of UN peacekeeping in the 1990s than its reluctance to distinguish victim from aggressor.'

The budget of the UN is shared by the member states on the basis of capacity to pay and the system has worked well, except when the US held back its contributions for political ends on the dictum that he who pays the piper should call the tune. The US made the UN starve of funds to force reform in the style of spending, prompting a comment that the US was not different from Cinderella's mother! But the payment argument has not prevented countries like India from playing an effective role though our share has been below one per cent of the cost. Nor have Germany and Japan gained any major advantages on account of their high contributions. India is one of the few countries, which have paid the contributions in full and on time.

The UN has contemplated changes in the funding mechanism of the UN, particularly in development funds, including the technical cooperation funds of the specialised agencies, such as the IAEA, as at present, such funds are voluntary and not apportioned among member states. Both, the developed and developing countries, have resisted change. Brave promises have been made by some countries to liberate the UN from the financial grip of the developed countries, but none has put their money where their mouths are.

The funding and budgeting methods of the UN are so complex and the checks and balances are so many that any reform is hard to accomplish. Apart from the Fifth Committee of the General Assembly, the Advisory Committee on Administrative Questions (ACABQ), a most powerful body of elected individuals, the Committee on Programme and Coordination (CPC) and the Committee on Contributions come into play before funding is found for any programme that is adopted by the UN. Even reducing expenditure on defunct organs, sunset operations or economy measures are hard to accomplish. The Trusteeship Council has very little to do, but its budget cannot be eliminated because of long-term contracts and service conditions of professionals employed by it. The moribund Military Staff Council still holds ceremonial dinners for delegates from thirty-nine countries. Once, the General Assembly decided to stop the supply of pitchers of water to each delegate at all meetings and set up drinking water fountains outside the halls, believing that more than a million USD could be saved. But when the expenditure statement for the year came, the expenditure was still there because the staff engaged in supply of water could not be sent home. No wonder when the secretary general was asked how many people worked in the UN, he said, 'about 50 per cent!'

A word must be said, in conclusion, about India and the United Nations. India is among the countries that take the UN very seriously. An investigative report on the oil for food programme in Iraq indicted the secretary general, but the SG survived and the then Indian foreign minister had to resign as his name was found in an annex to the report. Gone are the days when we took the Kashmir issue to the UN. We do not take any bilateral issue to the UN anymore, but we do our best to contribute to the growth of the UN. We do not think very deeply about the value of permanent membership, particularly if it is without the veto. We have been exaggerating our accomplishments as a non-permanent member and imagining that our claim to a permanent seat has been strengthened. The truth of the matter is that every country on the Council, whether permanent or non-permanent, will act in its own national interest even when it is elected regionally. No one, other than the candidate itself is, therefore, enthused by claims of permanent membership.

India has given much more to the UN by way of concepts,

seminal resolutions, conventions and the rest than it has gained by way of core interests. We have had to plough the lonely furrow on issues such as self-determination, non-proliferation, International Criminal Court and also on an Arms Trade Treaty. But we count our blessings from the UN not in terms of the concrete benefits it gives us, but on account of the hope it holds out for world peace and prosperity.

2

REFORM OF GLOBAL INSTITUTIONS

Global institutions, by their very nature, have to remain dynamic and ready for change. The mere change of membership, the entry and exit of member states, brings in changes in priorities, agenda and nature of functioning, as the sovereignty of member states continues to be the guiding principle in international relations. Changes in the global power structure, sometimes gradual and quiet and sometimes sudden and dramatic, also do force changes in global institutions. Continuous reform, therefore, is essential for global institutions to remain relevant, effective and efficient. History has shown that only resilient global bodies have survived.

Reforms are cyclical in nature for all global institutions and the process can never be completed once and for all. The challenges of the times impose reform to meet immediate needs, and it gets formalised only subsequently to bring the practice in line with the statutes of the organisations. The most significant restructuring of global institutions is the emergence of G-20 in the wake of the global economic crisis. The speed and efficiency with which this was accomplished should be a model for other global institutions. Even the financial institutions, which were considered extremely conservative, have begun to see changes sweeping through them, as a result of the transformation of the world economy.

The Commonwealth underwent a fundamental change when India decided to remain within it as a republic, and its agenda has also been flexible and responsive to the demands of the time.

The United Nations itself is the classic example of an international organisation, which has changed beyond recognition without any change in its Charter. The agenda of the UN and its priorities today were not dreamt of by the authors of the Charter. From peacekeeping to human rights, from terrorism to climate change, the UN has taken on tasks and responsibilities not envisaged in the Charter. They are subsumed in the general concept of maintenance of international peace and security. Fight against apartheid and the concept of humanitarian intervention have amended the basic tenet of non-interference in internal affairs of states. The existence in the Charter of outdated words and phrases, which make a mockery of the existing state of the world, has not inhibited the functioning of the UN.

The adoption of the Agenda for Peace and the Agenda for Development and the massive array of declarations, treaties and resolutions have made the UN richer and relevant. The changes in the working methods of the Security Council and the General Assembly are far-reaching enough to meet the aspirations of the members for change to a great extent.

The history of the UN has shown that one thing that cannot be changed without a formal amendment to the Charter is the composition of the Security Council. The UN went through the difficult process of amendment to the Charter in 1965 to raise the number of non-permanent members from six to ten. We have now reached a stage when a change in the Charter is necessary to reflect the realities, not only of the enhanced membership of the UN, but also of the power structure in the world, which is dramatically different from the days after the end of the Second World War.

India is of the view that time for concrete action has come after thirty years of discussions on this matter. On a personal note, I was at the UN as a young diplomat when India introduced the relevant agenda item in the General Assembly in 1979. Every aspect of the issue has been considered and there is now a consensus that expansion is necessary in both categories of Security Council membership. Today, we have reached text based negotiations with different formulas and numbers. What is required is political will to act here and now.

In his report 'In Larger Freedom', Secretary General Kofi Annan had brought down the options to two and in our view, Plan A is clearly preferable for the simple reason that creating a new category of members, as outlined in Plan B, will be clearly invidious. In discussing strategy, the one thing that we have to remember is that support to one country or another, however strongly worded, will not lead to a decision. Members, preferably the permanent members, should promote a formula, like Kofi Annan's Plan A, which has the potential for securing a two-thirds majority in the General Assembly. As for the identity of the new permanent members, India has held the view that criteria should be established for them. The UK is in a position to take the lead in this regard.

The G-4 countries, Japan, Germany, Brazil and India have taken certain initiatives to speed up the process of reform. The difficult question of veto can, perhaps, be tackled at a later stage. The India–UK Roundtable appears to be an ideal venue for reaching an understanding on this important issue.

3

INDIANS IN THE UN SYSTEM

You cannot throw a stone into the UN or its specialised agencies without hitting an Indian, but there are no Indians as chiefs in any of these bodies. Indians may do all the work and win approbation, but even today, none of the nearly twenty specialised agencies is headed by an Indian even though many Indians in key places may well be doing the work of these agencies. After Arcot Ramachandran headed the UN-Habitat in Nairobi many years ago, we have not been able to get a similar post even though we have highly qualified experts in many areas.

The reason for this sorry state of affairs is that we do not have a policy to create opportunities for deserving individuals to enable them to grow in the system. Even those who go fairly high do so by their own initiative and by pulling wires in the government to gain support for one post or another. Many posts in the UN system are the preserves of different countries and the countries concerned plan the careers of successors in such a way that the jobs remain within the countries concerned, or in the regional groups.

Even the Indian candidature for the post of the UN secretary general was at the initiative of the candidate himself. The Government of India did not give any thought to finding a winnable candidate for the post and merely made Shashi Tharoor India's candidate after he decided to make a bid and influenced high places in India. Even after he became the official candidate, he did not get the whole-hearted support of those in the field and many of them were happy that he lost, as was predicted. It was argued that his candidature would stand in the way of reform of the UN and India winning a permanent seat in the Security Council.

The Asian Group in the UN is so diverse that there is hardly any possibility of agreement on a common candidate, except on a rotational basis. There were already several Asian candidates, including Ban Ki-moon when the Indian candidate emerged. Countries like Japan and Korea are able to get posts considered preserves of other countries and groups by putting up candidates with relevant experience, by keeping them in the mainstream for years. In our system, rotation is so sacrosanct that no individual is allowed to grow in any organisation beyond a few years. Homi Bhabha helped establish the IAEA and his bust is still there outside the IAEA boardroom. But no Indian has risen to even the second level in the IAEA since then, though some of our scientists aspired to senior positions. Of course, our not signing the NPT had made several areas in the IAEA out of bounds for Indians.

The Indians who rise in the UN system are the objects of envy of their colleagues and every effort is made to get them back as soon as possible. Many diplomats have been forced to return to the country to protect their promotions in their own services, though now the government is a bit more liberal in extending their deputation to the UN and other organisations.

We do not subscribe to the dictum that having Indians in high places in the UN system is helpful to India. Those who rise to these positions go out of their way to erase their Indian identity to become truly international civil servants. This is one of the reasons why those in the government do not care to secure these jobs for Indians. Only personal networking enables them to get these jobs, and the next time they look for the Indian ambassador is when they are due for a promotion or an extension. Most Indians in the UN system are no assets to the Indian missions accredited to them.

Most Indian permanent representatives to the UN have managed to get positions in the UN, but not beyond under secretary general. None of them has contested for elected posts. Most heads of specialised agencies are elected and India is extremely reluctant to put up candidates. The myth is that contesting these posts will affect our chances for becoming a permanent member in the Security Council.

The World Bank and the IMF are even less democratic than the rest of the UN system because they operate on the basis of weighted votes. Even though we have good candidates and there is a general sentiment in favour of the highest jobs being made available to those outside the US or Europe, it will be very hard for India to get the top position in the IMF. India will be offered second or third positions as a compromise in the end.

There have been a few instances where it has suited the big powers to offer some high-level positions to Indians. A few years ago, India got a very important post, but we paid a very high price for it by helping to bring down a fellow developing country head from another organisation. Such deals may become increasingly possible, but we have to plan ahead and present acceptable candidates. No one gets top positions in the UN system by sheer merit. Major powers should be made to develop vested interests in India or in certain Indians, if Indians have to become chiefs in the UN system. Till then, Indians will be playing second fiddle or lead peacekeeping units under civilian bosses from the Western world.

4

UNSC: RESISTANCE TO REVOLUTIONARY CHANGE

UN reform is a continuous process, dictated by changes in the international situation. The Charter has been resilient enough to let the UN change with the times even without any amendment to its provisions. But the effort, launched since the end of the Cold War, to seek an expansion of the permanent membership of the Security Council, is nothing short of a demand for a revolution. The proponents of change are challenging the very foundation of an institution, born out of a World War, the winners of which gave themselves the responsibility of maintaining world peace and security by assuming extraordinary powers.

'Five countries are permanently placed at the core of the UN Security Council, which is the heart of the global security system,' Paul Kennedy said in his book, *The Parliament of Man*.

'Upon what they do or decide not to do, and upon what they agree to or veto, lies the fate of efforts to achieve peace through international covenants. Even more amazing and disturbing is that any single one of the Permanent Five, were its national government determined upon it, can paralyse Security Council action; moreover, it would be fully within its Charter right to do so. Some states are more equal than others.'

The UN Charter, which was crafted by them, has been embraced voluntarily by 193 nations. That there has not been a world war since and that the UN has served as a stabilising factor in the world is the strongest argument for continuing the status quo. But the contrary argument is stronger. The global equations have changed so much in the last sixty-six years that it is imperative that the UN must reflect those changes to maintain its representative character and moral strength. The struggle is on between those who wish to perpetuate their privileged positions and the forces of change that cannot but win. But no one can predict the time and nature of revolutions. They have their own logic and time.

The question today is whether a real change can be brought about by the provisions of the very Charter that established the institution. If history is any guide, major changes take place when the time is ripe, in unexpected ways, regardless of the strength of those who seek change and those who resist. The provisions of the law that seek to protect the establishment will be thrown to the winds and the old system will yield place to the new. A Malayalam poet declared many years ago, 'Change your outdated laws; if not, they will change you themselves.' We have many examples in history that those who conceded change lasted longer than those who resisted the forces of change. In 1979, the India-led demand was to add a few more non-permanent members, on the simple logic that the ratio between the strength of the General Assembly and that of the Security Council should be maintained.

This led to India's long absence from the Council from 1993 to 2010 after having been elected as a non-permanent member seven times in the earlier period. After India's bid for a non-permanent seat was thwarted by Japan, India decided not to contest against any of the countries which had announced candidature. In 2010, the withdrawal of the declared candidate, Kazakhstan, in India's favour led to the election of India as a non-permanent member. As the only candidate from the Asian Group, India won 187 out of the 192 possible votes.

Ismail Razali, the Malaysian president of the General Assembly in 1997, introduced a framework resolution to amend the Charter in several steps: First, the General Assembly would adopt a framework resolution to increase the size of the Security Council; second, the Assembly would vote for five candidates for the new permanent seats without veto, as follows: Two from the industrialised states, and one each from the developing countries of Africa, Asia and Latin America; third, two-thirds of the entire General Assembly would have to approve the amendment; fourth, two-thirds of all the member states, including the five original permanent members, would have to ratify the amendment; and finally, ten years after ratification, the UN would convene a review conference. The Razali formula was novel in the sense that it did not require two-thirds approval of the entire General Assembly during the first two steps, only two-thirds of the members present and voting. By circumventing Article 108 in the earliest and most problematic stages (Agreeing to reform and selecting the new permanent members), the Razali Plan was a good compromise, but it was never put to a vote. If it had been, it would not have passed due to opposition from the African states.

Efforts made outside the Working Group were also fruitless, like Secretary General Kofi Annan's proposed Plan A and Plan B.

Security Council Reform

Model A: Provides for six new permanent seats, with no veto being created and three new two-year term non-permanent seats, divided among the major regional areas as follows:

Regional Area	No. of States	Permanent Seats (Continuing)	Proposed New (Permanent)	Proposed Two-year (Non-permanent)	Total
Africa	53	0	2	4	6
Asia and Pacific	56	1	2	3	6
Europe	47	3	1	2	6
Americas	35	1	1	4	6
Total	191	5	6	13	24

Model B: Provides for no new permanent seats but creates a new category of eight four-year renewable-term seats and one new two-year non-permanent (and non-renewable) seat, divided among the major regional areas as follows:

Regional Area	No. of States	Permanent Seats (Continuing)	Proposed New (Permanent)	Proposed Two-year (Non-permanent)	Total
Africa	53	0	2	4	6
Asia and Pacific	56	1	2	3	6
Europe	47	3	2	1	6
Americas	35	1	2	3	6
Total	191	5	8	11	24

Although the secretary general included both the plans, Plan B had greater acceptability. It was at the insistence of General Satish Nambiar, the Indian member of the group, that Plan A was included. General Nambiar expressed his disagreement with the formulation and informed the chairman of the group that he would not be able to support just a Plan B recommendation. As a consequence of this, and because some of the other members would not accept Plan A, the final report included both the plans. General Nambiar received the support of the representatives of Brazil, Japan, Tanzania and Ghana as well as two members representing P-5 countries.

Another exercise undertaken by G-4 in July 2005 established a certain framework for expansion of the Security Council. G-4 had proposed that the General Assembly should adopt a resolution calling for an increase of six permanent members and four non-permanent members on the Security Council. It committed G-4 to seeking six permanent seats, increasing the size of the Council from fifteen to twenty-five. The six new permanent members would be two each from Asia and Africa, one from Latin America/Caribbean and one from West Europe and other states. G-4 also toned down the demand for veto by conceding that they were willing to be just permanent members 'with or without veto'. The resolution, which had twenty-three sponsors, was not put to a vote on account of African objections. Among other things, the African Group was not in favour of not demanding the veto.

India had never been in the forefront of the move for abolition of the veto as it had benefited from the Soviet veto at certain crucial moments, though it went along with the consensus within the Non-Aligned Movement in favour of its abolition. The original proposal for an expansion of permanent membership was on the basis that the new members would have the same privileges and obligations as the original permanent members. But it has become abundantly clear that there will be no expansion if the veto is insisted upon. Apart from the permanent members, a vast majority of the general membership may also not favour the veto for new members as they had pressed for abolition of the veto. As a Canadian representative put it, 'Five vetoes already impaired the good functioning of the Council. How would adding five more help, and who would it help?' For this reason, India went along with an idea of postponing the issue for fifteen years.

This was in recognition of the fact that the new permanent members would not have the veto in any event.

The General Assembly mandated intergovernmental negotiations on reform in 2008 when the Working Group failed to reach any agreement. The negotiations were meant to suggest a 'timeline perspective' to agree on reform in two stages on the basis of a draft text. But the participants were unable to shorten the compilation text, listing the position of all member states. The president of the General Assembly convened a new forum, 'Group of Friends on Security Council Reform', in 2011 to facilitate a compromise. A UK–France proposal for an intermediate solution that could provide a new category of members with a longer mandate than that of the members currently elected is under consideration. This proposal is similar to Plan B of Kofi Annan's proposal, except that on completion of the intermediate period, a review would be done to convert these new seats into permanent seats.

In 2011, G-4 canvassed support for a simple resolution to decide that both permanent and non-permanent membership will be expanded. This was a clever way to see whether the idea of expansion of permanent membership could be endorsed with the required two-thirds majority of the General Assembly.

The story, so far, of India's quest for a permanent seat on the Security Council is, as Ambassador Hardeep Puri described it, '*Kabhi khushi, kabhi gham*' (joy sometimes, despair at other times), the title of a Bollywood movie. In fact, there is more despair than joy in that saga. The reason for joy is that the need for expansion has been recognised by the entire membership but as of now, there is no formula for expansion which can command consensus or even secure two-thirds majority of the General Assembly, including the support of the P-5.

The framers of the UN Charter did not intend that it

should be amended easily. Article 108 of the Charter stipulates that any amendment should be adopted by a vote of two-thirds of the members of the General Assembly and ratified by two-thirds of the members, including all the permanent members of the Security Council. The alternate route prescribed in Article 109 is through a General Conference, but the majority required is equally stringent. But that has not prevented the UN from transforming itself to deal with new issues and new circumstances. Charter amendments have not been initiated even to remove anachronisms like the enemy countries clause (Article 107) and the changed name of one of the permanent members.

However, the most crucial article of the Charter on the veto itself has been changed in practice as abstention by a permanent member is considered a concurring vote under Article 27. The permanent members discovered fairly early that the Military Staff Committee, consisting of the chiefs of staff of the permanent members, envisaged in Article 47, would not work and the whole part of the Charter was set aside. The Committee was responsible under the Security Council for the strategic direction of any armed forces placed at the disposal of the Security Council. Such a responsibility could not have been carried out by the Committee during the Cold War. The Committee exists on paper even today, a skeleton in the cupboard, meeting regularly without an agenda. Boutros Ghali's reforms under Agenda for Peace were dealt with by a resolution of the General Assembly. But when it comes to an expansion of the Security Council, the only way is to bring a Charter amendment.

The P-5, for instance, consider that they only stand to lose by adding new permanent members with veto. No group outside the G-4 is actively campaigning for a formula. The idea of the African Group to rotate two permanent memberships within the Group itself a contradiction. At the minimum, Africa will have to choose one amongst their members as a permanent member for the reform process to begin.

The US, which had supported Japan and Germany in the early 1990s, now favours 'two or so' new permanent members, including Japan and 'two or three' non-permanent members, making an addition of only five to the Security Council. Such a formula is a non-starter. The support extended to India by President Obama during his visit to India is in the form of a wish without a commitment to bring it about. His words were, 'In the years ahead, I look forward to a reformed Security Council that includes India as a permanent member.' Though this is a significant departure from the previous US position, it is not enough for the US to extend support to India; it should shape a formula, which is acceptable to the membership. Its reservation over Germany and Brazil will itself deprive it of being decisive on the issue of expansion.

We did not need WikiLeaks to find the reasons for the United States' reluctance to bring about expansion of the Council. But we now have in black-and-white what we knew from the beginning. The US ambassador said in a cable in December 2007:

> We believe expansion of the Council along the lines of the models currently discussed will dilute US influence in the body.... On most important issues of the day—sanctions, human rights, Middle East etc.—Brazil, India and most African states are currently far less sympathetic to our views than our European allies.

The Council of Foreign Relations report, by Stewart M Patrick, senior fellow and director of the International Institutions and Global Governance Program at the CFR, has strongly argued the Indian case for permanent membership, as follows:

> The rationale of India's candidacy is obvious. The world's largest democracy with more than 1.2 billion people, India has a dynamic, fast growing economy, the

> world's fifth largest navy, and an impressive army with a distinguished role in international peacekeeping. India is increasingly at the forefront of efforts to police the global commons and combat transnational terrorism and, although not a member of the Nuclear Non-Proliferation Treaty regime, has established a strong record over the past decade in combating nuclear proliferation. India, simply put, has the assets to become a bulwark of world order. [A Moment for UN Security Council Reform, 8 November 2010, CFR website—ed.]

Patrick adds that the United States has geopolitical interest in expanding the UNSC's permanent membership, 'The time for a global dominant state to cede some power to rising ones is when it can still dictate the terms of the shift.' The United States can help relieve its strained resources by sharing some of the privileges and burdens of global leadership. Patrick has recommended establishing criteria for new permanent members so that they accept not only the privileges, but the weighty obligations of membership. However, the US administration does not seem to have accepted the logic as yet. Answering a question in Parliament in August 2011, Preneet Kaur, India's minister of state for external affairs stated that, 'Both India and the US are actively involved in the ongoing negotiations in the UN and seek an expansion in both permanent and non-permanent categories of membership of the Council.' There was no word about the two countries working together on a particular proposal.

China is reported to have advised a visiting Left leader from India, Sitaram Yechury, that India should part company with Japan in its quest for a seat in the UN Security Council if it expects China to back the proposal. 'China has no objection to backing India provided we come out of Japan's field.... They have a lot of historical baggage with Japan,' Yechury told the press in August 2011 (Report in Geopolitics, Vol II, Issue III, August 2011).

It will be difficult to accomplish the fundamental change India is seeking by way of the procedure laid down for change. India and the other aspirants for permanent membership, in the meantime, must maintain pressure for expansion. Making the support for India's permanent membership the litmus test of bilateral relations is untenable. India should appear more confident and secure even as it demands its rightful place in keeping with its status as the largest democracy with a dynamic, fast growing economy, an impressive record in UN peacekeeping, ability to protect the global commons and to combat transnational terrorism, and strong record against proliferation.

It may also be noted, without appearing to spurn the proverbial 'sour grapes', that permanent membership without veto is not an attractive trophy that India should expend unlimited resources and energy on it. As a permanent member of the Council, India will be called upon to take sides on every issue in the world, sometimes losing friends in the process, as India is fiercely independent and does not play second fiddle to anyone. India's positions in the Security Council from the beginning of 2011 have already caused suspicion that India has not yet got over its 'non-aligned mindset'. Lack of the veto may make India vulnerable as a result, if issues of crucial importance to it come up in the Council. India has been playing a significant role even without being on the Security Council for many years. A posture of its willingness to serve when required to do so rather than seeming desperate to secure a seat here and now may be a good strategy to adopt.

Paul Kennedy (*The Parliament of Man*) wrote in 2006:

> With the world still ravaged by the scourge of war and the threat of interstate and internal conflicts turning into open hostilities, and with the Great Powers bound to play the most dominant roles on the global stage, something

> like a UN Security Council is very much needed. Yet, is the existing Council, deep frozen in time and so often fractured, the body to provide genuine international security for all? There are few who think that. Yet, can the 1945 system be amended absent great turbulence, wars and the remaking of the world order? There are few who think that either. Hence we all live, whether we like it or not, with this giant conundrum. Everyone agrees that the existing structure is flawed; but a consensus on how to fix it remains out of reach.

The UN needs reform not to make one country or the other happy, but to make itself more relevant, credible and effective in the world and it will be ready for a revolution sooner rather than later. A time will come when global governance will not be possible without the participation of countries like Germany, Japan, India, Brazil and South Africa in the Security Council. When that happens, the provisions of the Charter will not stand in the way of restructuring the UN just as they did not stand in the way of expanding the agenda or ignoring anachronistic ideas and institutions. Fundamental changes cannot come like raindrops, they come like avalanches. The amendment route will, at best, create a third category of members with long or permanent terms in the Council, but without being equal to the original permanent members. What the UN requires is not a fix, but a fundamental change to reflect the realities of the present century.

5

UN GAFFES ARE NOT RARE

When the president of the UN Security Council for February 2011 invited the Indian minister of external affairs to speak at the horseshoe table, he began reading from a text placed before him and it turned out that it was the speech the Portuguese delegate had just delivered. No wonder only the Indian ambassador realised that the minister was reading the wrong speech. The others were not listening, not even the Portuguese delegate who authored the text. In the UN, delegates develop selective hearing, because no one can listen to the millions of words spoken every day. Everyone knows that the first few minutes of the speeches in the Security Council will be devoted to congratulating the present president on his assumption of the position even though it is by rotation and thanking the previous president for his accomplishments, even if he did not achieve anything during his month-long presidency. The members of the Council were waiting for our minister to come to the substance of the debate to give him some attention. If he had said anything new or original, it would not have gone unnoticed.

But what happened to the practice in our permanent mission in New York of one officer being assigned to every politician to keep a copy of the speech and to make sure that every word is delivered correctly? In the case of the minister of external affairs, this used to be done at the level of the deputy permanent representative himself. How could the officers occupying the four chairs behind the minister not know he was reading the wrong speech for full three minutes?

Has the good custom of having a heading and even a separate cover sheet for the speeches of the ministers been abandoned? Did the Portuguese mission also circulate the speech without a heading or a cover? We need to have answers to these questions if we are to understand where the system went wrong. Such things are too important to be left to the minister himself. After all, ministers have too many things on their mind to check whether the text placed before them is the right one.

I have had some experience of gaffes by our political delegates misreading or mispronouncing words. One distinguished minister of state read 'Namibia' as 'Nambiar' repeatedly from the podium of the General Assembly. Unlike in the Security Council, no one sits or stands behind the speaker when he speaks and there is no way to communicate with him quickly to correct any mistake. Another delegate, this time a lady, accustomed as she was during the decolonisation days to condemnations of various policies of imperial powers, decided to 'condemn' UNESCO for helping a non-self-governing territory to preserve its cultural heritage. The text, of course, meant to 'commend' the UN agency!

Speaking of pronunciation, an Indonesian colleague asked me once what language our delegate was speaking in. Normally, if a delegate does not speak in any of the six languages of the UN, someone would read the English text from the booth. Our delegate was actually speaking in his version of English!

On one occasion, we had a seriously ill external affairs minister, who should have ideally stayed at home and not travelled to New York, without any aide. Our minister insisted on doing everything that ministers were expected to do, like making speeches and holding bilateral meetings. He resented any suggestion that he might want to rest after a few meetings. There was one occasion when I had to park myself behind the podium with the permission of the chair when the minister spoke to help him, if necessary. In replying to the minister's comments on Jammu and Kashmir, a particularly vicious Pakistani delegate referred to India as 'the sick man of Asia', hitting somewhere below the belt.

The same minister, when he called on the secretary general described all the problems we had been having with Pakistan and repeatedly asked the secretary general to intervene in some way. The secretary general, who was very keen to intervene, knew the Indian policy too well to take the request seriously. Still, we did not feel comfortable till we wrote a letter to the secretary general, that the minister did not really mean to request for mediation.

We also had political delegates, who wanted to change policy when they were at the UN. A very senior delegate was convinced that our policy on Afghanistan was wrong. He was inclined to support the resolutions, which criticised the Soviet invasion of Afghanistan, but our policy was to abstain on them. We had abstained on the main resolution already, but in one of the committees, a similar resolution was introduced. When a roll call vote was announced and India's name was called, our delegate said 'yes', but I shouted loudly 'abstention' from behind him. The secretariat official, who knew the Indian position well, recorded our vote as abstention and our delegate was not any wiser. He was hard of hearing.

We had another delegate, who was convinced that our policy on East Timor was faulty. He was seen hobnobbing with the Portuguese delegation in the lounge occasionally. He tried to persuade me to change our position on East Timor and denounce Indonesian colonialism. I explained to him the rationale of our policy and said that he could take the matter up with Delhi, which he was not inclined to do. He watered down the language of the speech I gave him, but as long as the speech conformed to the established policy of the government, there wouldn't be a problem. I kept a close watch on him as he read the speech and, sure enough, he deliberately changed a phrase to dilute it further. The statement that the people of East Timor had already exercised their right to self-determination was changed to suggest that we were not convinced that it was so. I was astonished by his dishonesty, but without saying a word, I went to the secretariat and handed over a copy of the speech and said that it should be reflected faithfully, and the electronic recording should be ignored. The secretariat normally obliges in such cases, but it does insist occasionally on showing the original and the correction. If a delegation votes wrongly on a particular resolution, the original vote will be recorded together with the amendment submitted subsequently. In the case of the Security Council, I do not know whether the secretariat insisted on recording what he read from the wrong speech, expressing pleasure on seeing two countries of the Portuguese speaking community in the Security Council.

India is not the only country that generates such gaffes in the UN. Uganda had a big problem once when no Ugandan delegate was present in the General Assembly hall. When Uganda's name was called, someone walked to the podium and made a speech denouncing the reigning president of Uganda, Idi Amin. By the time the official delegates heard about it and rushed to the hall to challenge him, the damage was done and the news was already in the air. The whole Ugandan team was recalled and a new team was sent with instructions that the Ugandan chairs should never be left vacant. Pakistan had to contend with a politician, a member of the official delegation, who denounced the regime in Islamabad. Knowing his views, the mission had refused to print out his speech, but he managed to type it on the teleprinter. Once when the Iraqi delegate referred to the Kuwaitis as 'small people', the interpreter referred to them as 'pygmies'. The Zaire delegate protested and the Iraqi did not know why. 'Pygmies' is not a politically correct word in Zaire! A delegate was asked to repeat his vote four times till the secretariat was convinced that he was acting as instructed.

Gaffes in the UN create some red faces and send a few chuckles around, but do not harm anyone as each country's position is known and the situation can easily be retrieved. These add some entertainment to the rest of the dull proceedings and go down to the archives, which have plenty of faux pas recorded for posterity.

6

OPCW vs MALALA IN THE NOBEL RUN

The Nobel Prize nomination for Malala may have caused deep divisions across the globe but the importance of the 2013 award to OPCW, which has served the cause of peace by eliminating a weapon of mass destruction, should not be lost in the din about Malala.

Unpredictability is the hallmark of the Norwegian Nobel Committee, when it comes to awarding of the Nobel Peace Prize. With no appellate authority to restrain it, the committee revels in exercising its prerogative to choose the laureates, often redefining and expanding the concept of peace itself.

The most unforeseen selection in 2009 was that of President Barack Obama, who took a break from actually waging a couple of wars to travel to Oslo to receive the award. Awarding the Prize to 'a lover of trees' and to institutions like UN agencies and the European Union have raised eyebrows in the past as well. By denying the Prize to Gandhi and Nehru, the Committee lost credibility in India long ago. Though the Prize is often seen as a political instrument of the West, it is highly coveted and recognised.

This year, the popular vote was in favour of Malala Yousufzai, the teenager from Pakistan, who fought for the cause of women's education and nearly confronted death for doing so. The Taliban lived up to its reputation for irrationality and ruthlessness by making an attempt on her life. Her escape was providential and recovery, miraculous. Her contribution to the campaign for women's education was hailed before and after the gory incident. Many believed that her nomination for the Nobel Prize was logical and convincing. Groups with vested interests may have rallied around her to promote her, but the fact remains that she has become a symbol of courage and conviction.

The hit by the Taliban did not deter her from pursuing her ambition, instead magnified it by not limiting herself to educate the women in her country alone, but expanding her sphere of work on to global reach. By aspiring to be another Benazir Bhutto, she has even courted martyrdom.

For the first time, a Pakistani was the hot favourite for the Nobel in India. The disappointment was palpable when the announcement was made, as it was misinterpreted by some, as an ode to the Taliban's ambitions. The reaction to the award going to the Organisation for Prohibition of Chemical Weapons (OPCW) was not very positive mainly because of the expectations piled up on Malala. Many saw in it a conspiracy by the usual suspect, the US, which did not want to provoke the Taliban, while it was on its way to setting up a new government in Afghanistan.

The US had brought the OPCW to centre stage by entrusting it with the task of eliminating Syria's chemical arsenal. Vladimir Putin, the main architect of the plan for Syria, was also apparently a candidate, whom the US did not approve of. So the inanimate

OPCW prevailed over personalities like Malala and Putin because of US pressure, it was said.

The award of the Prize to UN bodies and even UN officials is nothing unusual. Mohamed El Baradei, the then director general, International Atomic Energy Agency, was awarded the 2001 Nobel Peace Prize, together with the IAEA and Kofi Annan, the then UN secretary general, was awarded together with the Department of Peacekeeping Operations. The 2007 Prize went to the International Panel on Climate Change, a scientific body. The name of OPCW was heard in this context ever since the Syria Accord was reached. The UN itself hinted at the possibility of this award, when it tweeted that several UN organisations had won the Nobel in the past. It had a premonition that the new fame the OPCW had acquired might win it the Nobel.

The Chemical Weapons Convention and the OPCW which resulted from its coming into force, have certain unique features. Unlike the NPT, the Chemical Weapons Convention is non-discriminatory in the sense that its provisions equally bind all countries. It is, thus, a model disarmament convention. Its objective is not only to eliminate, but also to prohibit chemical weapons, while in the case of nuclear weapons, the IAEA has to accept the reality of nuclear weapon states and also promote nuclear energy for peaceful purposes, knowing well that proliferation is still possible.

The mandate of OPCW is unambiguous. The members have undertaken to destroy all stockpiles and production of new weapons is strictly prohibited. Journalists characterised OPCW as 'little known' and, on the lines of the IAEA as a 'chemical weapons watchdog'. True, it was not well-known and the Nobel Prize was meant to focus attention on the Hague-based organisation and its mandate. Even without a specific authorisation, OPCW could have demanded destruction of the chemical weapons in Syria since Syria has just become the hundred and ninetieth member of the organisation. The Syria agreement made it mandatory for it to search out and destroy the arsenal. Armed with the Nobel Prize, it will be in a better position to do its task.

Why the Nobel Prize should be given to an organisation, which is simply doing its job, some ask. The answer is that it is doing its job well and it needs to do it even better. OPCW is not just a watchdog; it is mandated to verify the elimination of chemical weapons and to encourage all nations to adhere to the norm. Since 1997, the OPCW has helped to destroy 82 per cent of the chemical weapons in the world. The US and Russia are guilty of violating the convention as they are still in possession of these deadly weapons. The OPCW has severely criticised these countries.

The Prize is very much in keeping with Alfred Nobel's vision of disarmament, particularly weapons of mass destruction. Israel, Myanmar, Angola, Egypt, North Korea and South Sudan are the only countries, which have not become adherents to the Convention. 'We are conscious of the enormous trust that the international community has bestowed on us.... The recognition that the Peace Prize brings will spur us to untiring effort, even stronger commitment and greater dedication,' said Ahmet Uzumcu, OPCW director general, a former Turkish ambassador.

7

THE CLIMATE CHANGE CONUNDRUM

My involvement in environmental negotiations, particularly climate change, is rather ancient, beginning with the Rio summit in 1992 and the Berlin Conference of Parties (COP) of 1995, where I was the vice chairman of the Conference and spokesperson of the G-77. It was the Berlin Mandate, which was formulated under the chairmanship of the present Chancellor of Germany Angela Merkel, that later became the Kyoto Protocol. Since then, the basic issues relating to the subject have remained unchanged, though we have negotiated through many more sessions of the COP and the dramatis personae have changed several times. In fact, the battle that Indira Gandhi waged against environmental colonialism in Stockholm in 1972 still continues. The essential features of the Indian position and the position of the developing countries are the same today as they were at the time of Stockholm.

Here, I do not intend to deal with either the science or the economics of climate change; I shall only touch upon its political and diplomatic dimensions. As far as the science is concerned, the International Panel on Climate Change (IPCC), the Nobel Prize-winning body of scientists, headed by Rajendra Pachauri, has established beyond any reasonable doubt that human activity of various kinds do contribute to the concentration of greenhouse gases (GHG) in the atmosphere, leading to global warming. There are still some 'deniers' even among scientists, who believe that either there is no global warming at all or nature will find its own way of restoring the equilibrium in the atmosphere. The so-called 'climate gate' in Copenhagen, the leakage of some emails purporting to suggest that some scientists in the IPCC deliberately suppressed some scientific evidence to the effect that anthropogenic emissions had nothing to do with global warming, did muddy the atmosphere. Well, there are people who still believe that the earth is flat and that Darwin's theory of evolution is sheer fiction. There is no doubt that it is time that human beings, who have by their careless and extravagant consumption of the resources of the earth, caused damage to mother earth, must take corrective action to reverse the trend in climate change.

As stated earlier, Indira Gandhi had the vision and wisdom to go to Stockholm in 1972, the only prime minister to do so, and to influence the agenda that the Western world was setting to mitigate environmental problems. The theory being floated in Stockholm was that the developing countries should desist from using the energy resources of the earth for their economic development as the developed world did, but conserve them and preserve the forests and lakes, which have the capacity to sink greenhouse gases. The developing countries should also adopt environmentally friendly technologies in their development efforts. In Stockholm, Indira Gandhi declared, '...poverty the biggest polluter', by which she meant that the environmental problems of the developing countries are simply a reflection of their poverty. The Stockholm Conference finally resulted in an acknowledgement by the international community of the link between environment and development and also of the greater responsibility of the industrialised countries regarding the contamination of the planet. The 'polluters must pay,' said Indira Gandhi, to clean up the mess that they had created. The historic Earth Summit in Rio in 1992 refined these concepts further and formulated several programmes of action to deal with environment and development in an integrated manner.

The UN Framework Convention on Climate Change (FCC) was one of the two international conventions, which opened for signature in Rio. This landmark convention expressed concern that human activities have been substantially increasing the atmospheric concentrations of GHG, and that this will result in an additional warming of the earth's surface and atmosphere and may adversely affect natural ecosystems and humankind. But the basic premise in the Convention was that 'the largest share of historical and current global emissions of greenhouse gases has originated in developed countries, that per capita emissions in developing counties are still relatively low and that the share of global emissions originating in developing countries will grow to meet their social and development needs.' In other words, the 'luxury emissions' of developed countries should be reduced substantially, while the 'survival emissions' of developing countries should be allowed to grow in a controlled manner. The principles of the Convention were particularly significant as the protection of the climate should be 'on the basis of equity and in accordance with their common, but differentiated responsibilities and respective capabilities.' Specific commitments for reduction of GHG emissions by designated developed countries and for provision of new and additional resources were included in the Convention and the developing countries had no such commitments, in view of their need for economic growth. The vision of international cooperation contained in the Convention based on the balance between development needs and environment protection made the Convention universally acceptable. A new pact between the developed and developing countries raised new hopes for mankind.

The journey from Rio to Copenhagen and beyond, through Berlin, Kyoto, Bali and other cities, however, has turned out to be a great disappointment. The Rio commitments remained unimplemented both in terms of emission cuts, financing and technology transfer and each COP diluted the basic principles farther and farther till the Copenhagen COP moved away from those principles by excluding the whole concept of legally binding commitments altogether. The Copenhagen COP ended in a discordant note when it merely 'took note' of an Accord produced by the so-called major economies, the United States, India, China, Brazil and South Africa. Most developing countries condemned the Accord and even several developed countries expressed anguish that Copenhagen had moved away from the Rio and Kyoto commitments. Of course, the words of the Rio principles are scattered all over the Copenhagen document and the commitment of the parties to the Kyoto Protocol is reiterated to satisfy public opinion, but it contains only a pious wish 'to hold the increase in global temperature below two degrees Celsius, and take action to meet this objective.' As for commitment of new and additional resources, developed countries will provide an amount 'approaching US $30 billion for the period 2010-12', it said. They also committed to the goal of mobilising jointly US $100 billion a year by 2020 as part of the Copenhagen Green Climate Fund, subject to 'meaningful mitigation actions and transparency of implementation'. Some in the developing world called it 'Floppenhagen', some compared it to the holocaust and some even accused those developing countries which accepted it as having betrayed humanity for thirty pieces of silver.

India undoubtedly disappointed the developing world by breaking away from its ranks to bail out the United States and China, the highest GHG emitters. India went to Copenhagen with a negative mandate—no legally binding cuts in greenhouse gas emissions, no monitoring and no burying of Kyoto Protocol. When it came under pressure to accept new obligations, it found common cause with the worst polluters in the world, the US and China, and let down the other developing countries. The victor in the exercise was the United States, which changed the course of the climate change debate to a new direction, after having accomplished the three objectives of mitigation, transparency and financing in their sway. India, China, Brazil and South Africa let the US off the hook. Perhaps, this is the first time in the history of the UN that India is part of a consensus in a small group, which is being disowned by a majority of the developing countries. It is no great consolation that we are in the company of three other major developing countries. A new alliance between the 'emerging economies' and the US has been forged at Copenhagen, but its future remains in question as they begin to grapple with legally binding commitments, which will be absolutely essential in any action plan for climate. India and China will also come under pressure at that time as the concept of per capita emissions seems to have disappeared from the formulations in Copenhagen.

President Obama's insistence on transparency in actions by all states figures in the Copenhagen Accord, in the form of emerging economies reporting every two years to the United Nations, which will be subject to 'international consultation and analysis', a euphemism for international monitoring. A US spokesman has already claimed that China and India have set goals for mitigation and that they will be challenged if they do not reach those goals. The 'common but differentiated responsibilities' of the individual countries, one of the principles of Rio, has been forgotten as now all the major economies have the same common responsibilities.

In his speech to the conference, President Obama, with his characteristic mastery of juggling with words, changed the much negotiated principle into 'common but differentiated responses'. India would have been far better off without this Accord. Minister Jairam Ramesh did not carry conviction when he declared that the Copenhagen Accord was good for India and the world. His approach looked more like the way he himself described the typical Indian attitude towards the United States, 'Yankees go home, but take me along with you!' The prime minister, at his plenary speech, had opposed any dilution of the Convention signed in Rio, particularly the principle of equity and common but differentiated responsibilities and respective capabilities. 'To settle for something that would be seen as diminished expectations and diminished implementation would be the wrong message to emerge from this conference,' he had said. He went on to add, 'Those worst affected by climate change are the least responsible for it. Whatever emerges from our negotiations must address this glaring injustice, injustice to countries of Africa, injustice to the least developed countries, and injustice to the small developing states, whose survival as viable states is in jeopardy.' Unfortunately, the very countries that the prime minister mentioned felt betrayed by the Copenhagen Accord.

The Copenhagen Accord can be defended only on the ground that it prevented a complete breakdown of the negotiations. Instead of being a 'deal breaker', as India was rumoured to be before the conference, it become a 'deal maker'. The commitment to limit the rise in temperature to two degrees, with the possibility of even considering bringing it down to 1.5 degrees holds out some hope for mankind. The Accord retains much of the language of the past to show that the way forward is not a complete break from the past. The concept of a fund to finance mitigation of and adaptation to climate change has taken some concrete shape. The United States is now a partner rather than a target in the global effort to safeguard the environment. Cooperation rather than confrontation is the way to go and these are the days of multiple alliances rather than non-alignment.

These accomplishments must, however, be weighed against the price India will have to pay for the concession India has made by accepting some form of international monitoring of its voluntary commitments. India has taken a calculated risk by accepting what was essentially a US–China deal. The Copenhagen conference was remarkable for the demonstration of the grave anxiety of the world about the deterioration of the environment.

Mahabali
The Kerala Landscape

Mahabali—the legendary Asura king who is believed to have ruled over a large part of the Indian subcontinent, including the land of Kerala as we know it today, is considered the epitome of virtue, righteousness and generosity amongst all rulers. His utmost devotion to the governance of his state and welfare of his subjects made even the heavenly beings shake with envy. The legendary land of Mahabali is nothing short of a utopia. A prosperous land and peace-loving people where no vices or villains burgeoned, no ill will or ire emanated, and demonstrated no impudence or discordance. That was 'God's own country' in every sense, where even after the ruler of the land was exiled to the nether world, the Lord himself served him as the door-keeper, guarding his subjects.

The annual visit of Mahabali to his kingdom, granted to him as a reprieve by Vishnu, is celebrated as Onam, a virtual act of deception to convince Mahabali that the people of Kerala today are as happy as they were during the days of Mahabali. Swami Vivekananda, on visiting Kerala, infamously remarked that Kerala was a lunatic asylum. He was appalled at the state of society here, rife with communal conflicts and caste politics. Kerala is indeed a far cry from the land of Mahabali as, today, it is known for its regressive mindset even in the middle of progressive slogans, conspicuous consumption of alcohol, communalism, casteism and high suicide rate.

The section that follows brings together a bunch of articles on Kerala and its development. TP Sreenivasan is very much a son of the soil. Although he spent nearly forty years abroad, he returned to Kerala to return something to his homeland. The state has recognised his merit and entrusted him with various responsibilities. He is currently serving the Government of Kerala as the executive vice-chairman of the Kerala State Higher Education Council. With the increasingly active Kerala State Higher Education Council under his care, progress in the higher education sector is underway and is expected to transform the state into an educational hub. He is also a familiar face for every Malayalee news channel viewer through his weekly programme *Videsha Vicharam* on Asianet News, and he appears frequently in the news hour debates, providing balanced analysis on issues concerning foreign affairs and international relations. Kerala is and will always be proud of this great son of the state.

1

IN KERALA, FEASTING, SPLURGING AND MOLLYWOOD USHER IN ONAM

Visiting Kerala during the Onam week is like visiting New York during Christmas week, except for the scale. Both places have the festive atmosphere, illumination, feasting everywhere, high alcohol consumption and crass commercialisation, including a grand shopping festival. None of these have anything to do with the traditional Onam festival, but care is taken to do all these in the name of Mahabali, the legendary ruler of prehistoric times. His majestic and well-fed figure juts out of every hoarding like Santa Claus' in the West.

Onam, whose festivities centre around Thiru Onam, is a combination of the Kerala New Year and the harvesting festival, marking the end of torrential rain and misery associated with the previous months. The Onam legend of Mahabali is the best excuse for the feasting and the splurging. Keralites believe that they have to appear as happy and prosperous as they were in the days of Mahabali, the benevolent king, who returns to Kerala once a year to see his subjects. This was a boon he received from the Supreme God himself, Vishnu, who sent him to the netherworld out of envy for his popularity. The story goes; Vishnu appears disguised as a Brahmin boy, who seeks three feet of land to do his praying. Mahabali promises to provide that, but then Vishnu suddenly grows so large that he measures the earth with one foot, the heavens with another foot and demands that Mahabali find room for his third bit of land. Mahabali offers his own head as the third, and Vishnu pushes him down. However, Mahabali managed to negotiate a deal with Vishnu to visit Kerala once every year. The literature that describes his reign reads like the description of utopia, or the Promised Land: Socialist in concept but capitalist in terms of prosperity and plenty. Everyone was equal, no untruth or deceit, not even an iota of falsehood. No wonder the gods grew jealous as even in heaven they did not have such a paradise.

The regime change that Vishnu brought about may have had to do with more than jealousy. It was a just regime, but there is no talk of the empowerment of women or faith in God. Some believe that these were the tragic flaws that transported Mahabali to the netherworld. The legend of Mahabali and his kingdom may well be the primeval memory of a people, in jumbled up images of old times. But more likely, it is a vision, a dream that is difficult even to conceive of, not to speak of accomplishing. By portraying a dream as something that existed in the past, the creators of the legend gave it a touch of reality. The creation of the image of Mahabali was another master stroke to give form and content to the dream.

Keralites do not see deception in pretending to be content on Onam day. It is a legitimate way of pleasing their ruler. The deception gives the Keralites the license to indulge in luxuries. Even the sale of immovable property is permitted to celebrate the Onam festival. The government abets the splurging by giving salary advances, which will have to be repaid in subsequent months.

Onam, in the old days, meant ten days of feasting, flower decorations and traditional dances for women and martial arts and sports for men. Like Thanksgiving, Onam brought families together, even if it meant travel over long distances. Onam used to be very private and unostentatious, but today Onam is a street festival, with an eye on attracting tourists. Kerala is sold as a tourist and shopping package during Onam.

Today's Onam also revolves around Mollywood, the Malayalam movie industry, which has been exceptionally active. Superstars like Mammootty and Mohanlal still hold sway, and the dream of every television channel is to get them to talk about themselves on Onam day. If the networks can't get hold of them, every other star is lined up on Onam day.

Onam is not about a legend anymore. It is a contemporary festival to rejoice, to feast, to shop and to ogle at film stars. Mahabali is just an excuse for Keralites to deceive themselves that they are well. As long as remittances come from the Keralite workers in the Gulf, Onam can have all the glitter it has acquired.

For menial work in Kerala, people from West Bengal and Odisha come in large numbers. For them, Kerala is the Gulf, with jobs aplenty and good wages. In fact, chief minister of Kerala, Oommen Chandy, has had to greet migrant workers on Onam day in Hindi.

In the Onam season, everything is postponed till the long holidays are over. Once it emerges, bleary-eyed, from the Onam season, Kerala will return to its routine of hyper politics, high spending and the Kerala model of development, and Mahabali will return to his netherworld home in the belief that his subjects are happy.

2

UNCROWNED KING

If there ever was an uncrowned king, who commanded more respect and reverence than any ruler, hereditary or democratic, it was Uthradom Thirunal Marthanda Varma of Travancore, a princely state in British India, now part of Kerala state. Adulation and admiration for him were evident for many years, but the outpouring of grief over his demise at the age of ninety-one on 16 December 2013 broke all records of display of a sense of loss and grief.

Uthradom Thirunal did not rule Travancore even for a day. He remained in the shadow of his brother as his lieutenant and chief advisor, Maharaja Chithira Thirunal Balarama Varma, when the latter was the ruler. When duty beckoned him to abandon his business in Karnataka to return to Thiruvananthapuram as the chief servant of Lord Padmanabha (*Padmanabhadasa*), as the maharajas believed they were, he plunged into the major transformation that the state and the family were dealing with. Chithira Thirunal, having been a visionary maharaja and credited with the historic Temple Entry Proclamation, which threw open Kerala's temples to the Dalits in 1924-25 (the Vaikom satyagraha), was undoubtedly popular and revered, but Uthradom Thirunal had not experienced power and he had stayed away from home for some years. The blue blood in him came through fast enough to win the hearts of the public at large. The sprawling Padmnabha temple, with its inestimable wealth was at his command, but he was only its main caretaker and devotee. He respected the tradition of the maharajas by visiting the temple every day, not only to worship, but also to ensure that the property and the staff were taken care of.

By a combination of deep devotion to Padmanabha, vast scholarship, extreme humility and exceptional accessibility, Uthradom Thirunal recreated himself in the image of his elder brother and captured the hearts of the people, particularly of southern Kerala. In the earlier years, he was haughty at times and rude to the workers, according to his own autobiography. He was even chastised by his brother and made to apologise to an attendant, whom he had slapped in a fit of anger.

He and the members of the family were much sought after at social, cultural and religious functions, but no one, not even the Left, accused them of any political inclination. They did not vote in any election, not because they had no faith in democracy, but because they wanted to remain aloof from all parties. Their deep Hindu faith and participation in Hindu rituals did not detract from the secular approach that the monarchy had adopted right from the beginning.

Uthradom Thirunal did not shy away from public life. His philanthropy was well-known, but it was not showy. A modern hospital was built in his own palace compound, with the participation of private entrepreneurs. He had the usual problems of managing the assets of the palace, given the new regulations on land ownership. There were even moves on the part of the government to take over the Padmanabha temple. He fought these cases, defended by the best legal minds in the country, but remained within the law in all his battles. Some may have exploited his good nature and benefited themselves, but he closed his eyes to these inroads with generosity.

Uthradom Thirunal was an engaging conversationalist, not merely anecdotal but also scholarly, with the knowledge of contemporary affairs. He asked his interlocutors, of various professions and backgrounds, thought-provoking questions and left them enriched with his vision and wisdom. His punctuality and brevity were legendary. His speeches were known for their pithiness and deep meaning. He was adept in coining appropriate phrases to suit any occasion to delight the audiences with his keen sense of observation and inventiveness. Uthradom Thirunal's range of interests was astonishing. Photography was his passion, closely followed by vintage cars and classy watches. For him, old was gold. He used to wear old shirts and suits with panache and take pride in their class. Normally clothed in the most ordinary Kerala clothes, he would dress up in Western attire when the occasion demanded. He was seen last in an impeccable suit when he travelled to Kochi to meet Prince Charles, in keeping with his natural affinity to royalty anywhere. He was at a Masons function, decked in the most elaborate paraphernalia of a 'brother'. His royal grace and benevolent eyes came through any costume he wore, including the topless wrap he wore for temple functions. His duties at the temple were arduous in terms of the walking and long hours of meditation, but he performed all of them till the very end.

He lived in a modest palace, not far from the massive palace of the maharajas. The Pattom palace, as it is called because of its location, has a huge collection of art and other treasures meticulously curated by him. He enjoyed taking his guests around the palace and presenting them reproductions or photographs of the more valuable pieces. His massive collection of press clippings he had collected over the years was handed over to a local library. His memoirs and photographs, published only in 2010, tell not only his own story but the story of Travancore and its transformation.

Uthradom Thirunal's will, composure, patience and good humour were put to the severest test, when information on the extent of the treasures, locked up in different vaults in the sanctum sanctorum came into public domain in 2011 as a result of legal action two years ago. With estimates of the value of the wealth put around US $40 billion, the Padmanabha temple came to be known as the richest temple in the world. National and international attention focused on Uthradom Thirunal, as various suggestions were made to put the wealth to good use for the state. He may have grieved over the vulnerability of the temple on account of its new fame, but he calmly maintained that the treasure belonged to the deity and none else. He said nothing in response even to the allegation that he may have been carrying the treasures away during his daily visits to the temple. He tried through legal means to leave the treasures as they were without evaluating and exhibiting them, but on the orders of the Supreme Court, an evaluation process began, which is not complete yet at the time of writing. Security of the temple has been enhanced in the process, the number of visitors has increased and the fame of the temple has spread far and wide.

One of the rituals that every Maharaja performed after every temple visit was to leave behind even the smallest speck of sand from their feet after worshipping Padmanabha. So, there he went, leaving everything at the feet of his deity. His memory will remain fresh for a long time to come in the minds of the people who met him. The dynasty continues, as his nephew, Rama Varma, takes charge of the temple and the legacy, perhaps with less grandeur, but with equal humility, characteristic of the family.

3

IN GOLD'S OWN COUNTRY

Lord Padmanabha, the presiding deity of Thiruvananthapuram (also known as Trivandrum), the capital of Kerala, who is depicted as reclining on a gigantic snake, Anantha, suddenly went up in the estimation of his devotees when it was discovered that he has an inestimable treasure of gold in his custody.

Kerala values nothing more than gold, and it is comforting for the people of the state to know that their erstwhile rulers too had a fascination for the yellow metal, which they stored in the temple as an offering and as an insurance against famine. The innumerable jewellery shops around the temple and elsewhere in Kerala may be handling as much gold as the temple has accumulated. 'God's own country' is fast becoming 'Gold's own country'.

With only 3 per cent of India's population, Kerala gobbles up 20 per cent of the country's gold every year, and the World Gold Council estimates that India, the largest consumer of gold in the world, consumes 30 per cent of the global supply. 2,00,000 people are employed in the gold industry in this tiny state. Such is the love of gold in Kerala that there may be no household without some gold, tucked away as savings, either to be given away as wedding gifts for daughters or to raise cash by way of gold loans or outright sale.

Buying ornaments and investing in gold is an old tradition, but the proliferation of jewellery stores doing brisk business in gold, diamonds and platinum is a trending phenomenon in Kerala, coinciding with the rise in remittances from the Persian Gulf. While Indian migrants in the West keep their money in Swiss banks and other destinations, the Indians in the Gulf send their money back home either to purchase land in their villages or to buy gold for their women or simply as investment.

When the gold prices were favourable in the Gulf, they brought gold there, and many Kerala-based shops sprang up in the Gulf. Now that the international prices are the same, gold shops have come up in every city in Kerala. In small towns in Kerala, the most dazzling buildings are either jewellery stores or silk houses or combined 'wedding palaces'. Fashionable eating places or supermarkets are extremely rare even in prosperous towns.

Most film stars of repute are either partners or 'goodwill ambassadors' of these enterprises and appear on billboards or television commercials. One of them, Mohanlal, who has interests in different aspects of the gold business, advocates buying gold in various TV commercials throughout the day. He enticingly asks what his fans are doing in the evening and asserts that he cannot celebrate anything without them. He makes it appear as though gold makes the world go round.

If you want to see gold at its most ostentatious, go to a wedding. At these events, when it comes to the precious metal, the rule is—the more, the merrier. Many brides are covered in gold ornaments from neck to knee, not to speak of the weight placed on their heads. They resemble temple elephants, which are decked from top to bottom with golden decorations during festivals.

Since gold ornaments are highly desirable and they only increase in value, all available money is spent on them with no concern. Beg or borrow, the brides must be decked in gold. They are literally worth their weight in gold. The poorer the person, the greater is the desire to show off their wealth in gold.

As the lust for gold skyrockets, the demand for imitation gold jewellery also grows by leaps and bounds. Outside Lord Padmanabha's temple gates, as tall as the Joyalukkas jewellery retailer's building, is Kollam Supreme, a jeweller that freely displays intricate gold ornaments, with no care for security. The secret is that these are just gold-plated ornaments that look like the real thing, with just a gram of real gold used in each of them. The Kollam brides look as impressive as their richer counterparts at a fraction of the cost. This new brand of ornaments satisfies the intense desire of ordinary people to look as affluent as their rich neighbours.

Kerala is littered with small financial institutions that lend money instantly against gold deposits. Muthoot, one of the largest of these lenders, prides itself in completing a transaction within three minutes, and its branches can be seen on every corner in Kerala. The same family has competing businesses, with each brother advertising in a different colour, red being the most prominent of them. The owner of the red Muthoot was featured on the cover of Forbes magazine for running a big business empire in India based on gold loans. Hundreds of his branches are small establishments, with a simple, but elegant, counter in front and a big, fortified room behind.

Those who have feared a crash in gold prices have been proved wrong, as prices are escalating every day, even more than fuel prices. Those who have stocks of gold are overjoyed, and people buy up even at phenomenal prices in the expectation of even higher returns. Soaring prices of any commodity should normally cause concern and raise a hue and cry. But Keralites continue to buy gold in the full confidence that gold prices will never fall.

It's not as if Keralites don't have other avenues for investment. Land is another hot commodity that brings in steady profits. But land transactions are fairly transparent, land registration is cumbersome and expensive, and land holdings are hard to hide. Land transactions also require sound judgment as there is an element of speculation in them. For these reasons, when it comes to their money, Keralites put their faith in gold.

4

SWAMI VIVEKANANDA: THE SECOND COMING

The installation of a monumental statue of Swami Vivekananda right in front of the home of the erstwhile maharajas of Travancore in Thiruvananthapuram in 2014 by no less a person than the vice president of India conveyed several important messages. Most important of all, it is the message that Keralites have never resented Swamiji's characterisation of the land, which is now the state of Kerala, as a 'lunatic asylum'. The words he used were devastating. In 1897, Vivekananda remarked in a public address, 'Was there ever a sillier thing before in the world than what I saw in Malabar? The poor "Paraiah" is not allowed to pass through the same street as the high-caste man, but if he changes his name to a hodge-podge English name or to a Mohamedan name, it is alright. What inference would you draw except that these Malabaris are all lunatics, their homes are so many lunatic asylums and they are to be treated with derision by every race in India until they mend their manners and know better.

Shame upon them that such wicked and diabolical customs are allowed.'

In fact, many commentators of the social situation in the region at that time commended the Swamiji for pointing out untouchability as sheer madness. Today, by welcoming Vivekananda to the heart of the city with the erstwhile maharaja as the patron of the effort, Kerala is upholding the Temple Entry Proclamation as the response to the very evil that Swamiji found repugnant.

Secondly, the stern face of Vivekananda, exhorting us to awake, arise and stop not till the goal is reached, will be a constant reminder of what remains to be done in the state, not only in the area of caste and community, but also in matters of discipline and morality. The state of affairs today certainly needs to be dealt with in the light of the teachings of the Swamiji. His vision of India as the land of universal brotherhood and tolerance of all faiths is yet to be realised. Kerala has had a history of religious harmony and co-existence, which has been shattered by caste-based politics and emergence of fanaticism. The second coming of Vivekananda will admonish us and inspire us to work for the common good of the state and the country. He will remind us that calling the state 'God's own country' is not enough to instil godliness. We have to strive constantly to win the approbation of the world and justify our claim.

Kerala is the home of the most cosmopolitan and globalised people and it owes to Swamiji a great deal for being the ambassador extraordinary, who introduced India to the West and won acclaim for India's culture. The unveiling of the statue was timed to coincide with the exact moment when the Swamiji stood up in the Parliament of Religions in Chicago and addressed the Americans as 'Brothers and Sisters of America'. In a moment, he captured the imagination of Americans, who realised the wisdom of the Hindu religion as the guiding force of a secular state. They saw in the Hinduism he described, the very teachings of Christianity and Islam without any fundamentalist doctrine. Even today, Vivekananda's words reverberate in the councils of the world and Indians bask in the glory of Swamiji's personality. During the years that he spent in the West, he won admirers and disciples, who imbibed his teachings.

Vivekananda's views on education should be an inspiration as Kerala embarks on a thorough reform programme in education. He was himself the ideal teacher, who inspired men and women to manifest the wisdom innate in them. Education as a process of man-making, without ignoring the need for scientific advancement, should be at the heart of the education system that Kerala aspires to build to meet the challenges of the twenty-first century. Concentration is enough, he stressed, to acquire knowledge. Acquisition of facts will follow as a consequence. A meditation centre is being planned in the premises of the statue to practice concentration. The importance of teachers' education is being recognised in the state and by honouring the ideal teacher, we spread the message of reverence for the guru.

The significance of the grand memorial that has been erected in a historic point in Thiruvananthapuram is that it is a joint effort of people belonging to all religions and political parties. People came forward with effort and resources to build a monument that befits the grandeur of Swamiji. The best *vastu* experts designed the pedestal and the canopy according to Kerala's traditions of '*shilpa shastra*'. It will remain a vibrant symbol of India's unity and remind us of the remaining tasks of building the Indian nation he envisaged.

5

MALAYALEE MINDSET

Having had the unique privilege of interacting closely with Malayalees abroad and in their homeland, over the years, I have observed certain peculiar traits that characterises the Malayalee mind, which has made me look into what transformation is needed to make ourselves more modern, productive and closer to universal norms of behaviour. We are generally sharper in intellect, more creative and more innovative than many people. We have had the opportunity to interact with many cultures for centuries and even today we have greater global reach than many others. But the paradox is that there is much in our mindset that needs attention and correction, much in our ways that baffles others. It is said that any observation you make about India, the opposite of it will also be true and we should bear in mind that this is also true about Kerala.

The paradox is explained in a story of a bane and a boon. The bane of the Malayalees at the time of their creation was that they were dull, disorganised and lazy, although they were in an enchanting land. They complained bitterly to the Almighty, who gave them a boon that they would be perfect once they took off from Kerala and settled abroad. So we have two kinds of Malayalees, according to this tale, one that remains with the bane in Kerala, undisciplined and lazy; the other, the beneficiary of the boon, courteous and industrious, in other lands. The story may be apocryphal, but it underlines the fact that the Malayalees are capable of changing their mindset and mend their ways to be successful outside Kerala. They are trusted and depended upon in countries from Mauritius to Malaysia, from the Gulf to the Americas. The joke in Malaysia was that the name of their airline, MAS, stood for 'Malayalees are supreme'.

The story of the Kerala crabs is well-known. They are exported in open cans, as no crab will allow another to climb up in any circumstance. We are highly individualistic, incapable of working as a team. Our superb intellect and creative energy are frittered away in internal squabbles. We are all chiefs, not Indians, as Americans would say. For a society to develop, it has to operate within which each of us has a niche. We have to learn to wait for our turn, whether we are entering an elevator or waiting to help ourselves to a buffet. We must learn from our brethren, who patiently wait in line at the beverage corporation stalls.

Social graces are generally absent in our society. We may be the only people in the world, who do not greet each other as a matter of routine. Most societies develop set phrases, to greet when they meet. Japan has a whole set of traditional expressions for every occasion, to show courtesy and humility. But amongst us, the greeting is at best, a smile or at worst, a personal comment, which often shows lack of sensitivity. Gratitude is rarely expressed in Malayalam and at best, we resort to a casual thank you. No Malayalam word exists even for 'cheers', though we drink Indian made foreign liquor in huge quantities. The British talk about the weather to break the ice, but we do not do it, perhaps because we have no variety in weather conditions. We need to cultivate social graces within our own society, not just outside it.

Kerala women are liberated and control the purse strings in the family, but their place is in the home. Wives are not seen or heard in public. Given a choice, we will still make them walk thirty yards behind us. True liberation will come when women are able to come out of the homes safely and occupy positions beside their men in any area of activity. Michelle Obama should be the role model for Kerala women.

Malayalees have gone global, but we remain insular in our own state and resist the winds of change. Outsiders are uncomfortable here because we tend to ignore them on social occasions after an initial introduction and resume our gossip in the vernacular. Partly, it is the inadequacy of language; partly it is lack of confidence. For a people, who have been successful abroad in various professions, we are often tongue-tied when the conversation is in English. Our students have no opportunities to speak in English, not at home, not in class, not among friends and so we remain perpetually handicapped in articulation. Finishing schools and instant English courses do not seem to have raised the general level of proficiency in English. I have seen our people not being able to express themselves adequately even after living abroad for several years. This is more a matter of the mindset, which can be changed, not a mental block. We are not poor in learning languages; we remain poor in using them.

Swami Vivekananda's 'lunatic asylum' is alive and well in Kerala even today. Religions, castes and sub-castes still divide us and the trend is to perpetuate and deepen the divisions, not to discard them. How come that education, economic development and social growth do not erase caste prejudices and practices? Caste, which was once a tool to protect the social fabric and to foster traditional professions, appears to have penetrated the psyche of our being.

It strikes at the very root of democracy. We do not cast our votes, we vote our castes. The caste mindset will stay with us as long as it determines our social status, our job opportunities and our loyalties. But Kerala cannot become an egalitarian society, unless we get over our caste mindset.

There appears to be a new explosion of faith. Are we turning more and more to the gods as we have no faith in our fellow men? Temples, churches and mosques have sprung up everywhere, as if in competition. Religious rituals are no more private between man and his God, but conspicuous display of devotion, a few degrees higher than the competitors. The aim is not to reach heaven anymore, but the *Guinness Book of Records*. Religious tolerance, a hallmark of Kerala in the past, is fast disappearing from our land. Even Mahabali is greeted with splurging, drinking and Bollywood talk.

The quest for leadership and public recognition must be a weakness of all human beings, but Malayalees seem to have an overdose of it. That explains the proliferation of political parties, organisations and associations. The saying goes that where there are two Malayalees, there is an association, where there are three, there are two associations and where there are four, there is a federation of associations. It is the pursuit of positions that prompts this pointless proliferation of institutions. The waste of energy and resources in our society must be phenomenal in our quest for visibility. We have an infinite infatuation for the camera at every level and the media exploits it merrily. The new tendency to put up huge flex boards of leaders, big and small, in every square and circle, must be curbed. When everyone knows that the persons who are featured often finance the flex boards, what purpose do they serve? Thank God, we do not go for gigantic cut-outs of leaders like in a neighbouring state.

This is the same mindset that results in the immense waste of resources, time and money in our ritualistic public meetings.

Any occasion is good enough for a public meeting at any time of the day and you find enough people to line up on the stage and even to occupy the front seats as fodder for verbal canons. Long welcome speeches and several felicitation remarks detract from the substance of the occasion. Speakers are selected to give honourable appearances and not to make a contribution. Money is spent on flowers covered in plastic sheets and crude metal, glass and wood souvenirs. Unless a code of conduct is established for public meetings, much energy and resources will be wasted on them, as they do in authoritarian states. In Kenya, a hundred senior-most officials would go to every meeting that the president addresses and the state machinery came to a grinding halt. Should we have the same mindset? In power-hungry Kerala, do we need thousands of bulbs burning every time a festival passes by?

Civic sense is also a matter of mindset. Being clean ourselves, while polluting the neighbourhood is classic hypocrisy. Same is the case with polluting rivers, destroying forests or turning streets into toilets. Cleanliness must be as much in the mind as in our surroundings.

Another bane of our society is the overdose of ideologies. Some of us still open our umbrellas as soon as it rains in Beijing. We are the only people who closed our shops when Saddam Hussein and Osama bin Laden were killed. Strikes, *hartals* etc. are still common and the consciousness is only of the rights of workers, not their responsibilities. The institution of 'looking charges' should put any labour movement to shame.

Attachment to land is an obsession, not even a mindset. We kill each other for a strip of land. We are perpetually in narrow streets and inadequate civic facilities as no one parts with land even for the common good. The Malayalam University cannot get land in Ezhuthachan's village. The same mindset thwarts proposals for industrialisation. Every potential investor is suspected to be a land grabber. The lust for land skews land utilisation. It is true, as Mark

Twain said that, 'land is not made any more,' but judicious use of available land is essential for Kerala's development.

In making my case for transforming the Malayalee mindset, I may have exaggerated facts, generalised isolated tendencies and caused offence. But I have not spoken as an outsider, but someone who may have the same mindset that I am seeking to transform. This was more introspection than criticism. Changes in mindset are hard to accomplish in a clean sweep. In the meantime, Malayalees must be given tasks that suit their mindset and genius. Give them jobs that demand personal initiative, not collective action. Exploit them in ways that their intellectual talents and rich imagination is put to good use. Trust them to build a knowledge society and usher in a silent revolution. But if Malaylees can transform their mindset, the sky is the limit for them. If we add social graces such as courtesy, discipline and punctuality, social responsibility and industry to the other remarkable attributes of the Malayalees, we will get a productive work force, an impeccable society and a proud community. And then, as *Mahakavi* Vallathol said, 'When we hear the name Kerala, blood will simmer in our veins.'

6

CHALLENGES IN HIGHER EDUCATION: A KERALA PERSPECTIVE

Addressing the Kerala Legislative Assembly in 2012, the then Governor of Kerala HR Bharadwaj stated, 'My government recognises that higher education is a powerful instrument of economic and social transformation and will aim to ensure quality education based on access, equity and excellence. My government realises the importance of regaining the primacy of our state in the field of higher education. The thrust of our government will be on encouraging setting up of world class institutions and infrastructure in the state.'

Indeed, the challenge is to fashion an education system, which will provide access, ensure equity and maintain excellence. Today, none of the Indian universities figure in any list of a hundred or more world-class universities identified by different assessment agencies. The wide gap between our universities and world-class universities must be bridged so that our graduates can compete with their peers in India and abroad.

Higher education system in the state has succeeded in increasing quantity to meet the aspirations of the youth. The enrolment rate in Kerala is higher than the national average. No one needs to deny himself higher education for want of accessibility, though he may not get the course or college of his choice. Of late, even engineering colleges have vacancies. We have also risen to the occasion when it comes to offering new courses, including cutting edge technologies in some colleges and universities. Compared to the situation when I was a student at the Kerala University till 1966, there is a world of difference in quantity, diversity and quality in higher education today. Modern methods of teaching, including use of technology, have been introduced. Internet connectivity has opened a new world of knowledge. In other words, the system has much to claim credit for.

But Kerala seems to have lagged behind in competitiveness. This is evident from the fact that our graduates have only a small share of seats in specialised institutions in Kerala and outside, for which national competition is necessary. Similarly, the share of our graduates in the IT industry worldwide is low. We need to reform our higher education in such a way that it matches the highest standards in the world and makes our graduates competitive.

We should recognise that reform in the field of higher education will be slow and painful. Innovation gurus concede that it is hard to introduce innovation in the so-called 'mature enterprises' as innovations can be risky and expensive. Past successes can also be a disincentive. Higher education is in this category of enterprises. Any failed innovation may put a whole generation into jeopardy. The available teachers may not be well-equipped to impart the new system of education. Introduction of reforms should be after due deliberation and preparation. Any wrong step can be costly.

Inadequate infrastructure, particularly in the government institutions is an immediate challenge. Low living and high thinking may be a good dictum, but our educational institutions should have the minimum comforts and conveniences to enable teachers and students to perform at the optimum level. The disparities among the facilities available should also be a matter of concern. Libraries, laboratories and other facilities need modernisation and upgradation as new courses are introduced. Internet connectivity, which remains low, is also crucial in higher education. Massive infusion of funds is necessary to improve the infrastructural facilities.

Teachers are the backbone of any system of education. The better the teachers, the better the students. Much has been done to improve the wages of teachers, but the wages are not linked to performance and the security of service tends to make some of them lethargic. There should be a system of evaluation to provide incentives and disincentives to teachers. The strength of the faculty must also increase to give teachers time to learn more and take time off to reinvigorate themselves. They should also have enough time to evaluate answer books and interact with their students. The existing teacher–student ratio does not meet the basic academic requirements. Teachers training programmes and exchange programmes must be developed.

The basic weakness of our higher education system is that teaching and learning methods continue unchanged from schools to postgraduate studies. Teachers are the source of all knowledge and the students merely imbibe knowledge. In higher education, the initiative for learning should come from the students and the teachers should be guides, evaluators and motivators. The spirit of enquiry should be encouraged in planning the curriculum and prescribing textbooks. As the governor stated, 'Our universities must not only impart knowledge, but also create knowledge through research and innovation. New products and processes must emerge from our campuses, giving the industry a stake in our education system.' Today, industry merely recruits graduates. Instead, they should invest in education and participate in its planning so that the graduates meet the requirements of the industry without sacrificing the basic academic standards and overall development of their personalities.

Fluency in English language, particularly its spoken variety, is lacking among our graduates and it militates against the acceptability of our graduates outside Kerala. Stress should be given on articulation of ideas in English as well as in the mother tongue and opportunities should be given to them to use the language in everyday life. A special effort to develop linguistic skills must be made.

The Government of India is in the process of enacting laws to facilitate and regulate the operation of foreign universities in India. Since profit-making is prohibited, only those universities, which have an interest in Indian knowledge and talents, will come to India. Kerala should equip itself for the advent of foreign universities by establishing links with some of them in advance. Emulating the best practices in foreign education is the first step towards building world-class universities.

Continuous assessment of institutions and teachers is absolutely essential to determine the amount of autonomy that individual institutions should enjoy. Institutions of excellence can be developed in the state by identifying the potential of each institution. A state assessment and accreditation mechanism is being planned to meet this requirement.

Two reforms introduced in higher education have shown how problems develop in implementation of reforms, even when they are sound in objectives. The introduction of the semester system at the graduate level was long overdue in the state and it has proved valuable nationally and internationally. It aims at broader acquisition of knowledge, encourages the spirit of enquiry and transforms the relationship between teachers and students. It certainly increases the workload of the students and teachers, particularly since the number of examinations multiply. The system was introduced rather hastily and without consequential changes in the curricula and the student–teacher ratio. As a result, several anomalies have cropped up, raising the demand for a return to the old system, which would be a retrograde step. We are in the process of examining the problems through wide consultations among the stakeholders and close examination by experts. The semester system should stay, but with the necessary correctives to make it an instrument of improvement in higher education.

The other reform, which met a similar fate, was the introduction of a cluster of colleges, aimed at sharing of resources among the colleges in the same area. But it has not yet taken because of the reluctance of the private colleges to share their assets. The scheme is being examined to remove the apprehensions of the reluctant managements.

Everyone agrees with Swami Vivekananda that the purpose of education is 'man-making'. It should bring out the talents already inherent in every individual. Our own ancient system of education remains a guide and efforts are being made to revive the spirit of Nalanda and Takshashila. But in modern terms, man-making will also include equipping the students to stand on their own two feet, another point that Swami Vivekananda had stressed. As the saint Narayana Guru emphasised, education must develop the hand, the head and the heart. The challenge of higher education is to devise a system that will meet the multiple needs of our youth to meet the challenges of a rapidly changing world. They should be equipped to seize the opportunities of globalisation, without being swept away by its tumultuous impact.

7

HIGHER EDUCATION 2.0: A BLUEPRINT FOR KERALA

Two laments that we hear about higher education in Kerala are that it has remained static and that our universities and colleges do not figure in the lists of excellent institutions nationally or internationally. The first is contrary to facts and the second arises out of inadequate appreciation of the relevance, rationale and methodology of drawing up the lists by national and international entities.

In the forty-five years that I have been away from the education scene in Kerala, higher education has made rapid strides, in terms of establishment of new institutions in areas of special interest, new courses to teach emerging technologies and new methods of teaching. To cite just one instance, the Masters' degree course in English literature offered in the universities in Kerala today are very different from the course I did in the sixties. Gone are the days when considerable space was given for Old English and Chaucer. Today, communicative English, diaspora literature and Dalit literature are part of the curriculum.

As for the lists of world-class universities and others, it is true that such lists recognise the exceptional quality of education available around the world. In our quest for excellence, the institutions recognised become models to emulate. But the criteria used in identifying these institutions are such that they are beyond the reach of the majority of institutions, particularly in Kerala. The number of Nobel Prizes won, patents registered, industry support, teacher–student ratio, autonomy, the presence of international students and infrastructure are factors that go into the selection of institutions. While it is desirable to strive for recognition on the basis of these standards, our institutions must be assessed in the light of our own needs and capabilities.

A prerequisite for excellence in higher education is the high quality of the school graduates, who enter the universities. Near 100 per cent pass at the school level, the variety of syllabuses in use in the school and the system of all school graduates seeking to enter the universities have a bearing on the quality of higher education. More rigorous testing at the school level and diversion of school graduates to vocational courses on the basis of their capabilities and talents will ensure that our universities get a better corpus of students at the entrance level. If I were to cherry pick from Gandhi's views on education, as suggested by Amartya Sen, it should not be his rejection of Western education, but his emphasis on vocational education. Dignity of labour and the principle of higher pay for the tougher job should be the norm if we have to divert young people to productive professions without entering universities.

The blueprint that the Kerala State Higher Education Council (KSHEC) presented to the government last year has identified five areas for special attention: Infrastructure, use of technology, teachers' training, research and autonomy. The expectation is that the package of proposals that will emanate from the Council will constitute the emergence of a new generation of higher education in Kerala, which may be characterised as Higher Education 2.0.

An urgent issue that received the attention of the Council was a set of anomalies and difficulties in the Choice Based Credit and Semester System (CBCSS), introduced at the graduate level in 2014. Lack of the required working days in each semester, the teacher–student ratio, the five point gradation system and unimaginative selection of books and syllabus were identified as the issues and recommendations were made to rectify them. The government has approved the recommendations and it is for the universities to implement them without delay.

The Council also undertook a comprehensive review of the state policy on education. The government has already picked and chosen several recommendations from our report for implementation. Improvement of the working conditions of the administrative staff in the universities and colleges is one of the recommendations we have stressed. Use of technology is an absolute necessity today. Massive Open Online Courses (MOOC) have transformed the education scene in developed countries and the same is available free of cost to our teachers and students, provided we have the connectivity. Course content could be simply modified to suit our requirements.

Training of teachers is the highest priority in Higher Education 2.0. A Faculty Training Centre with the proportions of a university has already been designed. No teacher in any faculty should go to the classes without training in teaching methodology. Teachers of exceptional ability should be given incentives and dead wood should be eased out of our higher education institutions.

Multiple assessment institutions are being created all over India and Kerala will take the lead by establishing the first institution at the state level for accreditation and assessment. With the advent of the new Kerala State Accreditation and Assessment Council (KSAAC), the state of assessment of our institutions will see a sea change.

KSAAC assessments will be compulsory and it will include gradation of teachers to provide incentives and disincentives. The standards of assessment, already set by an expert group, will be second to none.

Kerala has a fairly large number of research projects in the universities, but not the kind of research that will produce new products and processes. Research institutions of the kind that exist outside the universities must be created in the departments that have the expertise and facilities. Even graduate and postgraduate students must engage in research, leading to entrepreneurships. Many schemes have been announced to incentivise innovation and entrepreneurship, but unless a research culture is developed, our universities cannot create knowledge.

Industries, the main beneficiaries of our higher education, must also become its benefactors. It is not enough that they recruit the graduates and declare them unemployable. They should work with the universities to design courses, invest in them and then insist on quality. The Narayana Murthy Committee had envisaged 50 per cent of the investment in higher education emanating from the industries. Kerala established its own committee to study the issue and framed its own constructive proposals for the linkages between industries and institutions.

Kerala does not have a single autonomous college in the state, though there are several which deserve autonomy, both academic and administrative. But autonomy entails higher responsibilities and accountability. Strict criteria should be observed in creating autonomous colleges. No less a person than Prof Madhava Menon is heading a group, which is laying down the rules for the implementation of a decision already taken by the government.

Internationalisation of education is a corollary to globalisation and the existing smattering of foreign collaborations should be expanded. We should also be able to attract foreign students to our universities by designing courses for which India has a particular capability. Indian semesters for foreign students should attract many universities abroad. The Council has been asked to coordinate efforts of the universities in Kerala for internationalisation.

Higher Education 2.0 in Kerala should have many more features. It should be developed into a new vision and a blueprint for the future. The resistance to change must change to realise that vision. True, as management gurus say, it is hard, expensive and risky to innovate in established enterprises, such as higher education. But with care, expertise and commitment, it should be possible to reform higher education in Kerala to meet our needs and to benefit from the demographic dividend. We may not find a place in the list of world-class institutions for another generation, but we will be able to equip our leaders of tomorrow for the challenges and opportunities of the twenty-first century in which India will be one of the power centres of a multipolar world.

Vyasa
The Master Storyteller

Vyasa, the revered sage and venerable storyteller, is credited with some of the central works of Hindu theology and traditions, namely the *Brahmasutras*, the *Srimad Bhagavatam*, the eighteen *Puranas* and the *Mahabharata*, and classification of the Vedas. The versatility of Vyasa is nearly unbelievable—many believe that there were as many as twenty-eight 'Vyasas' prior to the Sage Vyasa who composed the *Mahabharata* in the oral tradition. He was an unwavering champion of the Sanatana Dharma: The concept of universal brotherhood that India has presented to the world. The legacy of storytelling that he left behind is unmatched till date. Many an acclaimed author has conceded that no story which is not incorporated in the *Mahabharata* has ever been told to this world by anyone. All the venerable volumes of work by Vyasa were composed by him as a tool to enlighten the common man by revealing to them, the great philosophical knowledge of life and ethics, in the simplest manner possible. His works are equally appealing to all, irrespective of age, gender, occupation etc. That is precisely the hallmark of a popular author. His awe-inspiring acumen in narration is a unique ability that the current generation of writers should look up to. In fact, all communicators, authors, columnists, speakers, orators, academicians and storytellers bear this responsibility on their shoulders to ensure that wisdom and virtue are passed on to the coming generations.

Taking a cue from the amusing tales and complex constructs of Sage Vyasa, the next section consists of a peal of unexpected, amusing, yet profound set of articles and talks. Sailing on the sea of diplomacy, one often shores up to exotic locales and exciting adventures. This final section of the book takes the reader through a fascinating journey of several experiences, thoughts and opinions of the author, sprinkled with his wit. The master storyteller in him unfurls gracefully through this section, which is predominantly culled from his speech transcripts. To transition from some to awesome, we explore the inner sanctum of a writer, take a flight to the future on a sci-fi mode, jump the fence for some fashion sense, sing paeans to fascinating personalities, have kava and Chinese tea as we globetrot across continents, and get into the celebratory mode in a riot of colourful stances that take us from the paddy fields to the world parliament.

1

THE PAINS AND PLEASURES OF WRITING

I rarely get invited to speak on literary topics, as my long career in the Foreign Service and my present assignment in higher education have diminished my academic background in English literature. Having got this opportunity to speak in memory of a legendary teacher of English literature, I have chosen to speak on the pleasures and pains of writing—as all of us, at one time or another, have experienced both, whether we as students, teachers, professionals and most of all, creative writers. When I speak of creative writing, I refer not only to poetry and fiction, but all writing, which contains thoughts, feelings and emotions, not just information. We engage in creative writing at one time or another and experience its pleasures and pains.

Every educated person carries ideas for creative writing, irrespective of whether he ever puts pen to paper. Someone said that there are only two kinds of people on this earth, those who write and those who think they can write. Indeed, we believe that any of us can write a novel, short story, poem or autobiographical reflections, if only we tried. But it is like imagining that we can play the sitar like Ravi Shankar, if only we tried. We need extensive reading, intensive imagination, a compulsive urge and specialist training to create any kind of literature. A famous writer prosaically remarked that a literary creation is a piece of furniture, which has its own requirements. We have to learn the laws of construction before we go about creating it. 'Just because I had read plenty of novels did not mean I could write one, more than I could make a chair because I had sat on enough of them,' said Nigel Watts, author of *Write A Novel*. On the other hand, the director of a creative writing programme in a university for many years said that all creative writing programmes ought to be abolished by law, as creative writing cannot be taught.

Writers have their own reasons to write and many of them have explained why they write. Some do it to create a revolution. Friedrich Nietzsche believed in the old dictum that the pen is mightier than the sword. He said, 'All I need is a sheet of paper and something to write with, and then I can turn the world upside down.' I suppose Martin Luther King would have been reading Nietzsche when he inspired the masses by exhorting, 'If you want to change the world, pick up your pen and write.' Mahatma Gandhi brought a mighty empire to its knees by writing. Others write for their own satisfaction and pleasure, but not without pain. According to Thomas Mann, 'A writer is someone for whom writing is more difficult than it is for other people.' Writing is pain and pleasure in parallel proportions like the two sides of a coin. A young researcher collected for me what famous writers had to say as to why they wrote. Some remarkable explanations worth noting include poignant ones like Albert Camus', 'The purpose of a writer is to keep civilisation from destroying itself'; philosophical ones like Maya Angelou, who said, 'A bird doesn't sing because it has an answer, it sings because it has a song'; psychological ones like EL Doctorow, who said, 'Writing is a socially acceptable form of schizophrenia'; prudent ones like F Scott Fitzgerald, who said, 'You don't write because you want to say something, you write because you have something to say'; pragmatic ones like George Orwell, who came up with, 'I think there are four great motives for writing, at any rate, for writing prose. They exist in different degrees in every writer, and in any one writer the proportions will vary from time to time, according to the atmosphere in which he is living. They are: Sheer egoism, aesthetic enthusiasm, historical impulse and political purpose'; matter-of-fact ones like Somerset Maugham's, 'There are three rules for writing a novel. Unfortunately, no one knows what they are' and simply practical ones, like Toni Morrison said, 'If there's a book that you want to read, but it hasn't been written yet, then you must write it.' George Bernard Shaw is credited to have suggested that he writes for the same reason as a cow gives milk, 'It's inside me, it's got to come out, and in a real sense I would suffer if I couldn't.' The pain of milking is compensated by the pleasure of giving. But the most fascinating and simple reason for writing was given by my own guru, Ayyappa Paniker, who wrote, 'I cannot but bloom, as I am a flowering tree (*pookkathirikkan enikkavathille, kanikkonnayalle*).'

Writing is the simple exercise of translating a thought into an action through the chosen medium of words; though finding the right word is often a difficult task. Mark Twain said, 'The difference between the right word and the almost right word is the difference between lightning and a lightning bug.' Nonetheless, the writer must set his pen moving constantly as perfection is like chasing the horizon. Words leave behind indelible impressions that can be restrictive or resurrective in nature. The reader should be able to visualise a world of his own, rather look for real images in the mind of the writer. To sum it up, allow me to borrow these prescient words of Marcus Fabius Quintillions, a Roman rhetorician of the first century AD who wrote,

'We should not write so that it is possible for [the reader] to understand us, but so that it is impossible for him to misunderstand us.'

Needless to say, reading is the most essential requirement for writing. Some writers say that one needs to read a thousand sentences before writing one sentence. Reading gives you language, thoughts and experience, not to be copied, but to be imbibed to ignite your imagination and to express your thoughts in elegant language. The war with words ensues only if one has conquered the first battle; which is the drive to initiate writing. Blaise Pascal once prophesied, 'All of humanity's problems stem from man's inability to sit quietly in a room alone.' I would say that the solution to it is to engage in the art of writing. The ability to embrace the self in solitude and empathise with fellow human beings, either directly with the characters created or indirectly with the targeted reader, is essential for creative writing. Starting to write is often painful, but finishing it is pleasurable. It may be tedious, but the pure pleasure of writing is priceless, just like it is for a bird that sings in the wilderness. The sense of fulfilment that one derives out of writing is often compared with that of motherhood.

Language was the earliest and the best invention in human history. It arose not only from man's absolute necessity to convey his ideas, but also his enthusiasm to communicate in the best possible manner. Creative writers moulded the language, in its many manifestations, to change the world itself. The voice of the writers ought to be the voice of change and the collective voice of the society should bring about progress and betterment. The voluminous novels and scholastic tomes have determined the course of history in the past and micro writings on Twitter and Facebook create revolutions today.

Turning to my own experience of writing—which consisted initially of professional analyses of political events and personalities and now of newspaper columns and autobiographical narrations—

it is prompted by an urge to share experiences and shape opinions. I would not call it creative writing, but the sense of fulfilment in seeing my writings published gives me immense joy. Even after many years of public speaking, producing television programs and blogging, the thrill of seeing bylines in the leading publications of the world is unparalleled. Today, the writer has been liberated from the clutches of editors and publishers, as blogs and electronic publications are not subject to the scissors of editors and publishers. But the traditional interaction with editors, before a piece sees the light of day is an exercise I enjoy most. Most Indian publications carry columns either as they are written or edited for brevity or acceptability, but writing for the *New York Times*, the *Wall Street Journal* or the *Washington Quarterly* involves a dialogue with gifted editors, who do not leave any fact unchecked or views unexamined. The final product inevitably has the stamp of the publication in both language and content. The partnership between the author and the editor embellishes rather than diminish the value of writing.

The pleasure and pain of writing, I imagine, is more in poetry and fiction, but any writing that goes beyond conveying information carries the exhilaration of creation as well as the frustration of inadequacy. Like many others who believe that they can play the sitar like Ravi Shankar or sing like Yesudas if only they tried, I too dream of the day when I can create a masterpiece of classical proportions. But for the time being, I must be content with the lesser experience of expressing my thoughts in words for the pure joy of it.

(Dr EC Antony Memorial Lecture of Sri C Achutha Menon Government College, Thrissur, February 2013)

2

FLIGHTS OF FICTION

Distinguished Delegates,

I hope that you will forgive me if I read from my latest acquisition, an iPhone 55s. One feature that this iPhone has is the ability to transcribe your thoughts into a readable text. I merely thought about what I should say at this conference during my walk this morning and by the time I returned home, my speech was ready in readable form. But I still have to read the text from my iPhone. By the time the iPhone 56s is unveiled, we will be able to read the text from the air or our own palms as Pranav Mistry predicted in his TED talk more than fifty years ago. The real world and the virtual world will be totally merged and we will be able to move from one to the other soon.

I am a little disoriented today as I landed at the Nedumbassery 'spacedrome' only yesterday, after my three-day trip to the Moon by Chandrayan 54. Though the journey itself was only for three hours, the traffic was so heavy that we had to go three times around the

Earth before we could land. The Teresa 'people's mobile' was there and its pilot brought me to the Holiday Inn in two minutes, but the system was down at the hotel and hundreds of people were waiting. These are occasions when we feel nostalgic about the old ledgers and pens, which were used for registration of guests at hotels. They never failed. Today, we save time in travel, but spend it in long queues!

But what a joy it was when I finally reached my room and had access to the supernet and I was able to sign into my Superskype, which enabled me to see my near and dear ones in different parts of the world in three dimensions and reach out and touch them. All of them appeared to walk out of the monitor like the originals, but since they were busy, I could not spend more time with them. As soon as I said 'Hi!', they were ready to say 'Bye'. It seemed the blurred pictures of the old Skype were better. They spent more time trying to connect, and I felt that they were making an effort to connect with me. Now they walk in and out of the monitor in a desperate rush. The world has become even faster in 2064.

I am most delighted to be at the Teresa's College at this fifty-third International Conference on Science Fiction. When I was here at the third Conference in 2014, this hall was a dull place with standard furniture and decoration. But look at what nanotechnology has done to it. It has glittering colours and magnificent shapes, which can be changed every day, if you so wish. The invisible public address system is perfect and the acoustics are excellent. As for the audience, all of you looked older with grey hair and even no hair and with paunches of different sizes and shapes on that occasion. But today, though you are older by fifty years, all of you are trim, thanks to the medical technology available today. No more treatments, no more surgeries, but mere replacement of vital organs at frequent intervals. You can order your complexion, the colour and style of your hair and the size and shape of your whole body. That explains the spring in the air, the sparkle in your eyes and the style in your strides. We are in the days of ageless body and timeless mind, as the super guru, Deepak Chopra promised us fifty years ago. I believe he has migrated to Moon, with frequent trips to Mars by the ISRO Mangalyan Express.

I shall conclude with a little bit about my latest Moon journey. I went to participate in the annual celebrations of the Moon Malayalee Association. The usual suspects were all there, including the minister of cosmic Indian affairs. Dancers and singers were brought by a special spacecraft all the way from Kerala. We stayed at the Super Duper Nair Cosmic Hotel, which was a mere teashop run by the same Nair when Armstrong set foot on the Moon. Now, with daily flights to Moon, we can get the best Kerala cuisine every day.

On my Moon journey this time, I discovered the new Knowledge Infusion Machine fitted on the Moon Shuttle. You merely connect the gadget with a band around your head and the book you select out of the millions on offer will be infused directly into your brain. I chose the books I began reading several years ago, but could not finish. Tolstoy's *War and Peace*, Milton's *Paradise Lost* and Vikram Seth's *A Suitable Boy* are now in my head forever. Once this machine is commercially available, we shall all be scholars without having to find time to read and without ruining our eyesight.

Friends,

As you may have guessed, the speech I just delivered is ahead of its time by fifty years. I do not know whether you will call it flight of fancy, fantasy or science fiction. I thought I should present my own science fiction, rather than explain what science fiction is all about. Someone has said that science fiction is like pornography: You cannot define it, but when you see it, you know it. If science fiction is a genre of fiction dealing with imaginative content such as futuristic settings, futuristic science and technology, space travel, time travel, parallel universes and extraterrestrial life, my vision of the world of 2064 is science fiction. None of the innovations I envisaged is far beyond the frontiers of science, as we know them today.

Imagination is boundless, while science has its limitations. Science fiction shows the way, science follows. Today's science fiction is tomorrow's innovation. Our myths and prehistoric fiction had anticipated intercontinental flying (*Pushpakaviman*) and weapons of mass destruction (*Agneyastra*). Narad Muni had the capacity to move around the whole universe, carrying tales. Hanuman could leap across the oceans and turn a city into ashes. Lord Krishna could be with 16,008 women simultaneously, probably cloning himself with an ancient version of the 3D printer. None of these feats are unthinkable for man today. In fact, today, facts are stranger than fiction.

Finally, I must congratulate the literary fraternity for striking back at the scientific community by celebrating science fiction. Scientists are strutting around the globe showcasing astounding scientific inventions and innovations in every field. Innovate or perish, they say. This conference will show that the origin of these innovations are in the brains of men of letters, people like Jonathan Swift, Mary Shelley, Jules Verne, HG Wells, Isaac Asimov, Carl Sagan and Arthur Clarke, who had visions of a brave new world long, long before the scientists created it. Science fiction is indeed a harmonious blend of imagination and science, which helps the frontiers of science to expand beyond the wildest imagination of scientists.

(Science Fiction Speech at the Third International Conference on Science Fiction, February 2014)

3

THE FASHION STATEMENT

I am honoured to be invited to speak at the Convocation 2013 of National Institute of Fashion Technology (NIFT), Kannur. In fact, I was quite surprised about the invitation, because, even though I am responsible for advising the government on all aspects of higher education, I was never called upon to pay any attention to NIFT. Having come here and seen the institution, its ambience, its faculty and its students, I know why it requires no attention from the government. It is an institution of excellence that any other college in Kerala will be envious of. This is an institution that dreams are made of.

I said I was surprised to be invited to NIFT, but more than me, a young relative, passionate about fashion, was not only surprised but immensely amused that I should be speaking on fashion and design in clothes. In her eyes, I am the least fashionable, despite my using designer brands and wearing expensive attire. She even believes that I am colour blind, because of the way I choose shirts and ties. Now you know why I chose to wear a kurta today.

I told her, however, that being 'fashion-less' is also a fashion.

Nobody would associate Mahatma Gandhi with fashion, but he made the greatest fashion statement in history by graduating to the loincloth after donning Western suits for several years. It was a statement of identification with the masses of India and of revolt against Western ways. He went to the round table conference in London in 1931 in a loincloth. When asked whether he was wearing enough clothes to go before the king, he remarked, 'The king had enough on for both of us.' 'Truly fashionable is beyond fashion,' said artist, designer Cecil Bacon.

Addressing those who are about to enter the fashion industry to make it richer, more imaginative and more innovative, I should be speaking of the relevance and indispensability of the best minds devoting attention to what we wear. As Shakespeare said, 'Apparel oft proclaims the man.' Each person may make his or her own fashion statement, but your task is to offer a wide range of options to choose from. Your skills must be deployed to lead the fashion industry by using indigenous materials and world-class techniques to create your own fashions.

The power of fashion in today's world is incredible. As you fly out of this campus into the world to leave your footprint across the globe, I hope you will become the torchbearers of responsible fashion. Kannur is already famous for its traditional weaving and your creations will bring style and vibrancy to the Kannur school of fashion.

History shows, strangely, that the first purpose of clothing was not protection of the body or modesty, but ornament. People of the Stone Age wore no clothes, but tattooed their bodies and used twigs and other materials to adorn themselves. I have seen a cartoon of Adam and Eve standing under a tree with leaves aplenty. Eve says, 'I have nothing good to wear today.' Pharaohs used clothes to display wealth even in death, as we can see in the mummies of Egypt. Today, a dress or an accessory not only satisfies social and emotional needs, but also becomes part of our well-being. Clothes accentuate the body rather than conceal it. Even the most conservative clothes, designed to cover the entire body, are decorated with diamonds today.

Fashion is a medium of expression. It is poetry in fabric. The expressions of fashion and design are as delectable an art form as poetry is, mysterious and creative. Fashion incites emotions, evokes memories and excites aspirations. It is imperative that you send the right message across to your followers. Remember that by creating a piece of fashion product, you are not just expressing your own creativity, but you are enabling millions to express themselves through the clothes they choose to wear. They say that the most alluring curve of a woman's body is her smile. So, create clothes that enable her to wear her smile while she adorns your clothes.

Fashion is also the script of history. Fashion and style are not merely the hot trends of the day. The apparels that a population is clothed in and the accessories that a populace is adorned in, tells the story of their lives and etches it in the history of their glorious past, leaving indelible impressions. In any archaeological excavation, the depiction of the clothing, jewellery and accessories of a community are the most important clues for us to help rediscover the past and weave history of their lifestyle and even economic conditions. No time capsule will be buried without NIFT creations. Thus, fashion is enduring. A piece of your creation today sets the youth of today in the fashion groove and starts to write the history of tomorrow. Someone said that the moment a fashion trend becomes universal, it is out of date. Fashion trends hold on to its grip only when it is still tantalising. So, the moment your idea has received universal acceptance it is part of history, and it is time for you to move ahead and churn your brains. Thus, unlike other professions, you are constantly living in creating history of a culture. So ensure that you create fashion that narrates a beautiful story of our lives today depicting it in all its glory and simplicity to the coming generations.

Fashion is also a tool for empowerment. In a world where throes of affliction and exploitation hits the vulnerable constantly, where cries for emancipation of women continues to echo across the globe, fashion seems to have a role to play as a tool for empowerment. Fashion not only serves as an instrument to bring a person into the limelight, but also protects her from the dangers around. It is like a barbed wire fence around a house. I am not suggesting that you build an impenetrable fortress. I agree with Sophia Loren's comment that, 'A woman's dress should be like a barbed-wire fence: Serving its purpose without obstructing the view.' You are the originators of trends and styles of tomorrow. Keep in mind the safety and security of all men and women in the society while you do that. Bring out the heritage and culture of our nation through your designs and weave an adorable tapestry to be displayed in front of the world. Thus, you empower not just individuals, but also communities and nations.

Being a medium of expression, armed with the power to carve history and empower communities, fashion definitely stands in good stead as a tool for transformation. Fashion for change, for positive change, is the best contribution you can make to the society. Through your creative process, render voices to the voiceless and power to the powerless. A great advantage that you have bred in your technology is that innovation and creativity are your bread and butter, unlike other professions where they have a set norm and standard to follow. That gives you endless opportunities to spin changes in the society. There is also a hidden danger in that, because nothing is wrong in fashion. So your freedom to make grave errors is also limitless. Stories of transformation enabled by creative and innovative designs are aplenty today. From electronics to architecture, from jewellery to footwear, from perfume to pharmaceuticals—design is the key to change. In USA, mind-boggling statistical figures show that fashion industry does more business than music, movies and books combined. That is to tell you that you are entering a world filled with temptations and lucrative offers which gleam at you. It is for you to decide whether to embrace responsible fashion in an industry blinded by glitz and glamour. The annual Cannes Film Festival which is touted as the world's most popular fashion park where cultures intermingle seamlessly in the form of celebrities from the film world and fashion houses hits the top news every minute. What Aishwarya Rai, Vidya Balan or Amitabh Bachchan wear becomes more important and interesting to us than the gnawing problems of our country. Thus is the power of fashion to overpower everything else. So use your power diligently and responsibly in collaboration with your friends from other disciplines and create responsible fashion for tomorrow.

Finally, I would also like you to pay heed to the alarming deterioration of the environment around us. For the fashion industry to be sustainable economically, it must be sustainable socially and environmentally. Fashion should follow the trends of nature and not the other way round. Make sure that you create environment-friendly, sustainable fashion products in which the current generation can delight in, and the future generations can be proud of.

Aping the West has been a style in itself, probably as an adverse effect of globalisation and foray of foreign industries into our markets. We in India need to create our own niche in the world of fashion, which the rest of the world shall be eager to emulate. I am aware that we have many a great name in the fashion industry from India, of whom we can be proud. I would like to see many more of you join that elite club, while remaining rooted to our Indian identity and creating fashion that is environment-friendly and embraces nature. May you utilise your knowledge of design, management and technology for the glory of the institute, the progress of the country and mankind at large.

(Convocation Address at National Institute of Fashion Technology, Kannur, 2013)

4

FUNDAMENTALS OF DECISION-MAKING

The subject 'fundamentals of decision-making' is fascinating, though in my long career of public speaking, I was never asked to address this issue. In fact, like every other human being, I have been taking decisions of various kinds, both private and official, without bothering to study or codify the theoretical fundamentals of decision-making. I know now that volumes have been written by management gurus and public administration specialists about decision-making. I have no intention to present a scholarly study. I shall confine myself to my own experiences of decision-making, by myself and others, to throw some light on the process.

The eternal human dilemma on decision-making was most eloquently, but enigmatically described by Shakespeare, when he made Hamlet say, 'To be or not to be, that is the question.' The tragedy of Hamlet was not on account of a bad decision, but because he did not take decisions at the right time. Dead bodies piled upon the stage even as he was wondering how he should deal with people to avenge his father. Two prime ministers of India, Pandit Jawaharlal Nehru and PV Narasimha Rao, have been credited with an extra dose of Hamletian dilemma. But indecision arising out of deep intellectual analysis may have its own advantages. Impulsive decision-making, on the other hand, may have dangers, particularly when it involves national and international issues.

Decision-making, for the most part, depends on personal traits and experience and it is for this reason that people matter in any organisation, whether private or government. Choice of personnel for leadership, the function of Service Commissions, is crucial. It is not organisations that solve puzzles; it is the people who solve them. A surprisingly large number of people in any organisation make personal choices, which add up to make the policy of the organisation. Today, there are many proven methods to assess abilities of individuals for various positions, but in the ultimate analysis, it is the overall personality of the individual, as it evolves and develops. And the circumstances in which decisions are taken that determine the success of the organisation. Inevitably, luck plays a part in success, a factor that cannot be designed by any scientific method. The family a person is born in, the country in which he is brought up, his personal traits, his education and health and his opportunities, most of these a result of lucky or unlucky accidents, contribute to decision-making.

The choice of personnel can be scientific at executive levels in government and the private sector, but the political leadership, which determines the future of mankind, emerges in unpredictable ways. We seek consolation in the theory that nations get the leaderships they deserve, but how did the people of Germany, Cambodia, North Korea and Burma deserve Hitler, Pol Pot, Kim Il Sung or Ne Win? They are simply accidental creations of history, who brought about untold suffering to their own people and humankind in general. In democracies, the chances of creating such disasters are less, but ballot boxes too have brought in aberrations, which needed to be corrected by the people themselves.

Let us return for a moment to the record of decision-making of some of our prime ministers, who have shaped our history in modern times. It is indeed unfair to pick a few specific instances to test their decision-making skills, because such an exercise will not do justice to their larger contributions to the country. To characterise Pandit Nehru as indecisive is to be unjust to the architect of modern India. But his decisions relating to Jammu and Kashmir remain mysteries till this day. If he had the determination and practical wisdom of his daughter, the matter would not have gone to the United Nations and remained there today as an impediment to the full flowering of India in international affairs. Pandit Nehru's approach to China, which was openly criticised by Sardar Patel, turned out to be his own undoing in 1962. In his short stint as prime minister, Lal Bahadur Shastri proved himself to be decisive, but in Tashkent, the pressures of decision-making made him a martyr.

Indira Gandhi has already gone down in history as the ideal decision-maker, who balanced cool consideration of issues with a sense of precision in taking action. Bangladesh, Sikkim and nationalisation of banks are but a few shining examples that changed the course of history. But at the same time, the same Indian people, who adored her for several years, discarded her for her decision to declare national emergency for what was perceived to be a decision motivated by personal ambition. On her return to power, she took several admirable initiatives in foreign policy, but fell prey to her decision on the Golden Temple. A study of her decision-making alone can fill volumes.

The popular perception of Rajiv Gandhi as PM is of an impatient young man, who was determined to take India to the twenty-first century and did everything possible to bring about changes. He accomplished his mission to a great extent and made a mark on the international scene with his imaginative moves. But it was precisely his hasty decisions, on the basis of wrong advice, that led to the spiralling effects of his decisions on Sri Lanka.

The extraordinary caution and reflection that characterised Narasimha Rao as prime minister was perhaps a result of his perception of his predecessor. An astute diplomat wrote that Rao's 'great intellectual gifts were not, however, matched by an ability to hand down clear-cut decisions'. His usual response to a request for a specific initiative was to thrust his lips forward into a thoughtful pout and give utterance to something between a grunt and a 'hmmm'. Indecisiveness was an art for him in 'decision-making' and one cannot deny that it helped him not to be accused of major mistakes either in domestic or foreign policy. He may have underestimated the developments in the Soviet Union, but once the old order changed, he was very quick to adjust India to the new circumstances, thanks to advisers like Manmohan Singh and Mani Dixit.

A prime minister, whom I personally knew well as he was my ambassador in Moscow, was Inder Gujral. He was decisive in many ways and had no hesitation in pushing his agenda. The Gujral Doctrine, which he introduced in our neighbourhood policy, did not have popular support in the bureaucracy, but he pursued it with vigour. Atal Bihari Vajpayee's decision to go nuclear was a decision that several prime ministers before him were hesitant to take, but it reflected his extraordinary sense of the pulse of the people. No decision of his government had the kind of popular support that the making of the bomb enjoyed. We shall leave out the present dispensation from this analysis, but Manmohan Singh proved that he was capable of decisive action as well as deep reflection, bordering on indecision.

I drifted away into my reflections on India's prime ministers to illustrate how individual predilections in decision-making at that level can shape the future of the country. That is the level at which decisions become crucial. In the ultimate analysis, what matters are not the theories and established practices that our management gurus have compiled, but the circumstances, the nature of advice and finally, the personality of the decision-maker. Rationality is important, but it is 'bounded rationality', as one of the gurus, Herbert Simon, put it.

As my experience in the government has been in the field of diplomacy, I have been often asked who takes decisions on foreign policy and how. My answer has been that decisions in foreign policy are dictated by geography, history and circumstances. Pandit Nehru is undoubtedly the architect of Indian foreign policy, but could he have shaped a policy other than that of non-alignment at that particular moment in history? Emerging as it did from the yoke of colonialism and not too fascinated by communism, India had no choice but to take the middle path and what Nehru did was to give content and voice to the aspirations of the people. Geography has already determined who our neighbours are and we have no control over the feelings of our neighbours, whether it is envy, fear or sheer ambition to dominate. Freedom to formulate foreign policy, therefore, has its limitations. This must be true also of domestic policy, which is circumscribed by the constitution, law and precedents.

Another factor that determines decision-making is our assessment of our strengths. When India was not self-sufficient in food grains and had to depend on PL 480, it was not possible to be fiercely independent. It was the new freedom gained by self-sufficiency in food grains that led to the flourishing of Indian foreign policy in the late seventies and the eighties. With the end of the Cold War and the emergence of the new world order, India took a series of decisions to readjust ourselves to the emerging global context. We are once again at a decisive moment in history with the new assertiveness of China and the resulting rebalancing that the US has launched in the Asia-Pacific Region. The need for a dynamic foreign policy, necessitating constant decision-making is evident from this analysis.

At the diplomatic and functional level, decision-making is more routine and less demanding. The broad policy and approach are laid down in respect to most countries and we have to operate within the instructions from the government. It is said that there is never anything urgent in diplomacy that cannot await instructions unless there is a war with the host country or the host country decides to expel a diplomat. I have had no experience of the former, but I did go through the latter when a military regime in Fiji ordered me out of the country as India did not recognise the regime. But I still had the time to seek instructions from Delhi. The only occasion I had to act on my own was when communications were disrupted when the coup which established the regime took place. Although it was clear that the coup was against the interests of the Indian immigrants, I maintained our traditional position of neutrality between the communities till I received instructions to change our position and oppose the military regime.

Our decision-making was under particular stress in the UN in the period following the collapse of the Soviet Union. The changes in the UN were so radical and fundamental and it looked as though many diplomats suddenly had had a change of the software in their brains. Changes in our positions were not so fundamental, but fresh instructions needed to be sought on several issues. Establishment of diplomatic relations with Israel had its own impact on our policy. Since we continued to support the Arab position on Palestine, the change was gradual and nuanced. Another major shift for India was in the aftermath of the nuclear weapon tests in 1998.

If I were to draw some conclusions from the sketchy experiences of decision-making I have described, I would say that no hard and fast rule can be applied to decision-making. We are constantly taking decisions all our lives and whether they are personal or official, the decisions that we take, shape our lives. We would like to take good decisions, but it is easy to miss an important factor, miss a possible option or base the decision on false information. Indecision can lead to missed opportunities for individuals, institutions and nations. Different kinds of decision-making structures are available to consider context, objectives, options and criteria. But in actual practice, decisions are often taken impulsively and in an ad hoc manner.

An important fundamental factor is the nature of advice that decision-makers get from time to time. The bureaucratic steel frame was once free of corruption and nepotism. Moreover, it was apolitical. But today, the bureaucracy is often committed to the political masters at best and corrupt at worst. They often give the advice that the masters like to hear. One celebrated example was the way Indira Gandhi was misguided into thinking the Emergency had enhanced her standing in the country. Another instance was the conviction that the NDA government had that it would return to power in 2004 as India was shining under its rule. On both these occasions, the wrong advice resulted in disastrous decisions. The right assessment and advice are crucial in taking the right decisions.

Another conclusion we can draw is that decision-making is lonely at the top. All said and done, the buck stops there and the consequences of every decision go to the very top. That is the reason for indecision in many cases. History is replete with instances of bad decisions taken with good intentions. As I said before, luck plays an important role in taking the right decisions in any sphere of activity. Uncertainty is the only certainty in this world and as in other activities, uncertainty will remain, however systematic decision-making can be. But one can never escape decision-making.

The joke about a husband claiming that he takes only important decisions such as the family's approach to disarmament and climate change and he leaves unimportant decisions such as those on family budget and children's school to his wife reflects escapism. But none can escape decision-making and none can avoid its consequences, good or bad. The saying goes, 'If you take a decision, you may be a scapegoat, if you choose not to, you end up being an "escape-goat".'

I began with Shakespeare and I shall finish with the bard's wisdom. All of Shakespeare's tragedies deal with unintended or unexpected consequences of one's decisions and the need to take responsibility for them. This is so in *Hamlet*, *Julius Caesar*, *Romeo and Juliet* and *Othello*. Some of the plays actually detail the thought processes in the minds of the characters when a decision is made, allowing us to learn how we ourselves think. Hamlet remains a very rational decision-maker till the end, but he fails to see that while he waits for the right circumstances, the world is moving on, creating new circumstances. In *Macbeth*, the predicament is to feel moral responsibility for the choices that are illusory, because the future is predetermined. *Julius Caesar* is all about miscalculation. All the main characters have to make decisions under uncertainty. They are free to make their choices, but they are not masters of their destiny because history does not depend on their decisions alone, but on the interaction between all of them. Shakespeare believed that choice triggers changes that often transcend what was expected or could be expected by a decision-maker. Shakespearean tragedies are always about choice, effectiveness and moral responsibility. We too face these issues in decision-making at every stage.

Public Service Commission ought to be morally responsible for their choice of public servants. And your decisions are crucial in shaping the destiny of our nation. May I wish you the wisdom, judgment and luck to make the right decisions all the way.

(Address at a National Workshop hosted by the Kerala Public Service Commission for members of the Public Service Commissions, 2013)

5

A DIPLOMAT AHEAD OF HIS TIMES

Former Foreign Secretary Jagat Singh Mehta, who breathed his last in March 2014 in Udaipur at the ripe age of ninety-two, had a meteoric rise in the Foreign Service because of his intellectual prowess and strategic thinking. But he proved much too ahead of his times to complete his tenure at the helm of the service.

'Much maligned', 'much misunderstood' and 'more sinned against than sinning' are some apt descriptions of Jagat Mehta. For a diplomat and statesman (1922-2014), who made an immense contribution to foreign policy right from the time of Pandit Nehru in 1947 to Charan Singh in 1979 in various capacities in the service and later as a thinker and writer, the entry on him in Wikipedia is a meagre paragraph, which does no justice to his illustrious career.

He is described as an Indian 'politician and diplomat' who was foreign secretary from 1976 to 1979. His postings to China as charge d' affaires (1963-66) and Tanzania as high commissioner (1970-74), his books and Padma Bhushan (2002) are mentioned.

'I am not an exportable commodity,' Jagat Mehta used to quip when asked about his only ambassadorial assignment to Tanzania. The fact is that he had made himself indispensable in the ministry as a foreign policy thinker and negotiator.

He used to recall how he was the only undersecretary in the Ministry of External Affairs, reported to Pandit Nehru and stayed in the same house he occupied later as the foreign secretary.

He turned his innocuous posting to Tanzania into a major listening post in Africa and won the hearts of Africans and Indians in East Africa. Policymakers should reread one of his dispatches on the creeping Chinese influence in Africa, to understand Chinese methods today.

It seems the Tanzanians realised the size of the Chinese hordes, which had arrived only when they saw the quantity of noodles being imported into the country. Jagat Mehta returned to the ministry as joint secretary and was soon appointed by Indira Gandhi as foreign secretary, overlooking the claims of some of his seniors. He was considered Indira's blue-eyed boy during her term, even through the first nuclear tests, the Emergency and her defeat in the elections in 1977.

The change of government gave Mehta an opportunity to shape the Janata Party's foreign policy through 'genuine non-alignment'. Morarji Desai and Atal Bihari Vajpayee were inclined to accept his suggestions to improve relations with the US, China and Pakistan, while maintaining good relations with the Soviet Union.

He also recommended some changes in nuances of our nuclear policy, by entering into a dialogue with the US. The initiatives such as Morarji Desai's visit to the US and Vajpayee's visit to China were results of his prodding the Janata government to bring in subtle changes in foreign policy.

These initiatives, meticulously analysed and formulated for the political leadership, turned out to be much too ahead of the times and, therefore, did not make much headway and eventually led to Jagat Mehta's downfall.

The country was in too cozy an embrace with the Soviet Union to think in terms of diversifying its relations and the Janata government was particularly suspect on this matter.

The US initiative and signals of change in nuclear policy ended in a fiasco when President Carter cut short his visit and returned, after a disastrous conversation with Morarji Desai.

Vajpayee's China visit turned sour when China invaded Vietnam even when he was on Chinese soil. Many in the Congress party and the Soviet lobby sharpened their attack on the Janata government's foreign policy and focused on Jagat Mehta as its architect.

India's decision not to recognise the Vietnam-backed Kampuchea provoked the Soviet Union itself. Eventually, it was the Charan Singh government, which decided to appoint another foreign secretary even when Jagat Mehta had several months to go before his retirement.

Prime Minister Charan Singh explained that the change was necessary because Mehta had brought in changes in the US, China and Pakistan policies against the interests of the country.

A posting abroad was offered to him, but Indira Gandhi withdrew even that when she returned to power in 1980. But Mehta stayed on with the government till his retirement, doing various diplomatic errands.

As Jagat Mehta's special assistant during the last two years of his tenure as foreign secretary, I saw for myself how his conviction, courage and patriotism enabled him to fight against heavy odds.

A particularly painful experience for this veteran diplomat was the accusation that he had hurt India's prestige at the Lusaka CHOGM by promoting his own candidature as the secretary general of the Commonwealth.

I know for certain that it was the inept handling of the issue at the political level that led to the fiasco. Mehta took the moral responsibility on himself and submitted his resignation, but instead of letting him leave, he was kept on and later dismissed, partly on account of the Lusaka incident.

The government did not even inform him of the impending change till a few days before the new foreign secretary arrived to take over. None of these discourtesies provoked him and he countered my advice to react by asserting that he was a disciplined soldier.

Honest and upright, he met allegations and accusations in good humour, considering himself above suspicion.

Jagat Mehta was a perfectionist and kept revising his notes and speeches incessantly. In the pre-computer age, this meant typing and retyping papers by an army of stenographers, which I kept correcting before submission to him.

I remember counting more than fifty versions of the toast that Vajpayee was supposed to deliver in Beijing. The joke about him was that when someone went to him and said that he should look at a speech that was to be delivered that day, he said, 'What do you mean? I need to finish yesterday's speech first!'

Jagat Mehta has recounted a number of the tough negotiations he was involved in, particularly with the Chinese on many issues, including on the border. He had the habit of recording the minute details of these negotiations, just as he recorded the reasons for each of his decisions on every file.

His negotiations with Idi Amin and his men for compensation for the Indians, who left Uganda, were particularly tough. Apparently, Amin warned him that the body of the British negotiator, who came earlier, was found in a roadside gutter.

But Mehta managed to leave Uganda in one piece after getting a sizeable compensation by negotiating each case separately.

I saw how he handled Soviet diplomats during Morarji Desai's visit to Moscow, when it became difficult to find a compromise on a reference to the Indo-Soviet Treaty in the Joint Statement.

It is to Jagat Mehta's credit that he was fully vindicated, when India pursued subsequently the same policies he had advocated towards the US, China and Pakistan. He had even anticipated the understanding we reached with the Americans on nuclear issues in 2005 by signalling that we would be flexible on non-proliferation.

Vajpayee as prime minister, made amends for the injustice done to him by seeking his advice and conferring the Padma Bhushan on him.

Apart from his policy frustrations, it pained Jagat Mehta that many of his colleagues in the Foreign Service were extremely critical of some of his administrative decisions, even though they were taken in the best interest of the service.

His exhortation to women officers to accept difficult postings caused a virtual revolt and resulted even in a court case. When he sought to expand the IFS, ulterior motives were attributed to him.

If only he was allowed to expand the service at that time, we would not have faced the acute shortage of officers in later years. None of these caused him any rancour as his mind was constantly focused on India and its future.

What he lamented in one of his last books was not his personal frustrations, but 'The Tryst Betrayed'.

Jagat Mehta's lasting legacy will be his intellectual contribution to the making of India's foreign policy and his humanism as exemplified in his social work in Rajasthan in the evening of his life.

(Rediff.com)

6

REFLECTIONS ON LEARNING ENGLISH LITERATURE

I could not have expected a greater honour from the Department of English of the Government College for Women, Thiruvananthapuram, than being invited to deliver the Prof Hrdya Kumari Endowment Guest Lecture 2011-2012. I had dreamt as a teenager that I would speak English like her one day. Today, at least, I speak in her name, though not like her. I bow my head to this extraordinary teacher and an exceptional human being.

The topic of this talk to honour Prof Hrdya Kumari could not be anything other than 'Reflections on Learning English Literature' as she was a towering presence in my five years as a student in the University College. But I must say that the final title of the lecture is a product of hard negotiations with the organisers. The process reminded me of an old Egyptian story of a fish vendor, who put up a board, 'Fresh Fish Sold Here', but ended up without a board as each wise man who passed by suggested one word after the other as redundant. In my case, I managed to retain the main part of the title, though I had to change the scope of the talk each time a word was dropped!

Believe it or not, it was precisely half-a-century ago that I made a crucial decision in my life. Instead of pursuing a professional course with a clear career option, I decided to chase a Foreign Service dream my father had by joining a course of study in English language and literature. I had no idea how it would help me reach my goal and I did not know how it would help in a Foreign Service career itself. I was happy to be rid of science subjects, particularly Mathematics, and nothing else bothered me as I registered myself in the University College for BA (English), which not many others seemed to want. At that time, as of now, the best and the brightest went to professional studies; our protestations that we joined English for the love of literature and to compete for the Civil Services did not carry any conviction. But we claimed elitism over our poor brethren in history and economics and gloated over our central location in the college and the attention we received by the abundance of the female of the species in our midst. Some of us also dabbled in student politics and became prominent.

Looking back at those years, 1961 to 1966, memories of events, personalities and experiences come to mind in an endless procession. As the most decisive years in shaping our lives, philosophies and thoughts, recalling them is an adventure in itself. Recording them after half a century is hazardous in the extreme, as events and people merge into each other and separating the different strands is difficult to accomplish. I can share only the overall impressions, fully aware that the important events may be hazy and the less consequential ones may get exaggerated. Personalities may emerge in black and white, though they were actually in colour, like the bewitching shades of an artist's palette.

My overwhelming recollection about those times is that none of us, neither students, nor teachers, appeared to have a vision or mission about the knowledge imparted to us. The prescribed books for both the bachelors and masters' courses belonged to different genres and different ages and there were no efforts to establish historic interlinkages either in terms of movements or literary crafts. We focused on texts without their contexts and we were unaware of the vast world of knowledge out there, outside our books.

The biggest weakness of teaching a course in English language and literature was that there was no effort to develop communicative English in the classrooms. We lived in two distinct linguistic worlds. We spoke in Malayalam the whole day except when we spoke to the teachers during lectures. Private conversations were strictly in the mother tongue and we were quite proud that neither our mother nor our tongue was English. In the process, the felicity of spoken English eluded us even after finishing five years of English language and literature. No group discussions were ever organised either to develop the language or the analytical ability of the students either at the graduate or post graduate level. The English associations, which were supposed to provide such opportunities were mired in politics and were used by the student organisations to bring their favourite people to interact with the students. In fact, the language aspect received no attention. Grammar, usage and idiom were unheard of. We developed a bookish form of English, which should have been conducive to literary writing. But creative writing was totally outside the curriculum. One of them, Mani Jacob, who became an educationist, had the skill to add cadence and colour to the most prosaic statements. For instance, I recall that when he had to say that Bacon made skilful use of aphorisms, he wrote, 'Bacon was not inept in the art of incubating aphorisms.' I do not think he developed his creative writing skills in later life. Creative writing, perhaps, had no place in his career as an educationist. I wonder whether ours was the only university in the world, where a student could become a Master in English literature, without writing a dissertation or a literary piece or acquiring proficiency in spoken English.

The focus was on prescribed texts at both the graduate and postgraduate level and there was no incentive to read. The library was stocked with literature and literary criticism of an earlier era and we did not know the contemporary literature in English. The infamous question, supposed to have been asked by a professor of English, 'Who on earth is TS Eliot?' may be apocryphal, but reflected the reality of the impression that English literature came to a close with the Victorian period. We had a book on British history in the BA class, but it was not linked to the literary movements or the nature of the society in which those movements flourished. How could we understand Shakespeare without the knowledge of what shaped his mind and what his preoccupations were as a playwright?

We had the most talented of teachers in the University College at the time, but we did not have the ability to understand them in the early years. With one year of English medium of instruction behind us, we did not grasp much of what they tried to convey. But they helpfully gave us notes on various topics both at the BA and MA levels to prepare us for the examination. This reduced our involvement further in the learning process. By the time we discovered the talents of our teachers, it was too late to benefit from their abilities.

The English teachers at that time were not anonymous, but people with established reputations. Two established poets among them taught us most prosaic subjects like British history, English phonetics and old English. The senior professor, who taught us Shakespeare, was rather prosaic and depended heavily on his old notebook, neatly covered in brown paper and labelled. He was totally lost without his notebook. We tested it by hiding the notebook for a day! At one time we had a head of department, whose passion was not poetry, but ornithology on which he was an authority. He knew who Eliot was, but when I suggested to him that the English Association must meet to condole the passing away of the famous poet, he did not see any point in it.

When I reflect on the faculty that we had at that time, I distinctly recall what we admired best in each one of them. A teacher with the eloquence of Hrdya Kumari, the depth of knowledge of Ayyappa Paniker, the creativity of G Kumara Pillai, the friendliness of Sudhakaran Nair, the motherliness of Chellamma Joseph, the sprightliness of Santhakumari, the smile of 'Punchiri Mathai', the good looks of Gopakumar and the simplicity of K Srinivasan would be a perfect model. But one thing common for all of them was their enthusiasm for teaching. Their sincerity was beyond question. But the system of learning and teaching was such that there was no scope for innovation. They taught us the way they learnt, as no thought was given to the nature of the professions for which the graduates were being educated. The skills which we acquired were good enough only to turn us into teachers without the special talents our teachers had.

One person, who seemed to care as to whether we will fit into the wide world, was not in the English Department, but our Principal NS Warrier. I remember him calling some of us to his room one day in 1964 to ask whether we had understood the full implications of the Chinese nuclear test that had taken place that day. We had not, and we had not cared. Today, we know how that single incident had transformed the world we would live in. Even our policymakers in Delhi had not grasped its impact as Dr Warrier had done! The space age had just begun and Dr Warrier appeared bewildered by it. He asked me once whether I had ever thought of flying in space and landing in a country I knew nothing about. Would I be equipped to deal with that situation, with the education I was receiving, he asked. Indeed, I lived in a dozen countries in different continents and discovered that it is important to develop a global view even when one is young.

The variety among us, the students who spent five years together, was great. They ranged from hard working and ambitious men and women to those with no particular goals in life. Those who came from the Thiruvananthapuram aristocracy had airs about them till the 'outsiders' overtook them in the university examinations. I remember a classmate, who was confident about facing an exam on the basis of what I could tell him precisely five minutes before entering the examination hall. He asked me to tell him the story of *The Twelfth Night* so that he could take the examination. He had neither read the play, nor listened to the lectures on it. I obliged, but when he began telling the story in answer to a specific question, he could not remember what the respective genders of Orsino and Olivia were. The way out he found was to describe them not as 'he' or 'she', but as 'it', much to the consternation of the evaluator.

College was a pastime for some of the students and they fell by the wayside, but found their own way of making a living. We know from experience that dropping out of college need not necessarily be a tragedy. Honorary degrees have been awarded to dropouts by the same universities when some of them became millionaires or political leaders. Some among my classmates, who may not have been good students, turned out to be reputed teachers as the years went by. The 'glorification' course in the university Department of English gave them a second chance to qualify themselves as teachers.

One thing that puzzled me most was why we were taught old English as part of the Master's Programme. The effort was as strenuous as learning a new language with no possibility of the dead language being used. If learning of the old literature was important, it could be done in modern English. The option that the university offered to study American literature in lieu of old English was not exercised in the University College. The other irony was that Ayyappa Paniker, the most modern of Malayalam poets, taught us *Beowulf*. We were unaware that even as he was teaching us old English, he was creating a revolution in Malayalam poetry with his *Kurukshetram*. We only heard that he recreated *The Wasteland* in Malayalam and we were not even inquisitive about his contribution. Now, many years later, we are discovering Ayyappa Paniker and finding the meaning of what he said to us half a century ago.

Learning literature for the joy of it was rare those days. It turned out that our graduation coincided with the advent of junior colleges in the state and all of us found jobs as lecturers even without applying for them. I was invited to teach in the Mar Ivanios College even before the results of my MA examination came out for a princely sum of Rs125 per month. Privately, I taught a group of school teachers, most of them double my age, who wanted to move from school to college with a Master's degree in English. English MA degree was an employment bonanza without much learning of literature. If employability was the purpose of a Master's degree, nothing was better than an English degree at that time.

In my Foreign Service career, I often wished I had done politics, economics or international law in college, as these were the disciplines one needed on a daily basis in the business of diplomacy. But it is also true that many inadequacies can be covered with felicity of language. To speak without saying much, an art that is the hall mark of diplomacy, one can resort to flowery language and quotes from Milton and Shakespeare. Moreover, learning of literature expands your vocabulary and linguistic skills to your advantage. I can recall many situations in which I got away with language what I could not have accomplished with substance. But I have also seen an ambassador, who filled his dispatches with literary embellishments, being considered a man without substance.

I have no doubt that learning of English literature in Kerala has undergone many changes since 1966. I understand that there is greater emphasis on spoken English and creative writing. Modern Indian writing in English, rather than old English, is part of the curriculum. Amitav Ghosh and Vikram Seth should be part of any English literature course. I would go further and say that contemporary writing in Malayalam should also be familiar to the students of literature. The focus should be on research and innovative thinking.

The Kerala Higher Education Council intends to promote clustering of colleges in different cities and one of the activities that we are planning is to encourage lectures by outstanding teachers and men of letters for all postgraduate students. To make a beginning in sharing of intellectual resources among students and teachers, I have invited the heads of departments of English in the city to discuss ways and means of collective learning. The programme will be extended to other departments also. Our 'Erudite Programme' will be redesigned in such a way that the availability of renowned scholars benefits as many students as possible. Students and teachers exchange programmes with foreign universities are also on the cards. Prof Hrdya Kumari herself is heading a committee to remove the anomalies in the semester system at the undergraduate level.

In my view, the semester system, which has stabilised elsewhere in India and abroad, permits a broad perspective on the subjects of choice and stimulates thinking and the spirit of enquiry. I had found our system of intensive studies of a few works, instead of a comprehensive knowledge about each author, a liability in answering questions in the Civil Services examination. The semester system does impose higher responsibilities on the teachers and the students, but the new teacher–student relationship envisaged in the system will be beneficial to both. I would like to see the system implemented in the state with the necessary correctives that we are in the process of shaping education for the future generations.

I shared my reflections on my own days in the university,

not only to savour the old days, but also to show how much we have moved forward in higher education and how much more we have to do to give our students world class education.

(Prof Hrdya Kumari Endowment Guest Lecture at Government College for Women, Thiruvananthapuram, 2012)

7

FROM PADDY FIELDS TO THE WORLD PARLIAMENT

From some to awesome; from the ordinary to the extraordinary; from the mundane to the memorable; from man to superman is the law of evolution. The transformation is slow and gradual for humanity, but for individuals it is dramatic, a revolution in a single lifetime. It is the evolution of an individual human being that adds up to the transformation of humanity. As Armstrong said, 'A small step for a man, a giant leap for mankind.'

Imagine a boy, born in a village with no electricity, whose playgrounds were paddy fields, flooded in certain seasons and dry in others, whose toys were made out of coconut leaves and used bicycle tires. Subsistence farming ensured that there was plenty of food, but not much else. He had one pair of clothes for the school and a topless outfit for the home, either a tattered pair of shorts or a coarse loincloth.

He walked barefoot to school, balancing himself on the

slippery, narrow tracks in the fields, rain or shine, and read with the help of a kerosene lamp. His ambition was only to do well in class, with hardly any competition in a village school. What guided him was a dream that his father had, that he should conquer the world, not just be the best in the state or India. The widest horizon he could visualise was the Foreign Service, a magic wand, he thought, that would transform a village boy into a globetrotter. His father's dream became his own, though he did not know what it meant, or how to accomplish it. But he toiled on, from school to college, in frustration and excitement, in failure and victory.

He went through college with the singular objective of competing for the diplomatic service, chose literature rather than science, read everything that he could get hold of from the libraries, read newspapers and meticulously took notes that filled many notebooks. The Hindu editorials were the staple of his learning, both for language and information. Academic success gave him the courage to tackle the Civil Services examination. Pursuit of a dream energised him even when there were setbacks.

And finally, the fairy arrived with her magic wand in the form of success in an examination, which literally transformed him from being one in a billion struggling Indians into one in less than a thousand diplomats, consisting mainly of princes and other privileged men and women from Oxford and Cambridge. It was truly turning from some to awesome. It was an intoxicating experience as he moved from one world capital to the other, initially as a minor functionary of the Indian Foreign Service, but eventually as an ambassador extraordinary and plenipotentiary, authorised by the president of India to speak on behalf of a billion people. His identity merged with the identity of India, his voice became one with the voice of the motherland. He became an excellency, not just a simple human being.

The glamorous places on the political, cultural and tourist

maps of the world became part of his daily routine, driving past the Imperial Palace in Tokyo, the Dzong in Thimphu, the Red Square in Moscow, the Empire State Building in New York, the Lions Park in Nairobi, the fabulous beaches of Fiji, the White House in Washington and the Hoffburg Palace in Vienna. He sat across the table with world leaders, Brezhnev and Clinton, Castro and Tito, negotiated with world class diplomats and signed agreements that served the best interests of the country. Even when he was expelled from a country and hurt in an armed attack, the feeling was of elation that he went through them for his country. Having pledged to do whatever was required to be done, a few drops of spilt blood or a couple of metal pieces in the bones made no difference.

He turned every challenge into an opportunity and treated every experience as part of the learning process. He sipped bitter green tea with relish at tea ceremonies with the geisha, gulped down yak buttered and salted tea not to offend the Bhutanese monarch, burnt the gullet with undiluted vodka to celebrate India–Soviet friendship and drank kava, which tasted no better than gutter water to savour the bliss of the lotus-eaters of the South Pacific Islands. He ate raw fish in Japan, ate raw meat in Moscow, tasteless corn meal in Kenya and flourished on burgers and hot dogs in the US and relished schnitzel and wines in Austria. He watched the kabuki theatre in Tokyo, the Nutcracker in the Bolshoi Theatre, heard Jazz in Greenwich Village and enjoyed opera in Vienna. He wandered in the Metropolitan Museum of Art in New York, the Hermitage in Leningrad, the Space Museum in Washington and the Museum Quartier in Vienna. He lived in temperatures ranging from minus thirty degrees in Moscow to plus forty degrees in Delhi. Magnificent libraries, high domed Cathedrals and manicured parks were daily fare for him. Could anyone wish for more, having been born and brought up beside the muddy waters of the paddy fields?

Every time our man stood up in the magnificent hall of the General Assembly or addressed the mightiest around the horseshoe table of the UN Security Council on issues of international importance to India, he marvelled at his own journey from the paddy fields of Kayamkulam to the parliament of the world.

Our hero did not know whether he made a difference to the world, as achievements in the IFS are nebulous. There are no bridges to be built except in the minds of men. No accomplishments can be attributed to individuals. It is more a matter of intellectual satisfaction. On rare occasions, one gets a chance to play a crucial role in a crisis or shape a consensus among warring factions. None of these bothered our man, as he saw his work as a mission to be accomplished to his own satisfaction.

The evolution from some to awesome continues. Both his sons, who had better living conditions and better education than him, had their own accomplishments. One, who went to school in Manhattan near the famous Metropolitan Museum of Art, today leads the Met's efforts to turn its marvellous collection of art into a digital resource for global education. The other is a connoisseur of popular Western music, even while managing a business concern. Happily, even the next generation is showing signs of evolution.

Believe me, friends, there is no exaggeration, no hyperbole, no fiction in this tale. The person who transformed himself from 'some to awesome' was none other than the speaker, now back in the back waters with a fund of memories to recall and to relish with malice to none and goodwill for all.

(Talk at TEDx, January 2014)

EPILOGUE

AN UNSCRIPTED SCREENPLAY

The themes, thoughts and conclusions of my writings in the last decade are inevitably rooted in the place I lived in, the work I did, the people I met and the state of my mind and my preoccupations. Living in Kerala as an evangelist of the Foreign Service and analyst of foreign policy, teaching international relations, building a think tank, traveling, reforming higher education in Kerala and playing golf triggered them. I wrote when I needed to and when asked to. Writing enriched me and its acceptance rewarded me. While my writings of the previous decades languish in the archives of the Ministry of External Affairs, my work from the last decade is in the public domain, earning bouquets and brickbats. The publication of a selection of my writings in an anthology is an occasion to reminisce over the last decade.

It has been a decade as rich in experience as the previous ones. Those, who wondered, like the late Mani Dixit, how we would live in the narrow confines of Thiruvananthapuram after strutting around the globe, told me later that it was a wise decision. In the present world of internet and international travel, what you do is more important than where you live. The world itself and the friends around the globe are within reach of your fingertips.

Retirement and death are destined for every human being, but most of us are not fully prepared for either, as we think that there will be sufficient time to prepare to confront both. In the summer of 1967, when I joined the Indian Foreign Service, 2002 seemed very distant and the prospect of a new career was too exciting to make me think of its termination. Those were the days when we could run into the prime minister and other high dignitaries in the corridors of the South Block and even in the elevators. We were imagining more about making diplomatic history in the years ahead than about looking beyond superannuation.

Life came in blocks of three years each time with a clear beginning and an end and the chain did not seem to end. A new country, a new home, a new car, a new office, new colleagues and friends every three years added variety and verve to life. By the time 2004 came, the age of retirement having been raised to sixty, it was more a sense of elation rather than a fear of the unknown that gripped me. I was quite happy following an unscripted screenplay, which turned out to be as interesting as the choreographed career behind me.

One reason for complacency was an offer I had received from the director general of the United Nations Industrial Development Organisation (UNIDO) to serve in New York for two years in its office. I had turned down UN offers more than once in my career, but it appeared perfect to have two years in New York with children and grandchildren. But the head of the UNIDO withdrew the offer to accommodate a fellow Argentinian.

Coming back to the backwaters of Kerala after my years with the government was a decision I had taken when I left home to join the elite Foreign Service in 1967. Delhi, with 'its freezing cold of the sepulchre and the searing heat of the cremation ground,' as an eminent writer put it, where a majority of my colleagues settled down to be on the fringes of power and diplomatic life, did not attract me. So I returned to Kerala with no specific plan for the future, except a vague idea of starting a foreign policy think tank, which would offer consultancy services and training for Foreign Service aspirants. But I have not been without an assignment even for a single day after I landed in Delhi, though I never asked for anything from anyone. Every offer came spontaneously and every assignment had its triumphant and frustrating moments.

A big yellow hoarding with blue lettering at the arrival lounge in the Delhi airport about Amity University had attracted my attention, but I had not imagined that the same evening I would receive an offer from Amity to be its representative in Kerala, with a mandate to open a campus there. I plunged straight into the job of building a university till Amity lost its permission to operate anywhere in India on account of a court action at the behest of the University Grants Commission. I started an Amity Centre for International Studies, but Amity itself had lost interest in the project after the idea of a university was dropped. A bonus from that experience was the opportunity it gave me to work with Air Vice-Marshal Bipin Kurup of the Mannath Padmanabhan family, who became a trusted and true friend.

An unexpected offer from Asianet to be its managing director was bewildering as I had no experience of media management, but Chairman Reji Menon persuaded me to accept it. But by the time I received the government's permission to accept the offer, some internal complications made it difficult for the chairman to run his writ. But I became an adviser to Asianet, with little to do except to run a weekly show on foreign affairs. Producing that programme remained a passion. *Videsha Vicharam*, the show, came to be a part of my routine every week ever since. I brought to Malayalam television a unique programme on international affairs, in which diplomats, scholars and celebrities from all over the world shared their thoughts on intricate global issues. Keeping *Videsha Vicharam* going week after week by finding a topic, an interlocutor, slots for shooting and airing it needed dedication and commitment. Asianet and its editors gave me a free hand and its crew cooperated heartily throughout. To be recognised as a TV star far away from home was a thrill in itself.

Within months of my return from Vienna, a call from the director general of the International Atomic Energy Agency (IAEA), Mohamed El Baradei, to invite me to be the executive director of an Eminent Persons Group to set the agenda for the IAEA till 2020. The Group was extremely diverse, with people like R Chidambaram, who were enthusiastic about nuclear power, Wolfgang Schussel, the former chancellor of Austria, who was a nuclear sceptic and others, who insisted that the IAEA should turn to nuclear disarmament as a core activity. The discussions over four meetings in Vienna were extremely interesting and I was entrusted to draft the report of the Group on use of nuclear power. The mood in the report was upbeat as we felt that there was a nuclear renaissance in the offing and that it would reach a peak in 2020. We had not anticipated that an accident like the one in Fukushima would alter the power scenario drastically, as it happened in 2011. The IAEA had to change its mandate, which the Group had suggested. Safety became a fundamental preoccupation and the enthusiasm for nuclear power waned substantially. A number of pieces on nuclear power in the anthology emerged from my work at the IAEA.

Thiruvananthapuram, the capital of Kerala, was only a 'Three ambassador town' as only KPS Menon, Thomas Abraham and I had decided to settle there after retirement. Many others chose to live in

Delhi, Bengaluru or Chennai. With the support of the other former ambassadors and others, we established the Kerala International Centre (KIC), the only foreign affairs think tank in Kerala in 2007. About 200 people from different walks of life joined the KIC. The Centre, though not a think tank in the true sense of the term, has created a group of people with interest in foreign and strategic affairs. We meet once in a fortnight in the conference room in my own house to discuss international issues of current interest, either with a guest speaker or without. The discussions are always lively and interesting. We have also sent our consensus views to the Ministry of External Affairs, which has been appreciative of our efforts to provide inputs from outside New Delhi.

The Shashi Tharoor campaign for the Lok Sabha elections was a whirlwind, which kept me busy for several months in 2009. Having known and admired him for several years in New York, I took it upon myself to introduce Tharoor to the people in Thiruvananthapuram, my hometown. We put our heart and soul into the campaign and put together a group of intellectuals, writers, artists and thinkers to support him. The hopes he raised of being a new kind of politician, learned, committed and free of corruption, energised us. His impressive victory was a matter of immense satisfaction. His appointment as a minister of state for external affairs was a foregone conclusion.

Four years in the National Security Advisory Board (NSAB) gave me an opportunity to meet and interact with some of the best minds in India and it was interesting that I was once again with my former boss, Ambassador Naresh Chandra. The NSAB was quite exciting in the first two years under Ambassador Shankar Bajpai, when foreign policy issues were quite active on the Board. I had the responsibility for nuclear issues, soon after the signing of the Civil Nuclear Agreement between India and the United States and I maintained a stream of articles and broadcasts in support of the Agreement. The Nuclear Liability Bill was referred to us and if the Parliament had accepted our advice, the problems that arose subsequently could have been avoided.

During my second term on the NSAB, the focus shifted to internal issues and, except for some odd discussions on China and Pakistan, the debates were on the North East and other security concerns of the country. We had a never-ending exercise of drafting a Security Doctrine for the country without reaching a conclusion. The NSAB, even after several years of its existence, is still in search for a role for itself as its views are seldom sought and its reports disappear into the entrails of the gargantuan bureaucracy.

Reading and writing, a habit from childhood, maintained throughout my diplomatic career, not only stayed with me in retirement, but also gained momentum, with the sense of liberation felt after retirement. My first book, *Words, Words, Words—Adventures in Diplomacy* (Pearson) was a diplomatic autobiography, not just my story, but also the story of my professional life right up to 2004. Vice-President Hamid Ansari, my former boss in New York, released the book at his residence. Nikhil Lakshman of Rediff.com had encouraged me to write a regular column for him soon after my return to India. I am still addicted to writing for Rediff, which has a global audience, which reacts instantly to every column. A number of my columns on Rediff.com were published in book form by a Malaysian publisher, Rhythm House, with the title, 'Encounters', as they were accounts of my meetings with celebrities, from Leonid Brezhnev to Ayyappa Paniker. My pieces appeared in international and national journals frequently. Tunku Varadarajan introduced me to the *Asian Wall Street Journal* and Vikas Bajaj to the *New York Times*. I wrote in Malayalam also for various journals.

The announcement of the India–US nuclear deal and related developments gave me an extraordinary opportunity to read, write and speak to educate the public about the deal. The combination of my familiarity with nuclear issues from my IAEA days and my long association with the US gave me an edge over others as a commentator on the topic. Another topic of general interest was the expansion of the UN Security Council, which, many had believed, was about to happen. I injected a sense of realism into the debate. I maintained that permanent membership of the Security Council with veto is unthinkable for India or any other country and that there was no formula which would command consensus in the UN. My advice was that we should not appear to be over anxious in this matter and should refrain from holding our bilateral relationship with any country hostage to this issue. I spoke and wrote that President Obama's statement in 2010 expressing a wish to see India as a permanent member had no substance unless he put forward a formula, which would command two-thirds majority in the General Assembly with the concurrent votes of the permanent members.

My two months as a senior fellow at the Brookings Institution in Washington under Prof Stephen Cohen gave me an opportunity to study the making of the nuclear deal. Sreedhar Menon, former deputy president of the American Express was instrumental in organising the fellowship. A virtual bank of the intellectual talent of the world, Brookings is unrivalled as a think tank. Ashley Tellis, next door at the Carnegie was also an inspiring guide. A number of articles I wrote from Brookings have found place in the anthology.

My experience of campaigning for Shashi Tharoor was captured in another book, *Mattering to India—the Shashi Tharoor Campaign*. As the only book in the world on the campaign of a single candidate, it drew the attention of several institutions of learning, including the London School of Economics. The noted journalist, Pranay Gupte, listed it among the best books he read in 2012.

After my younger days, when I saw the workings of the Nair

Service Society (NSS) at the grass roots level, I had no contacts with it till I was invited to speak at its annual session in 2009. Later, I went to see General Secretary G Sukumaran Nair to compliment him on his stand on some critical issues and that was the beginning of my close association with the NSS. Out of the blue, I was invited to help set up the NSS Academy of Civil Services. It turned out that the general secretary's dream of starting an academy and my own dream of training as many young people for the Civil Services as possible happily coincided. The opening of the Academy coincided with an upsurge in the number of Civil Services aspirants in Kerala. The academy is yet to prove itself, but it began a new era in the work of the NSS in Education. Since 1975, the NSS had not opened any new educational institution.

My interest in education evidenced by the opening of the Academy led to an offer from the newly formed UDF government of Chief Minister Oommen Chandy for me to head the Kerala State Higher Education Council (KSHEC). I had occasion to interact with the chief minister and KPCC President Ramesh Chennithala at the time of the India–US nuclear deal and the Shashi Tharoor campaign. This was the first time ever that the Kerala government had decided to make use of a retired IFS officer at a crucial position in the state.

I had only a year of teaching experience at the Mar Ivanios College to do the work earmarked for 'an eminent educationist, preferably a former vice chancellor'. But I remembered that several former diplomats had done well in education and waded into the sea of issues that haunted the higher education scene.

There was no dearth of ideas for educational reform and there were role models to emulate. I did not take long to identify six areas that needed attention to build, what I called 'Higher Education 2.0'—infrastructure, use of technology, teachers' training, research, autonomy and internationalisation. Studies were done in each of these areas and proposals were submitted to the government. Apart from making recommendations to the government, the KSHEC assumed a proactive role in promoting the implementation of its recommendations and monitoring progress. With the advent of RUSA, an initiative by the Government of India to enliven the higher education scene in India, the Council is poised to assume additional responsibilities, as a planning, funding and monitoring agency. What inhibits progress in higher education in Kerala is the mindset of the people, which is not amenable to change. This permeates the entire spectrum of stakeholders. Among the many ideas my Council has proposed after wide consultations with experts and different groups, only one or two have been implemented so far. As evangelists do, I spread the gospel of reform in higher education, but much of it falls on deaf ears.

I welcomed the opportunity offered by the vice-chancellor of the Central University in Kasaragod, Jancy James, to be a visiting professor of international relations. In my teaching at the university, I practice what I preach. I prepared myself thoroughly for the lectures, with the latest developments covered, used technology and devoted time for discussions and debates.

I travelled to many of the cities we lived in for one reason or another—New York, Washington, Yangon and Vienna. But visiting Fiji this year, after I was expelled from there twenty-five years ago for fighting for the Fiji Indians after a military coup, was a unique experience. Inviting me back as the chief guest of the annual convention of the largest Indian organisation there, 'Sangam' was an act of gratitude by the Fiji Indians to India and me for standing by them at a time of travail for them in 1987. I met Sitiveni Rabuka, the coup leader, on the very golf club we played together just two days before the coup. I could not reconcile with the immense damage his coup brought to his country, particularly to Fiji Indians, but I accepted his logic that both of us were acting under instructions, and therefore, no personal animosity was necessary between us.

The idyllic golf course in the heart of Thiruvananthapuram had beckoned me back here. Even after playing in some of the famous golf courses around the world, the charm of the little nine-hole course, where I played at the beginning of my golfing career, never left me. When there was a threat to the existence of the golf course soon after I returned, I went to the then chief minister of Kerala to say that one consequence of the closing of the golf course would be my having to leave the city. I thought that he would say that my departure would be good for the city, but he told me then that whatever may be the decisions taken by the government with regard to the course, it would remain open for golfers. He kept his word, despite the machinations of those who thought that chasing a white ball on acres of land was crazy when it could be used to build a concrete jungle. I played with many foursomes on the course during the decade, but Brigadier Laxman Vijayan is the one person who shared the joys and frustrations of the game with me from day one till this day.

Our return to Kerala brought us closer to my favourite deity, Durga, in our family temple in Chettikulangara. She was a living presence wherever I lived and I believe that her unseen hand protected my dear ones and me from the dangers we faced, like the armed attack on my wife and me in Nairobi. Durga's blessings and my mother's prayers were the anchor of my life. Being able to visit the temple frequently, not only to pray, but also to reminisce over my childhood is a blessing.

I lost my mother two years after I returned to Kerala, but having her with us in Vienna and later in Thiruvananthapuram was a great boon. An extraordinary woman, a fighter all her life against financial and familial adversities, she spent the last years of her life in peace and prayers after seeing all her children settled well in life.

She was a contented person when she breathed her last at the age of ninety-three at her ancestral home. My father, whose dream it was that I join the Indian Foreign Service, had passed away when we were in Washington. Apart from the passing of my father, a tragedy she faced was the untimely demise of her granddaughter, Sangeeta, at an early age. But her unshakeable faith in God gave her exemplary courage.

By the grace of God, the members of my family have successfully pursued their interests in the last decade. Lekha, my wife, has nurtured Karuna, a charity, which she had set up in New York in 1992. A short stay home she started in Thiruvananthapuram has been serving the poor with dedication. She has simultaneously continued her classical dancing and painting careers in Kerala. Sreenath, my elder son, moved from the Columbia University to the New York Metropolitan Museum of Art as the chief digital officer and his wife, Roopa Unnikrishnan, a Rhodes Scholar and an Arjuna Award winner, has started up her own consulting firm. Their twin children, Durga and Krishna, born when we were in Vienna, bring us much joy by growing up as well-mannered and talented children. My younger son, Sreekanth, joined KEF Holdings in Dubai. His wife, Sharavati Choksi, a media professional and former anchor of Headlines Today, is now a full-time mother to their son, Shivaay, a bundle of joy.

Divya Iyer is a spiritual daughter I discovered in the early years of her preparation for the Civil Service. With her brilliant academic record and her extraordinary talent for speaking and writing, I had expected her to get the service of her choice long ago. It is a happy coincidence that her dream has come true, together with this book, on which she worked tirelessly.

The seven sets of articles that Dr Divya Iyer has put together with diligence and affection in this volume are picked up from the wide repertoire of my writings during the decade 2004-14. Most of them were written in response to requests from journals and newspapers.

I made an extraordinary number of speeches in universities, colleges, clubs and schools, but I had prepared texts only of some of them. The subjects ranged from international affairs to education, science fiction and even fashion technology. Some of them also have been included in this volume. My friend in Washington, Ambassador Rick Inderfurth, had suggested that the sequel to my first book, *Words, Words, Words* should be 'Speeches, Speeches, Speeches'!

Divya has found a novel way of editing this book by linking diplomacy to mythology in a way only she could accomplish, with her deep study of mythology and politics. She has seen in each of the seven sets of essays the unseen hands of a sage. It was unusual to think of the linkage, but her explanations in each section will convince the readers that indeed the parallel streams of diplomacy and mythology do meet like the way the invisible Saraswathi merges into the Ganga and the Yamuna. I affectionately accept her offering as a gurudakshina in acknowledgment of the role I played in her education. This is the second book we have done together. The first one—*Pathfinder*—a boon to Civil Services aspirants across the country, which revealed her talent for writing books, was a national bestseller on amazon.in for several weeks.

Lekha, who was keen that my writings should be published in the form of a book and our children and grandchildren join in the celebrations of my seventieth birthday, occasioned by Divya's anthology of my work. We are indebted to her for bringing out this book in time for my seventieth birthday.

Shobit Arya, who discovered that wisdom also grows on trees, is an exceptionally talented publisher and guide. He was involved in the exercise of producing this book right from the beginning and he has done a marvellous job. We were so preoccupied with the book that even the formality of a book contract was not insisted upon! The book may well have created history in that sense. Thank you, Shobit.

Robert Browning's famous dictum, 'Grow old along with me, the best is yet to be', guides me at the present stage of my life. Every extra day you get beyond seventy should be relished and put to good use in every way. The twilight hours are as beautiful as the dawn. Whether I can accomplish anything tangible in my days ahead is uncertain, but if I do not, it will not be for the lack of effort. Gone are the days when wisdom and knowledge came with age. Today, we need to learn from the younger generation. The young people of today give me reason to believe that the evolution of man into superman is well on its way. I feel fortunate to have been part of a generation that linked two centuries and made a significant contribution to the evolution of mankind.

TP Sreenivasan
Thiruvananthapuram
June 2014

INDEX